# AN OAK SPRING POMONA

# AN OAK SPRING

# POMONA

## A SELECTION OF
## THE RARE BOOKS ON FRUIT IN THE
## OAK SPRING GARDEN LIBRARY

DESCRIBED BY

SANDRA RAPHAEL

OAK SPRING GARDEN LIBRARY

UPPERVILLE VIRGINIA

1990

DISTRIBUTED BY YALE UNIVERSITY PRESS, NEW HAVEN & LONDON

PRINTED IN THE UNITED STATES OF AMERICA

LIBRARY OF CONGRESS CATALOG CARD NUMBER 90–62575

ISBN 0–300–04936–6

FRONTISPIECE:

B. R. DIETZSCH  TWO QUINCES ON A BRANCH, *c.* 1750

*For*

PAUL MELLON

# CONTENTS

# CONTENTS

# LIST OF ILLUSTRATIONS

# LIST OF ILLUSTRATIONS

x

## LIST OF ILLUSTRATIONS

xii

# LIST OF ILLUSTRATIONS

# LIST OF ILLUSTRATIONS

xvi

# LIST OF ILLUSTRATIONS

xvii

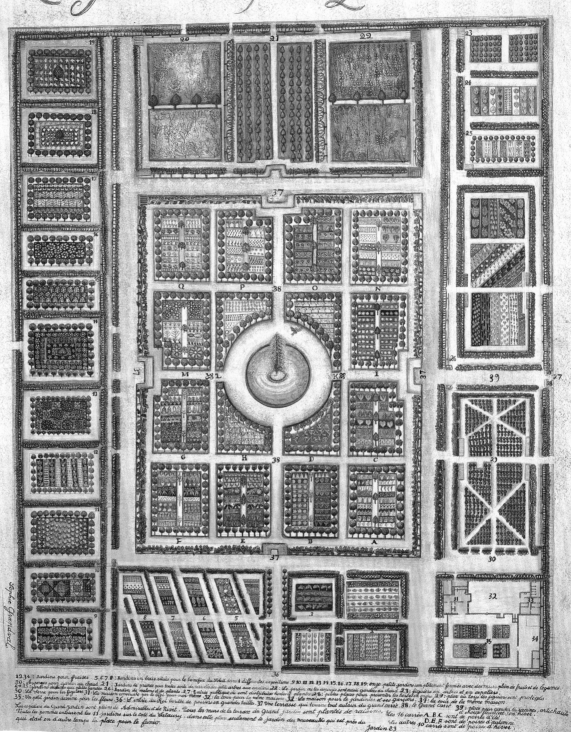

**SOPHIE GRANDVAL**
Le Jardin potager du roi à
Versailles *c.* 1984  A re-
interpretation in water-
colour and pencil of the
plan first printed in
J. de La Quintinie *In-
struction pour les Jardins
fruitiers* (1690), made for
the Oak Spring Garden
Library. The artist,
magnifying the print by
about ten, added appro-
priate fruit and vege-
tables to the beds and
borders

*Le Jardin Potager du Roi à Versailles*

# PREFACE

FRUIT — the subject of the second volume of the Oak Spring Garden Library catalogues — takes up a larger space on the shelf than some of its companions.

Children often find their symbols of stability and peace among the daily presence of things they love. For me they were apple trees. The driveway to our house was lined with apple trees. Leaving early in the morning for school and returning in the afternoon they were always there to welcome me. I knew their shapes by heart. Spring came with blossoms and wild violets that crept into the grass around them, followed by summer's heavy shade and autumn's red and yellow apples. Winter had a magic way of creating blue shadows on the snow that moved with the sun.

S. W. COLE
*The American Fruit Book* 1849 page 81
An apple tree

When the time came to plant my own fruit trees I made a search for books of instruction on this special subject, but there were no contemporary books to be had in the twenties and thirties. Turning to book-stores handling old and rare books I found my prize, which is still my favourite: the 1821 *Jardin fruitier* by Louis Claude Noisette (1772–1849). The inspiring illustrations and sheer beauty of the book in the beginning were balanced by the difficulty of translation, so the search continued and now, many years later, we have this catalogue — one might say the fruit of curiosity and love that started with an apple tree.

One cannot leave the subject of fruit without bringing to this preface the name of Jean de La Quintinie (1626–1688), the extraordinary seventeenth-century gardener who introduced methods of fruit culture and pruning that are still followed today throughout Europe. His study and practice of this subject caused him to be sought after as a gardener by many owners of large estates, including Charles II, King of England. Although he visited that country several times he chose to remain in France, loyal to Louis XIV for whom he designed the *Potager du Roi* at Versailles. This garden planned three hundred years ago still exists today, a living witness to the wisdom and theories of La Quintinie, where acres of espalier fruit trees are protected by the Government of France.

# PREFACE

I am profoundly grateful to the staff of the Oak Spring Garden Library—Tony Willis, Eugene Howard, Dorothy Tines, Fred Wines, and Mary Ann Thompson—who, with the guidance and encouragement of my dear friend and librarian, Dita Amory, have continued for the past eleven years to preserve the special spirit and atmosphere of this country library.

Without the sensitive and talented design of Mark Argetsinger and the perfection of the photography of Greg Heins this book would not have captured the true images of individual books. As a historian and writer Sandra Raphael has told with humour and intelligence the story of each volume, creating a book of garden history on the pattern of a book of short stories.

RACHEL LAMBERT MELLON
*Oak Spring*
*May* 1990

J. C. VOLKAMER
*Nürnbergische Hesperides*
1708 page 19  Vignette
of a citrus tree in a
garden

# ACKNOWLEDGEMENTS

THANKS once again to Niall Hobhouse, who first introduced me to Oak Spring and continues to foster both my work there and my parallel interest in botanical illustration. John Saumarez Smith, after constant encouragement as the book grew, coped with galley proofs and the aftermath of an invasion of builders in the same crowded week. Two other booksellers, William Patrick Watson in London and William Wyer in New York, found occasional books for the collection and shared a great deal of bibliomaniacal pleasure in looking at fine books and less imposing ones and discussing their various peculiarities.

In London John Barr at the British Library and Dr Brent Elliott at the Lindley Library of the Royal Horticultural Society made sure I found what I was seeking, and Jacques Paviot settled a few queries in the Bibliothèque Nationale in Paris. For translations from Flemish and Italian I am grateful to Dr Hanneke Wirtjes, Sharon Sage, and my nephew, Dr Gerard Duveen.

At home in Oxford Dr Richard Sharpe and Dr David Howlett joined in the Bodleian game of tracking down, translating, and sometimes correcting classical epigraphs. I must also thank them for taking care of more domestic concerns while I am away in Virginia, from sorting the mail to cutting the grass.

Mark Argetsinger looked after the book's design and production, and his colleagues at the Meriden-Stinehour Press in Lunenburg printed it. All the photographs for the illustrations were taken by Greg Heins of Boston, who also checked the proofs of those in colour. Drawings for the endpaper pattern (based on a design by Stephen Harvard) and the pear on the front cover were made by Ian Stephens, a wood engraver from Northampton (England). The care and skill of all these contributors have helped to make the book a fitting reflection of the library it represents.

As for the library itself, it is the only one I know in which a day of examining books may be finished off by helping with a little urgent pruning to trim an over-enthusiastic shrub back to its proper shape. The garden tools in the hall are not just for show. Describing fruit books in a library surrounded by apple trees made it seem right for the *Pomona* to be published in autumn as the fruit is being picked, but it has grown through all seasons in Virginia or Oxford. Mrs Mellon continues to preside over my exploration of her library, sharing the exhilaration of unexpected discoveries, the difficulties of choosing illustrations from such a profusion of possibilities, and the never-ending enjoyment of books large and small.

SANDRA RAPHAEL
*Oak Spring/Oxford*
*May/June* 1990

# INTRODUCTION

Then let the Learned Gard'ner mark with care
The Kinds of Stocks, and what those Kinds will bear.
Explore the Nature of each sev'ral Tree;
And known, improve with artful Industry.

VIRGIL *Georgics* II
translated by John Dryden, 1697

THE PROCESS described by Virgil and given English words by Dryden will serve as a reminder that the nurture of trees bearing edible fruit has been going on almost as long as gardening itself. In Rome the goddess of orchards and gardens, Pomona, had her own special priest, as well as a sacred grove of trees, which makes it rather appropriate that the oldest book described in *An Oak Spring Pomona* should be an Italian one, Bussato's *Giardino di Agricoltura* of 1592, with its earliest illustrations of methods of grafting and pruning. The tools shown in this book look quite familiar even now, and similar ones appear among the necessary equipment in fruit books during all the centuries since the sixteenth. Many of these books are quite modest and approachable. In the words of E. A. Bunyard (*Journal of the Royal Horticultural Society*, 1915, volume 40, page 424), 'It is the small books which have done most to create an interest in fruit culture, as they have reached the gardener directly.' From these little books it seems that fruit-growing has always attracted a particularly devoted group of gardeners, constantly ready to pounce on slightly improved trees and nurse them into stable varieties.

Though Italy produced the oldest book in this *Pomona*, the influence of that country, at least in English gardens, was soon surpassed by that of France, thanks to John Evelyn's translations of Bonnefons' *French Gardiner* in 1658 and La Quintinie's *Compleat Gard'ner* in 1693. He had travelled in both France and Italy, and his Bonnefons translation introduced the word *espalier* to his native language, with a definition of it for the benefit of his readers. Neither the word nor the manner of cultivation it described was adopted quickly in England, though the 1659 *Garden Book* of Sir Thomas Hanmer—a friend of Evelyn's—shows that he knew them well enough, as 'Hedges of Palissades, under 10 foote high commonly':

> The manner of making the hedges is either with streight poles set upright with others acrosse, about a foote or two asunder, bound together, or with tymber and crosse rayles. Some make the Fruite trees to spread their boughes by cutting them, and to grow without helpe of rayles or poles . . . These Hedges they set about great square Quarters in large Gardens in France. Fruite against Palissades or Hedges must bee grafted very low.

*Castagna Marrona*

Bianca Mojon dipinse in Genova 1831.          Franco. Corsi incise in Firenze nel 1834.

The Restoration of Charles II in 1660 brought many French fashions back to England with the Court, but fruit trees were already being imported from France or Holland. Hanmer's lists of fruit are thickly scattered with French names, some still in use, like 'Pearemaines' among the apples and 'Sommer Bon Chretien' and 'Beurré' among the pears. Sometimes the names are unknown, like 'The King peare soe called by Rose [that is, John Rose, gardener to Charles II] because the King liked it, but it is a French peare, I know not the name, it is a browne, round, moyst, musky peare, ripe with mee in Sept. very good.' The King's taste in fruit sounds rather good too.

Gardens in Scotland were also well supplied with fruit, especially the grand ones with protective walls, like that of Hamilton Palace near Glasgow and the river Clyde. The late seventeenth-century garden here is described by Rosalind K. Marshall in her book *The Days of Duchess Anne* (1973, pages 53–55), quoting from family archives. A visitor in 1668 saw 'Great abundance of as good vines, peaches, apricots, figs, walnuts, chestnuts, philberts etc. in it as in any part of France: excellent Bon Crestien pears . . . The walls are built of brick, which conduces much to the ripening of the fruits.' The first Duke of Hamilton, early in the century, bought small nails to fasten trees to brick walls, and the third Duke, who was particularly fond of cherries, continued the planting.

> The Duke extended the expanse of wall available, hiring brickmakers to come to the Palace and produce thousands of bricks for new walls. Against these, the Duke grew his peaches, apricots, and cherries. His success with these fruits became well known, and in 1682 the Earl of Callander was eagerly making arrangements to find out 'at what distance My Lord Duke plants the trees on his walls.'
>
> Some of his trees were obtained from other Scottish gardens. Two of the pear trees at Hamilton had come from Struthers, and some of the cherry trees had originated in the laird of Ormiston's East Lothian garden. Peaches and apricots were normally brought from London, and grafts, which were highly popular, were imported from the continent: on one occasion the Duke had a Bo'ness shipmaster bring over from Holland '5 peaches upon apricots, 4 peaches upon plums and 2 apricots.' At the same time, he ordered vines, mulberries and nut trees from the south.

The old alliance between France and Scotland may have been quite literally a fruitful one.

The 'great square Quarters' that Sir Thomas Hanmer had seen in French gardens sound just like the ones La Quintinie used in the *potager* at Versailles, the most famous of the fruit and vegetable gardens established by him in the second half of the seventeenth century. His book on the subject, though it was not published until 1690, two years after his death, was in such demand that only a handful of copies of the first French edition are known today, possibly because most of them were used to death. The Oak Spring copy is in a royal binding with the coat of arms of Philippe d'Orléans, the brother of Louis XIV. The book's circulation was maintained in the 1690s by several more French editions and a series of pirated ones produced in Amsterdam, as well as Evelyn's English translation and a second one by London and Wise, which pruned the text of a good deal of the first translator's characteristic verbosity. Whatever the form in which they were transmitted, La Quintinie's instructions on the training of fruit trees and his descriptions of preferred varieties of them were frequently referred to thereafter by his successors.

By now home-grown English manuals, like the little books by Ralph Austen, William Lawson, and T. Langford were also available, supplemented in 1699 by a treatise on sloping fruit walls, published in London by a Huguenot mathematician, Nicholas Fatio de Duillier. His theory about sloping walls trapping more sunlight to ripen fruit earlier was squashed flat by John Laurence, the country clergyman who wrote three more practical books on the subject about twenty years later, but Fatio's idea may not have been such a *bêtise*. In one garden in Cornwall, Trengwainton near Penzance, wedge-shaped beds were constructed by Sir Rose Price about 1820, when a series of very cold winters made extra heat especially desirable for early vegetables. The beds, facing south-west and sloping at an angle of about fifteen degrees, are still in the walled gardens at Trengwainton, which is now in the care of the National Trust. Perhaps Fatio's idea was more effective with smaller plants than with fruit trees. During most of the seventeenth and eighteenth centuries it was very cold in Europe, so cold that this period is sometimes called the Little Ice Age. Then there was a milder spell from about 1790 to 1810, before more extra cold winters. With this background the development of protected cultivation, walls and espaliers outdoors or orangeries and greenhouses for plants to be completely enclosed, is given a set of sound reasons.

The next group of major French writers on fruit, Duhamel, Le Berryais, and Noisette, are inter-related, the first two as collaborators in research and recording precise descriptions of trees—Le Berryais also contributed many illustrations to Duhamel's *Traité des Arbres fruitiers*—while Noisette used the coloured engravings from Duhamel's book as the source of most of the pictures in his own *Jardin fruitier*, first published about fifty years later, in 1821. Le Berryais' *Traité des Jardins*, which appeared in the 1780s, was sub-titled 'le nouveau de la Quintinye', borrowing the mantle of this great gardener nearly a century after the first appearance of his book.

François de La Rochefoucauld, a visitor to Suffolk in 1784, thought the English had not made the most of French examples. His journal has been newly translated and edited by Norman Scarfe (*A Frenchman's Year in Suffolk*, 1988, page 35) and he looked at kitchen gardens as well as landscaping:

> Kitchen-gardens are not as well-kept as ours: the gardeners are not so fully trained in their work. I've noticed that often their trees were not well-pruned. They seem to like long branches that decorate the whole wall with leaves, and which naturally bear nothing like so much fruit as ours do. They are not familiar with the use of wire, and attach each branch with a small piece of cloth and a nail. In general, all that they know about the cultivation of kitchen-gardens and the various kinds of fruit they have, comes from France.

NÉFLIER A GROS FRUITS.

A. BIVORT *Album de Pomologie* volume II 1849 [plate 25] Large-fruited medlar

A handful of encyclopaedic catalogues of cultivated fruit are among the most beautiful books in the Oak Spring collection. First the *Nouveau Duhamel*, which kept the great man's name for a compilation made by a group of botanists and published in the first twenty years of the nineteenth century. It was illustrated by Redouté and Bessa and described trees and shrubs growing out of doors in France, among them many bearing edible fruit. Giorgio Gallesio's *Pomona Italiana*, with its fine aquatint illustrations, worked through fruit in Italy from 1817 to 1839, omitting citrus fruit, which the author had already described (without pictures) in his *Traité du Citrus* of 1811. Alexandre Bivort's *Album de Pomologie* came from Belgium a little later, from 1847 to 1851, illustrating and describing the increasing number of varieties becoming available. Less grand books on the fruit grown in Austria, Germany, and the Netherlands had already appeared in the eighteenth century, the Dutch one by Knoop, dated 1758, with the earliest accurate coloured illustrations. Each of the main printing processes, from engravings of various kinds, printed in colour or hand-coloured, to lithography, with or without hand-colouring, is represented in the fruit books, often with very decorative results. So attractive are they that many of the larger books have sometimes been dismembered to allow their plates to be sold individually. The same hazard has affected smaller books too, like Lindley's *Pomologia Britannica* or its earlier version, the *Pomological Magazine*. Extra copies of other specially attractive plates, like those from Furber's fruit calendar or Brookshaw's gigantic *Pomona Britannica*, have been made by reprinting them, particularly Furber's monthly broadsheet catalogues of the fruit in season, which are still in demand two hundred and fifty years after their first appearance.

Many of the less showy eighteenth-century English fruit books had their popularity underlined by being pirated in Dublin editions, a brisk way to multiply copies before the restrictions of copyright law made the process more difficult. John Laurence's books received this dubious compliment in the second decade of the century, and later writers had their work borrowed in the same way, which at least confirms the desire of readers for information about fruit-growing. William Forsyth's best-seller on the subject went into edition after edition from 1802, adding two American versions to its success at home.

These American adaptations, made immediately by William Cobbett, were the first books to make allowances for different conditions across the Atlantic, though fruit trees had long been imported from Europe and by about 1820 American varieties were beginning to be sent back to nurserymen and connoisseurs in the Old World. From its foundation in 1804 the Horticultural Society in London was the centre of a great deal of interest in new varieties, and similar organizations elsewhere in Europe were also hospitable. The early *Transactions* of the (Royal) Horticultural Society contain a series of fine fruit plates, mostly by William Hooker, illustrating the varieties being described. Once again, they are often found singly in print shops, detached from their context.

William Coxe published one of the first purely American fruit books in 1817, but the long run of editions of Andrew Jackson Downing's *Fruits and Fruit Trees of America*, beginning in 1845 and supervised by his brother after A. J. Downing's early death, leave no doubt about the outstanding member of this group. It would be quite possible to make a small collection of fruit books by authors who were themselves the sons of nursery gardeners and presumably began to learn about their subject earlier than most—not only the Downing brothers but their English contemporary John Lindley and their predecessor Batty Langley, whose fine *Pomona* was published in 1729, though he is better known as an architect. C. M. Hovey's well illustrated *Fruits of America* (1852–56) suffered in comparison with the popularity of Downing and was never finished. From the 1850s to the 1880s the brightly coloured fruit shown in nurserymen's plates, an American way of producing illustrated catalogues for travelling salesmen representing nursery gardens, gives another record of varieties available in this country, both imported ones and those raised at home.

The American books are not generally remarkable for their beauty, but when one turns to books on individual families of fruits one is back among more elegant examples of printing. This section of *An Oak Spring Pomona* begins with the citrus fruits, from Ferrari's *Hesperides* of 1646, an Italian book, across Europe via Commelin in Holland (1676), Sterbeeck in Belgium

J. C. VOLKAMER
*Nürnbergische Hesperides*
1708 page 220c Detail
of a room looking into
an orangery

(1682), Morin, Gallesio, Risso and Poiteau in France (1692 to 1818) and, among the most beautiful, Volkamer's *Nürnbergische Hesperides* of 1708 and 1714, an intriguing mixture of German and Italian gardening. Oranges and lemons, with their need for warmth, were a challenge to richer gardeners in northern Europe in the same way that pineapples and melons were, for all these fruits needed constant skilled care in carefully planned surroundings. Lady Mary Wortley Montagu, writing to her sister from Blankenburg, not far from Kassel in Germany, on 17 December 1716, was startled by the orange trees at Herrenhausen, the Elector of Hanover's garden, and even more surprised by the fruit on the royal table, until she found out about the Germans' skill in heating the necessary glasshouses:

The ill weather did not permit me to see Herrenhausen in all its beauty, but . . . I was particularly surprised at the vast number of orange trees, much larger than any I have ever seen in England, though this climate is certainly colder. But I had more reason to wonder that night at the King's table. There was brought to him from a gentleman of this country two large baskets full of ripe oranges and lemons of different sorts, many of which were quite new to me, and what I thought

J. C. VOLKAMER
*Nürnbergische Hesperides*
1708 page 190b  An
orange with crimped
leaves and the garden of
a house in Mögeldorf

Aranzo con foglia rizza.

Das Obere Schlößlein und
Garten in Mögeldorf.

worth all the rest, two ripe ananas [that is, pineapples], which to my taste are a fruit perfectly delicious. You know they are naturally the growth of Brazil, and I could not imagine how they could come there but by enchantment. Upon enquiry I learnt that they have brought their stoves [that is, very warm greenhouses] to such perfection, they lengthen their summer as long as they please, giving to every plant the degree of heat it would receive from the sun in its native soil.

That accounts very neatly for Volkamer's enthusiasm for citrus fruit, when it is added to his travels in Italy and his delight in the gardens he saw there.

Next come the apples and pears, beginning with some seventeenth-century English books about growing apples and making cider of them. Worlidge's *Vinetum Britannicum* of 1691 refers to cider rather than wine, but the title shows how important cider was at the time, even having a didactic poem, John Philips's *Cyder* (1708) to itself. It was no less important in America in the eighteenth and nineteenth centuries, but somewhere between the Old World and the New the European habit of cultivating particular varieties of apple for cider-making seems to have been abandoned, as the Americans were and remain far less selective about which apples they press for cider. Thomas Andrew Knight's *Pomona Herefordiensis* (1811), a book about the apples of a great cider county by a man who bred many new varieties of fruit, explains the different qualities of cider apples. From the same county came the most exhaustive book on apples and pears and their history, Robert Hogg's and H. G. Bull's *Herefordshire Pomona* (1876–85), organized by the local Woolhope Club 'to restore Herefordshire to its fruit-growing supremacy'. The contributors to this thorough account of apples and pears and the drinks made from them would probably be pleased to know that there is now a Museum of Cider in Hereford.

In most of the general fruit books there are more pears than any other fruit, with flocks of varieties for different seasons. Once again they may have a special appeal to the connoisseur, if only because they must be picked and eaten at their peak of perfection to be tasted at their best, and that moment is easily missed. Pears were particular favourites in France and the Low Countries, so much so that the Huguenots have sometimes been given credit for taking this preference to America, though it was much later, between about 1820 and 1870, that pears became what U. P. Hedrick called a 'mild mania' there, thanks largely to the importation of Jean Baptiste Van Mons' new varieties from his nursery in Louvain. American nurseries followed the fashion, while the Massachusetts Horticultural Society and others exhibited the fruit of literally hundreds of different kinds. The craze is recorded in two books, the *Illustrated Pear Culturist* (1858) by 'An Amateur' and Thomas Field's *Pear Culture* of the following year.

A couple of little books on peaches, one French, one English, are followed by two on soft fruit—strawberries, raspberries, and gooseberries. A native fruit unique to America, the cranberry, also has a little book to itself before it is followed by Jacquin's *Monographie du Melon*, a small octavo in spite of its imposing title, and several books on grape-vines, covering the period from 1727 to 1830. Kerner's *Le Raisin*, a large folio full of his own exquisitely coloured drawings of the fruit of many varieties of grape, published in parts from 1803 to 1815, is easily the rarest and most beautiful of this group. The printed version of John Locke's manuscript advice on vines and olives, intended to encourage settlers in Georgia, is at the other extreme in terms of size, but its historical interest is great, as it recalls American efforts to naturalize European vines before people began to look at native ones to see how they could be used. William Prince's *Treatise on the Vine* (1830), the first important American book on the subject, described eighty native varieties and two hundred European ones, but the American vines were welcome enough about fifty years later, when some of them were exported to France as stocks to help vineyards there recover from the ravages of the plant louse, *Phylloxera vastatrix*. The little pest was inadvertently imported to France in a shipment of fruit from America, but its terrible effects were partially healed by American vines, in a neatly balanced solution.

The last section of *An Oak Spring Pomona* deals with tropical fruit. Two books and a large part of a third are devoted to the pineapple, that exceedingly fashionable fruit whose successful cultivation in England was one of the less obvious side-effects of the arrival of a Dutch king, William III, and his wife Mary, the daughter of James II, in 1688. A new style of garden design came in with other Dutch influences, and so did Dutch skills in horticulture, hence the passion for growing pineapples which spread among English gardeners in the eighteenth century, once the plants and the use of brick-lined hot-beds covered with tanners' bark to cultivate them had been introduced from Holland.

The first examples of this strange fruit arrived in London from the West Indies in 1657 with Richard Ligon, whose *True and Exact History . . . of Barbados*, published the same year, contained a glowing description of it. John Evelyn, writing on 9 August 1661, 'first saw the famous *Queene-pine* brought from *Barbados* presented to his *Majestie*, but the first that were ever seene here in England, were those sent to *Cromwell*, foure-yeares since.' He had to wait another seven years to taste the fruit, until 19 August 1668, when another imported pineapple was served at a banquet given by Charles II for Jean-Baptiste Colbert, Louis XIV's minister, who was visiting London:

> Standing by his Majestie at dinner in the Presence, There was of that rare fruite called the *King-Pine*, (growing in *Barbados* & W. Indies), the first of them [that is, this variety of pineapple] I had ever seen; His Majestie having cut it up, was pleased to give me a piece off his owne plate to taste of, but in my opinion it falls short of those ravishing varieties of deliciousnesse, describ'd in *Cap: Liggons* history & others; but possibly it might be, (& certainly was) much impaired in coming so farr: It has yet a gratefull acidity, but tasts more of the Quince and Melon, than of any other fruite.

A picture doubtfully attributed to Hendrik Danckerts, now in the possession of the Marquess of Cholmondeley, shows the King's gardener, John Rose, presenting a pineapple to Charles II, that enthusiastic connoisseur. Several copies of the picture exist, but the question of the pineapple's provenance remains unsettled, though it is unlikely that it was home-grown. Rose died in 1677. One of his apprentices and his successor as royal gardener was George London. Working for him at Hampton Court in 1693 Tilleman Bobart, a gardener from Oxford, saw a pineapple ripening and reported it in a letter of 16 October to the keeper of the Ashmolean Museum: 'Here is at this time a very fine Ananas near ripe in the stove which is to be presented to ye Queen in a few days.' Jan Commelin, whose catalogue of the contents of the Amsterdam botanic garden was published in 1697, complete with a fine pineapple plate, said the fruit was ripening in that garden from 1692, while Agnes Block, another Dutch gardener, had a ripe pineapple at her estate of Vijverhof five years before that. She even had a special medal struck to mark the occasion of the first fruit. Given the traffic in plants between Dutch and English gardens, it seems certain that London's 1693 pineapples came from Holland, along with advice on how to manage the greenhouses in which they had to be grown, in spite of the traditional belief that the picture shows a proud Rose offering his royal master the first English pineapple.

Pieter de La Court of Leiden worked out the most promising way of making pineapple plants comfortable enough to bear fruit, using extra warm hot-beds. His methods were transmitted early in the eighteenth century to Sir Matthew Decker, a transplanted Dutchman living in Richmond, where Peter Collinson saw what he thought was 'the first pineapple grown in England' in 1712. Decker's gardener, Henry Telende, is usually given credit for the first English pineapple. Once his treatment of the plants was described in print, by Richard Bradley in his *General Treatise of Husbandry and Gardening* in 1724, the pineapple became an essential plant in gardens able to provide the heated greenhouses and skilled attention it demanded.

Changing fashions in the design of gardens have been studied and explained at great length, but fashion is just as evident in the contents of gardens, the plants used to furnish them. Even the choice of fruit reflects contemporary crazes—evergreen orange and lemon trees in the seventeenth century made way for even more exotic melons and pineapples in the eighteenth, for example—but the more everyday kinds, with apples and pears in the lead, have never been neglected. The zeal of the gardeners and their enthusiastic descriptions of favourite varieties and skilful methods of growing them remain constant themes of most of the books described in *An Oak Spring Pomona*.

J. C. VOLKAMER
*Continuation der Nürn-
bergischen Hesperidum*
1714 page 207 An
angel tail-piece

# DESCRIPTIVE METHOD

EACH DESCRIPTION of a book begins with a simple transcription of the title-page, keeping initial capitals when they are appropriate but ignoring other variations in type or size. Oddities in spelling or accents have also been kept, and only the most peculiar ones have been labelled *sic*, as tagging them all would have produced a very speckled text. Rules and decorations are mentioned and measured; a rule of unspecified length stretches right across the title-page. Variants on the title-pages of multi-volume works are indicated volume by volume, as briefly as possible. A collation follows, with bare details of the book's construction but no systematic analysis of its components, though occasional eccentricities are mentioned. Unnumbered preliminary pages before a sequence with Arabic figures have been given Roman numbers in italics, which also indicate any other figures that make an obvious part of a series but are not printed on the relevant page. Individual leaves of a gathering are designated A1, A2, and so on, or in the case of numerical signatures 20:1, 20:2, etcetera, using a colon to avoid possible confusion.

Bindings are described briefly, with a record of inscriptions, bookplates, or any other indications of a book's provenance. Plates are also given a section to themselves in a description of an illustrated book, with details of artists and engravers, as well as any other relevant information. Then comes an account of the book's background and contents, varying in length from a paragraph or two to several pages, depending on the interest and complexity of the volume concerned.

Manuscripts and single drawings are also given brief physical descriptions, followed by comments on their contents and background.

No one working on historic books about plants and gardens should fail to be grateful for a handful of reference books that are constantly being used. Three in particular, Claus Nissen's *Die botanische Buchillustration* (1951; second edition and supplement, 1966), Blanche Henrey's *British Botanical and Horticultural Literature before 1800* (1975), and the *Catalogue of Botanical Books in the Collection of Rachel McMasters Miller Hunt*, compiled by Jane Quinby and Allan Stevenson (1958–61) may be described as so essential that it is hard to imagine how our predecessors managed without them. Other occasional sources of information are mentioned in the text, but there is no collected list of them.

# FRUIT IN FRANCE & BRITAIN

I  *The Seventeenth Century*

J. DE LA QUINTINIE
*Instruction pour les Jardins fruitiers* third edition 1697
volume 1 The author's
portrait, drawn by
F. de la Mare Richart
and engraved by
C. Vermeulen

F. de la Mare Richart pinx acad.    C. Vermeulen Sculp.

Hanc decorate Deæ, quot quot regnatis in hortis,
Floribus e vestris supráque infráque. tabellam:
Hic dedit arboribus florere, & ædibus herbis,
Et se mirata est tanto Pomona colono. Santolius Victorinus

# 1. LA QUINTINIE, Jean de (1626–1688)

Instruction pour les Jardins Fruitiers et Potagers, Avec un Traité des Orangers, suivy de quelques Réflexions sur l'Agriculture, Par feu M^r de la Quintinye, Directeur de tous les Jardins Fruitiers et Potagers du Roy. Tome I. [woodcut decoration of fruit, flowers, and foliage 6 x 6.5 cm.] A Paris, Chez Claude Barbin, sur le second Perron de la sainte Chapelle. [rule 7 cm.] M. DC. LXXXX. Avec Privilege de Sa Majesté.

4° 26 x 19 cm. a⁴ A–B⁴ A–3T⁴ 3V² *i–viii 1 2–16 1–522 523–524* (412 numbered 312, 416 as 316, 472 as 462, 481–488 as 471–478) including 3 (of 4) engraved vignettes at start of sections and 3 engraved garden plans, plus an engraved portrait frontispiece and 2 double-page engravings, one of 'Le Jardin Potager du Roy a Versailles' the other of grafting.

. . . Tome II. [woodcut decoration of putti, fruit, and foliage 6 x 6.5 cm.] . . .

A–4C⁴ *1–3 4–104 101–394 393–566* (i.e. 572) *573–574* (283 numbered 263, 380 as 038, 398 as 198, 399 as 299, 408 unnumbered, 422 as 442, 550 as 450, 553 as 535) including 5 engraved vignettes, plus 11 engravings of pruning patterns and tools.

BINDING: Red morocco, gilt borders and decoration, arms of Philippe d'Orléans (1640–1701), brother of Louis XIV, on sides; all edges gilt.

PLATES: The portrait frontispiece was drawn by Florent de la Mare Richart and engraved by Abraham de Blois. The four lines of verse beneath it come from Jean de Santeul's *Pomona* (see below). The plates are unsigned, but among the artists working at Versailles during La Quintinie's years there was Sébastien Le Clerc (1637–1714), a *graveur du roi* whose drawings of the Labyrinth were published in 1679. It seems possible that he might have recorded the *potager* too. The first double plate is the plan of the *potager* at Versailles, which has been reprinted so often, while the second shows grafting and the remaining plates pruning diagrams, except for three illustrating tools. Each section of the text, the six main books, the treatise on oranges, and the reflections on agriculture, begins with an engraved vignette, though one which should

appear on page 135 of volume I, showing ground being prepared for a garden, was not printed in this copy. The one beginning the treatise on oranges is specially interesting, as it shows orange trees being tucked into the containers now known as Versailles tubs. Woodcut decorations and bands of printers' flowers are scattered through both volumes.

*The first Amsterdam edition:*

. . . Tome I. Seconde Edition revûë & corrigée. [vignette 7 x 5.5 cm.] Sur l'imprimé de Paris. A Amsterdam, Chez Henri Desbordes, dans le Kalver-straat, prés le Dam. [rule] M. DC. LXXXXII.

4° 23 x 16.5 cm. ★–4★⁴ A–2L⁴ 2M² *i–xxxii 1–276* and a portrait frontispiece and 2 folding plans.

. . . Tome II. Seconde Edition Reveuë & Corrigée . . . Suivant la Copie de Paris. A Amsterdam, Chez Henry Desbordes, dans le Kalverstraat pres le Dam. [rule] M DC LXXXXII.

A–2V⁴ *1–2 3–344* (numbered 244) and 11 engravings.

BINDING: Two volumes in one; contemporary calf, rebacked. John Evelyn the younger's copy, inscribed on the title-page 'John Evelyn Durate &c. Virg: Æn: 1.1.'

PLATES: Reversed copies of those in the first Paris edition, 1690.

The 'Fautes survenuës dans l'impression', that is, the misprints, listed at the end of each volume of the first edition, have been corrected in this edition.

*The third edition:*

Instruction pour les Jardins fruitiers et potagers. Avec un Traité des Orangers, suivy de quelques Refléxions sur l'Agriculture. Par feu Mr. de la Quintinye, Directeur de tous les Jardins Fruitiers & Potagers du Roy. Tome I. [vignette 5 x 5 cm.] A Paris, Par la Compagnie des Libraires. [rule 7.5 cm.] M. DC. XCVII. Avec Privilege de Sa Majesté.

4° 24.5 x 18 cm. a⁴ A–B⁴ A–3T⁴ 3V² *i–viii 1 2–16 1–18 23 20–302 383 304–480 471–478 489–522 523–524* and an engraved portrait frontispiece and 5 engravings.

3

J. DE LA QUINTINIE
*Instruction pour les Jardins fruitiers* 1690 Twin bindings, with the arms of Philippe, duc d'Orléans

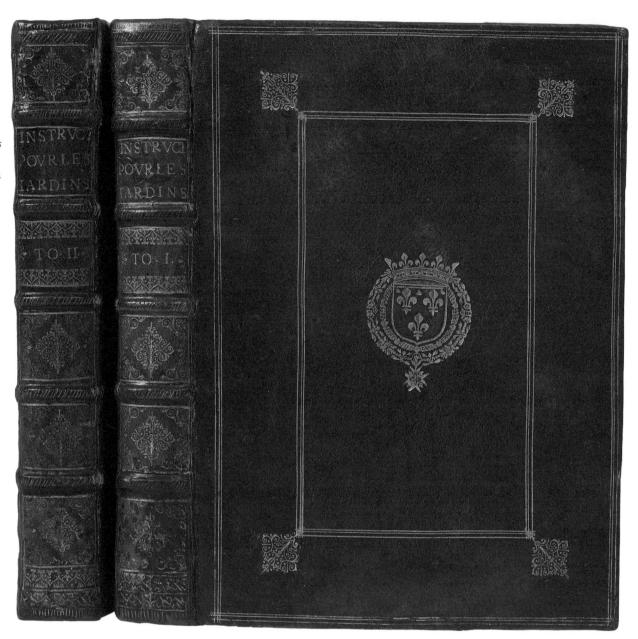

. . . Réflexions . . . Tome II. [BE monogram 4 x 4.5 .cm.] A Paris, Chez Claude Barbin, sur le second Perron de la sainte Chapelle. [rule 7.5 cm.] M. DC. XCVII. Avec Privilege de Sa Majesté.

A–4C⁴ (2H1 signed Dd) *1–3* 4–104 101–180 179–409 [2] 410–549 *450* 551–566 *527 568* and 8 plates.

BINDING: Contemporary calf, arms of La Rochefoucauld in gilt on sides. Stamp of 'Château La Roche-Guyon Bibliothèque' on both title-pages. This family library was sold by Sotheby's in Monaco on 8 and 9 December 1987.

'La Compagnie des Libraires', twelve of them, including Claude Barbin, is listed on the back of the title-page of volume I. The licence or *privilège* dated 18 October 1689 and printed on page *523* gave fifteen years' copyright to La Quintinie's son, with a postscript:

Et ledit Sieur de la Quintinye a cedé & transporté son droit

4

de Privilege à Claude Barbin, Marchand Libraire à Paris, pour en joüir pendant le temps porté par iceluy, suivant l'accord fait entr'eux.

This *privilège* is repeated in volume II, with the addition of a date in March 1697 and 'Les Sieurs Aubouin, Charpentier, & Compagnie ont acquis ledit droit pour en joüir pendant ledit temps', but the title-page of this volume bears only Barbin's name.

*An expanded Dutch edition:*

. . . Tome I. Troisiéme Edition. Reveuë, Corrigée, & Augmentée d'un Traité de la Culture des Melons, & de nouvelles Instructions pour cultiver les Fleurs. [decoration 5.5 x 7 cm.] Suivant la copie de Paris. A Amsterdam, Chez Henri Desbordes, dans le Kalverstraet, prés le Dam. [rule 9.5cm.] M. DC. XCVII.
4° 24 x 18.5 cm. ★–3★⁴ 4★² A–2L⁴ 2M² i–xxviii 1–276 (269 as 296) and an engraved portrait frontispiece and 2 folding engravings.

. . . Tome II . . .
A–2V⁴ 1–2 3–344 and 11 engravings.
Nouveau Traité de la Culture des Melons. Sous un climat tel qu'est celui des Provinces Unies. [decoration as main title-page] A Amsterdam. Chez Henri Desbordes, dans le Kalverstraet, prés le Dam. [rule 6.5 cm.] M. DC. XCVII.
A⁴(A4+1) B–R⁴ S²(S2+1) 1–2 3–8 [2] 9–140 141–142 including 2 engraved vignettes.

*Between pages 8 and 9 is a title-page for:*

Nouvelle Instruction pour la Culture des Fleurs. Contenant la Maniere de les cultiver, & les Ouvrages qu'il faut faire chaque Mois de l'Année selon leurs differentes Especes. Avec un Catalogue des Fleurs les plus belles & les plus Rares. [decoration as main title-page] Suivant la Copie de Paris. A Amsterdam. Chez Henri Desbordes, dans le Kalverstraet, prés le Dam. [rule 6 cm.] M. DC. XCVII.

BINDING: Two volumes and additions in one; dark brown calf. Incomplete list of editions of La Quintinie's book in French, German, and English, from 1690 to 1739, on front pastedown. Bookplate of Rachel McMasters Miller Hunt (1883–1963) on fly-leaf, marked in pencil 'HBL withdrawn', that is, withdrawn from the Hunt Botanical Library in Pittsburgh. An eighteenth-century inscription quotes Virgil at the top of the leaf, followed by a German inscription referring to another Virgil quotation. Scattered notes in ink or pencil, French or German, throughout the text.

This edition added the melon directions first included in Evelyn's English translation of the book in 1693 (see page 11–12) and based on letters La Quintinie had sent him. The manual of flower gardening also added to this edition is not the work of La Quintinie, though it was sheltering under his name.

J. DE LA QUINTINIE
*Instruction pour les Jardins fruitiers* 1690 volume I page 134 Pomegranate tail-piece

JEAN DE LA QUINTINIE, the leading French gardener of the seventeenth century, came from the Angoumois and studied law and philosophy at Poitiers before becoming a lawyer in Paris. He was then engaged as tutor to the son of Jean Tambonneau, president of the Chambre des Comptes. The Tambonneau house in the Faubourg Saint-Germain (rue de l'Université) had a large garden, in which the tutor was able to indulge his taste for botany. He escorted

J. DE LA QUINTINIE
*Instruction pour les Jardins fruitiers* second edition
1692 Title-page with
the signature of John
Evelyn the younger

# INSTRUCTION
## POUR LES
## JARDINS FRUITIERS
### ET POTAGERS,

Avec un Traité des Orangers, fuivy de quelques Reflexions
fur l'Agriculture,

Par feu *M. DE LA QUINTINYE*, *Directeur de
tous les Jardins Fruitiers & Potagers du ROY.*

### TOME I.

*Seconde Edition revüe & corrigée.*

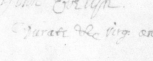

*Sur l'imprimé de Paris.*

A AMSTERDAM;

Chez HENRI DESBORDES, dans le Kalver-ftraat, prés le Dam.

M. DC. LXXXXII.

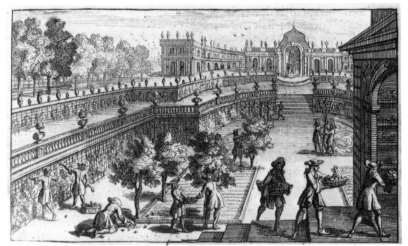

his pupil to Italy about 1656, visiting Montpellier and its botanic garden, the oldest in France, *en route*. Once back in Paris he continued his studies of plant physiology, concentrating on the growth of trees and the functions of roots. In 1665 he began work as a gardener for Louis XIV and also for the Prince de Condé, at Chantilly. Soon after this change in his career, some time in the late 1660s, he visited England, where he met John Evelyn and presumably others who shared his interests. Charles II is said to have tried to keep him in England, but he remained a servant of the French monarch, Charles's first cousin, rising steadily, with ever-expanding titles, to become eventually the man in charge of fruit and kitchen gardens in all the royal houses. The *potager* at Versailles, constructed in the years 1677 to 1683 to meet the needs of a larger court, was perhaps the most famous of them—a large patchwork of square plots around an even larger central one, well supplied with walls for espaliers. La Quintinie's skilful management kept up a supply of fruit and vegetables in and out of season: asparagus in December and strawberries in April, as well as the King's favourite figs. The degree of royal favour in which he lived is shown by the commission given to Jules Hardouin-Mansart to build a house for him, presumably when the architect had time to spare from his grander plans for Versailles.

La Quintinie also made *potagers* for other patrons, among them Fouquet at Vaux-le-Vicomte and Colbert at Sceaux, where Claude Perrault designed a Pavillon d'Aurore as its centrepiece.

The book that gave La Quintinie's directions to a larger audience was first published posthumously by his son Michel, in Paris in 1690. The gardener was in good company, for his publisher, Claude Barbin, was a leader in his field, whose authors included Molière, La Fontaine, La Rochefoucauld, and Madame de Sévigné. The *Instruction*, dedicated to the King, was so popular that the first of several pirated editions appeared in Amsterdam only two years later, in 1692. The dedication, after praising the King's knowledge of his gardens, points out the author's systematic presentation of directions for pruning, 'mes principes de la taille des Arbres (matiere jusqu'à present assez vague & assez inconnuë', in the hope that his book will help to educate

J. DE LA QUINTINIE
*Instruction pour les Jardins
fruitiers* 1690 volume II
plate facing page 159
Pruning to thin out
tangled branches

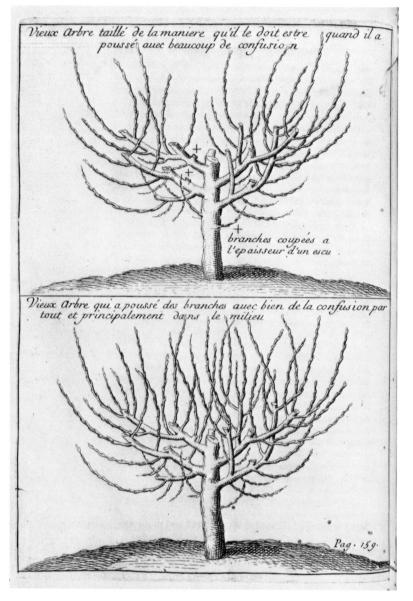

*Vieux Arbre taillé de la maniere qu'il le doit estre quand il a poussé auec beaucoup de confusion*

*branches coupées a l'epaisseur d'un escu.*

*Vieux Arbre qui a poussé des branches auec bien de la confusion par tout et principalement dans le milieu*

*Pag. 159.*

future gardeners. 'Je pourray au moins me flater de cette esperance, que le Traité, que j'ay aujourd'huy l'honneur de luy presenter, contribûra a lui former des Jardiniers.' Later editions, both French and Dutch, added sections on melons (via Evelyn's English translation in 1693) and flowers (not the work of La Quintinie) to the basic six books, five of them on the cultivation of fruit trees, with more detailed directions than any known before, and the last an account of a kitchen garden, with a month-by-month almanac of necessary work. Among fruit trees, pears are given more attention than any others. La Quintinie's advice on dealing with orange trees and his reflections on agriculture were also added to the six main sections. The advice on pruning and thinning out buds, especially the latter, was novel, and patience was recommended: 'Retarder vos jouissances pour en jouir plus longtemps.' Parts IV and V hold most of the relevant instructions, with the aim of making beautiful, shapely trees with fine, large fruit, that is, seeking quality as well as quantity. Pruning at the right time must take out useless branches, trim those that are too long, and be adapted to the state of the tree in order to keep it in good health year by year. 'Je suis persuadé que la Taille est une chose non seulement fort utile, mais aussi fort curieuse, & capable de donner du plaisir à qui l'entend: Mais en même temps il faut convenir qu'elle est assez pernicieuse, quand elle est faite par des mains ignorantes.' As Stephen Switzer said later in his *Practical Fruit-Gardener* (second edition, 1731, page 235), 'Monsieur de la Quintinie may be justly said to be one of the first that ever wrote distinctly of pruning.' La Quintinie praised his own predecessors too, among them Antoine Le Gendre, the 'curé d'Hénouville', who published *La Manière de cultiver les arbres fruitiers* in 1652. Le Gendre was 'inspecteur des jardins' to Louis XIII before becoming a country priest near Rouen, where he was visited by Pierre Corneille, the playwright, who enjoyed the fruit from his garden. La Quintinie gives him credit for being the first to suggest training fruit trees as espaliers and grafting pears on quince stocks.

The book was prefaced by a Latin poem, *Pomona*, by Jean de Santeul, celebrating La Quintinie's work at Versailles, and a French one in couplets by Charles Perrault, a brother of the architect Claude and better known now for his fairy tales. The repetition and discursiveness that might have been trimmed if the author had lived to put the finishing touches to his book did not diminish its authority, which was so great that nearly a hundred years later René Le Berryais sub-titled his *Traité des Jardins* 'le nouveau La Quintinye'.

As well as Evelyn's 1693 English version and its later abbreviation by London and Wise, the book was also translated into Italian and Dutch, while French editions appeared over and over again well into the next century, as late as 1756.

J. DE LA QUINTINIE
*Instruction pour les Jardins fruitiers* 1690 volume II page 237 A tail-piece of flowers

J. DE LA QUINTINIE
*The Compleat Gard'ner* translated by John Evelyn 1693 plate facing page 15 of part IV Pruning tools (combining three plates from the French editions, two from part IV, the third from part V)

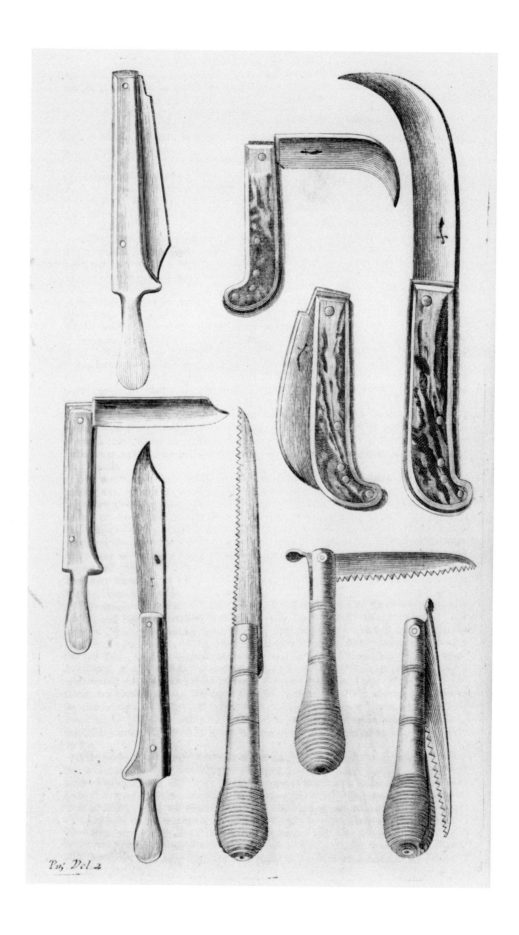

## 2. LA QUINTINIE, Jean de (1626–1688)

[within a border of double rules] The Compleat Gard'ner; or, Directions for Cultivating and Right Ordering of Fruit-Gardens and Kitchen-Gardens; With Divers Reflections On several Parts of Husbandry. [rule] In Six Books. [rule] By the Famous Mon<sup>sr.</sup> De La Quintinye, Chief director of all the Gardens of the French-King. [rule] To which is added His Treatise of Orange-Trees, with the Raising of Melons, omitted in the French Editions. [rule] Made English by John Evelyn Esquire, Illustrated with Copper Plates. [rule] London, Printed for Matthew Gillyflower, at the Spread Eagle in Westminster-Hall, and James Partridge, at the Post-house at Charing-Cross, M DC XCIII.

4° 32 x 20 cm. a★–b★⁴ b★★²(–b★★2) c★⁴ [a]⁴ [b]⁴(–[b]4) B–O⁴ P–Q⁶ R–2A⁴ 2B² B–P⁴ Q²T–2D⁴ [a]² A–K⁴ i–xlii 1–106 106 (i.e. 107) () 108 () 109 () 110 () 111–115 () 116 () 117 () 116 (i.e. 118) () 119–184 185–188 1–116 137–204 (but no text missing) 205–208 1–4 1–80 and a frontispiece, a folding plan, and 10 engravings.

BINDING: Two volumes in one; panelled calf, rebacked and repaired. Book label of Charles Milsom on front and back pastedowns; armorial bookplate of Laurence Williams 'Major 1894' also on back pastedown, with the signature of M. Williams on the front one.

PLATES: The engraved plates and vignettes are copies (sometimes reversed) of those in the first French edition (see page 3). The portrait frontispiece is engraved by William Elder after the French one, and the plan of 'The Kings Kitchen Garden at Versailles' is also copied. Two of the plates are signed 'MB' and 'M. Burg.' for Michael Burghers, a Dutch engraver who worked in Oxford from 1676 to 1699, as in London and Wise's later version of this translation (see page 12). There is a new engraved figure of a melon plant at the start of 'Directions concerning Melons', which appeared for the first time in this translation.

JOHN EVELYN is better known as the author of *Sylva* than as a translator, although he published an anonymous version of Bonnefons's *Le Jardinier françois* as early as 1658 and another of Le Gendre's *La Manière de cultiver les arbres fruitiers* in 1660 (see page 15). A third translation, *Instructions concerning erecting of a Library* (1661), rendering into English Gabriel Naudé's treatise on Cardinal Mazarin's library, is remembered for its dedication to the Earl of Clarendon, in which the Royal Society—founded in 1660—was given its name in print for the first time. Evelyn, of course, was a founder member. Stephen Switzer, in the first volume of his *Ichnographia Rustica* (1715, page 45), praised Evelyn's gardening translations:

Neither was his Labour less in Matters nearer relating to Gard'ning, in his Translations, and in his *Kalendarium Hortense* . . . He translated *Quintinye's Compleat Gardener*, with another smaller Tract, from French; was in his time the best Linguist, and to him it is owing that Gardening can speak proper English.

Travels in France and Italy had helped to encourage Evelyn's interest in gardening, and he must have appreciated the value of La Quintinie's book. The French gardener had visited Evelyn's garden at Sayes Court, Deptford, on the Kent side of London, during his stay in that town in the 1660s, though this meeting is not recorded in Evelyn's *Diary*. One result of the encounter was some advice on growing melons, which Evelyn translated for his friends. It is similar to, 'though somewhat more ample', than the letters from La Quintinie on the same subject published in the *Philosophical Transactions* run by Henry Oldenburg, the secretary of the Royal Society, in 1669 (volume 4, pages 901–03 and 923–24). These 'directions concerning the ordering of melons' were published as an addition to Evelyn's translation of La Quintinie's book, which also included the treatise on orange trees and the reflections on agriculture appended to the first edition.

A letter sent to Evelyn's brother George with a copy of *The Compleat Gard'ner* says: 'I do not attribute the whole to my selfe; the toile of meere translating would have been very ungrateful to one who had not so much time to spend thrashing: but as a considerable part of it was, and the rest under my care, the publishers & printers will have it go under my name.' The style certainly has echoes of Evelyn's voice, and public knowledge of his interest in gardening and his *Elysium Britannicum*, an encyclopaedic work on all aspects of gardening, begun in the 1650s, announced as being prepared for the press in 1669, but never published in its entirety, must have made his name a useful second to that of La Quintinie.

The dedication of Evelyn's version, signed by the publishers Matthew Gillyflower and James Partridge, is addressed to Henry, Baron Capel, whose garden at Kew is mentioned in Evelyn's *Diary* on 27 August 1678: 'His garden has certainly the choicest fruits of any plantation in England, as he is the most industrious, & understanding of it.' Lord Capel belonged to a family of gardeners, for his brother Arthur, Earl of Essex, had a famous garden at Cassiobury, Hertfordshire, and his sister Mary, Duchess of Beaufort, made her garden at Badminton, Gloucestershire, a rich collection of exotic plants, as well as extending her patronage to many seventeenth-century naturalists.

Mrs Gillyflower showed her enterprise by squeezing in an advertisement (b3 verso) for 'the best Pruning-knives, and other Instruments for Gard'ning, made according to the Directions of Mouns.ʳ de la Quintinye when last in London', which could be bought from her shop. This economical use of a blank space on a page of a thoroughly chaotic piece of printing seems to fit in well enough with the muddle of the book's construction.

## 3. LA QUINTINIE, Jean de (1626–1688)

[within a border of double rules] The Compleat Gard'ner: or, Directions for Cultivating and Right Ordering of Fruit-Gardens, and Kitchen-Gardens. [rule] By Mounsieur De la Quintinye. [rule] Now Compendiously Abridg'd, and made of more Use, with very Considerable Improvements. [rule] By George London, and Henry Wise. [rule] London, Printed for M. Gillyflower, at the Spread Eagle in Westminster-Hall, M DC XCIX.

8° 19 x 12 cm. π² (−π2) a–b⁸ c² B–C⁸ D⁸(D1+⋆1.2.3.4 +⋆⋆1.2+⋆⋆⋆1.2) E–U⁸ X⁴ Y² [2] *i–xxxv* xxxvi 1–43 [7] 35–309 *310–316* (the material in the double sequence is not repeated) and a frontispiece and 9 engravings.

J. DE LA QUINTINIE
*The Compleat Gard'ner*
translated by London
and Wise 1699 Frontis-
piece and title-page

BINDING: Contemporary panelled calf, inscribed 'Mark-nach' on torn fly-leaf and 'R. Gee' on page *i*, with occasional annotations in the latter hand throughout.

PLATES: The unsigned engraved frontispiece uses some of the elements from La Quintinie's original vignettes, with additional parterres, to form a garden scene. The other engraved plates repeat most of those of Evelyn's earlier translation; one of them is signed 'MB' and another 'M. Burg.', presumably for Michael Burghers. An engraved vignette of two garden plans on page 22 is still numbered 'p. 34' as in the Evelyn version, while the melon vignette on page 207 is another echo.

EVELYN'S 1693 translation of *The Compleat Gard'ner* was never reprinted, but a shorter version, 'Compendiously Abridg'd, and made of more Use, with very Considerable Improvements' by George London and Henry Wise, was issued by the same publisher, Matthew Gillyflower, in 1699. This revision was explained by its authors: 'In the first place we think fit to remark that we have gone through the Works of our learned Author with all the exactness we possibly could, abstracting . . . all that is useful; and have reduc'd into a proper method, that in which the Original is so prolix and interwoven, that the Reader was rather tir'd than inform'd.'

This condensed version, concentrating on practical information, had a much wider popular appeal, running through seven editions in the next twenty years. Evelyn's name did not appear on the title-page, though his signed 'Advertisement' for London and Wise's Brompton Park nursery, the leading one of its time, was reprinted from the 1693 translation in the abridgement, except for a part of the first edition of it, including this copy. Evelyn's translation of La Quintinie's notes on melons are moved from an appendix to their correct place in an alphabetical sequence of kitchen-garden plants. Geoffrey Keynes, Evelyn's bibliographer, has suggested that George London, who had travelled in France and was well acquainted with the most important French gardens, might have been the other translator concerned in the 1693 version (see page 12), an explanation that would account very neatly for his control of the abridgement. This shorter version was obviously the main vehicle for the spread of La Quintinie's methods in England, where his influence lasted well into the next century.

## 4. [BONNEFONS, Nicolas de (*fl.* 1651–1661)]

The French Gardiner: Instructing How to Cultivate all sorts of Fruit-Trees, and Herbs for the Garden: Together With directions to dry and conserve them in their Natural; [rule] Six times printed in France, and once in Holland. [rule] An accomplished Piece, [rule] First written by R.D.C.D.W.B.D.N. [that is, Nicolas de Bonnefons, valet du chambre du Roi] And now transplanted into Euglish [*sic*] by Philocepos. [that is, John Evelyn; rule] Illustrated with Sculptures. [rule] London, Printed for John Crooke at the Ship in St. Pauls Church-yard. 1658.
12° 14.5 x 8.5 cm. A–M¹² N⁸ O⁴ P⁴(P4+1) *i–x* 1–294

295–312 (page numbers 180 and 181 transposed) and a frontispiece and 3 other engravings.

BINDING: Dark brown calf, rebacked.

PLATES: All four are copies of those by François Chauveau (1613–1676) in the original French edition. A. Hertochs, a Dutch engraver who worked in England from 1626 until 1672, signed the frontispiece and the first plate, both showing garden scenes, and initialled the last plate, a kitchen picture. The second plate, of a kitchen garden and a parterre, is unsigned.

ALTHOUGH EVELYN used the pseudonym Philocepos ('a lover of gardens') on the first edition of this translation, he signed the dedication to Thomas Henshaw with his initials and later editions of the book printed the translator's name in full on the title-page. The Oak Spring copy is the third issue of the 1658 first edition, according to the criteria described in Geoffrey Keynes's Evelyn bibliography (second edition, 1968, page 51). The library of the Hunt Institute in Pittsburgh has the dedication copy (also the third issue) of the translation, inscribed to Henshaw (1618–1700), Evelyn's friend and travelling companion in Italy in 1644 and 1645, who had suggested an English version of the book. Both Henshaw and Evelyn were founder members of the Royal Society, Henshaw serving as its secretary from 1668 to 1672, when he was succeeded in this office by Evelyn. The dedication displays Evelyn's most orotund tone of voice:

NICOLAS DE BONNE-FONS *The French Gardiner* translated by John Evelyn 1658 plate facing page 1 Building an espalier frame, an engraving by A. Hertochs

Be pleased, Sir, to accept the *productions* of your own *Commands*; as a *Lover* of *Gardens* you did *promote* it, as a *Lover* of *you* I have *translated* it . . . For it is impossible that he who is a true *Virtuoso*, and has attain'd to the felicity of being a good *Gardener*, should give jealousie to the *State* where he lives. This is not *Advice* to *you* who know so well how to *cultivate* both your *self* and your *Garden*: But because it is the only way to enjoy a Garden, and to preserve its Reputation.

The dedication also mentions the garden encyclopaedia, *Elysium Britannicum*, that Evelyn was working on during the 1650s, describing its planned contents and saying: 'This . . . I intended to have published for the benefit or divertisement of our *Country*, had not some other things unexpectedly intervened, which as yet hinder the birth and maturity of that Embryo.' The difficulties were never removed and the *Elysium* remained unpublished, apart from a few chapters which were issued separately. During the same decade, when King Charles II was in exile and Evelyn was not in sympathy with the Commonwealth government, he probably translated another French book too, Le Gendre's *La Manière de cultiver les arbres fruitiers*, which was published in London in 1660 as *The Manner of Ordering Fruit-Trees*, without the name of its translator being printed in it. The title-page describes it as 'A piece so highly approved of in France, that it hath been divers times printed there', first in 1652, with later editions in 1653 and 1661.

*The French Gardiner* devotes its first part to fruit trees, their choice and cultivation, diseases and pests. The second begins with melons, cucumbers, and pumpkins before going on to other vegetables, salads, and herbs, followed by strawberries, raspberries, gooseberries, and mushrooms. There is an appendix about keeping, drying, pickling, or otherwise preserving fruit (in wine, cider, or honey) but the cooking instructions in the French editions are omitted. An entry in Evelyn's diary on 6 December 1658 records: 'Now was published my *French Gardiner* the first & best of that kind that introduced the use of the *Olitorie Garden* to any purpose.' He introduced the rare word olitory to the English language too, referring to a kitchen garden, but *The French Gardiner* also contains the earliest use in English of a much more common word, espalier. On page 14 there is an odd spelling of it in a section 'Concerning Esphaliers (which I will English Palisades)', accompanied by a definition in a marginal note, 'Pole-hedges set up against a wall, much used in France'. As French ways of growing fruit influenced English practice so much, it is natural enough that we should have borrowed the words to describe them.

The first French edition of Bonnefons's book appeared in 1651, but Evelyn revised and added to it as he translated, so his version is sometimes a fair way from the original, especially as he had more than one French edition at his disposal. After the three variant issues of his translation that appeared in 1658 there were four more editions in 1669, 1672, 1675, and 1691, all with Evelyn's name on the title-page and all usually bound with John Rose's *The English Vineyard Vindicated*, which was published in 1666. Although Rose, the royal gardener at St. James's, supplied the raw material for the book, it was organized and written by Evelyn, who signed the preface as Philocepos, the pseudonym he had used before in the first edition of *The French Gardiner*.

## 5. MASCALL, Leonard (d. 1589)

[small leaf] A Booke of the Arte and manner how to plant and Graffe all sorts of Trees, how to sette Stones and sow Pipins, to make Wild Trees to graffe on, as also remedies and medicines. With divers other new practises, by one of the Abbey of S. Vincent in Fraunce, Practised with his owne hands: devided into vii. Chapters, as here after more plainly shall appeare with an addition in the end of this booke, of certaine Dutch practises set forth and Englished, by Leonard Mascall. [woodcut of grafting 6 x 8 cm.] In laudem incisionis distichon, Hesperidum Campi quicquid Romanaque tellus. Fructificat nobis, incisione datur. ['In praise of grafting just two lines of verse: All that the western fields and Roman earth Bring forth is given us by the grafter's art.'] [small leaf] Imprinted at London. 1596. 4° 17 x 13.5 cm. A–D⁴ E⁴(E3 wrongly lettered D3) F–O⁴ P⁴(–P4) i–xxiv 1 2–84 85–94 (17 numbered 24 and corrected by hand; 24 numbered 17; 63 numbered 65) including one full-page woodcut and several smaller ones.

BINDING: Modern panelled calf by Zaehnsdorf, London; all edges gilt, but savagely trimmed.

PLATES: The full-page woodcut on page *xxiii* shows an

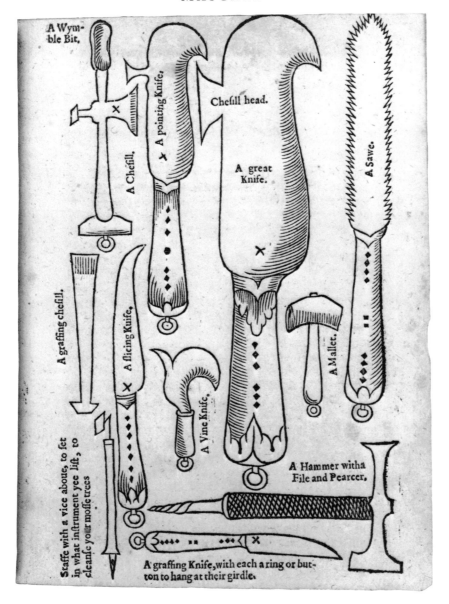

LEONARD MASCALL
*A Booke of the Arte and
Manner how to Plant and
Graffe . . .* seventh issue
1596 plate following
preface  Tools for plant-
ing and grafting

assortment of tools, most of them used for grafting. The woodcut of three grafted trees, with a gardener at work on the middle one, is printed on both the title-page and page 58. A diagram of a grafted apple tree is on page 73, a guide to planting vines on page 74, and an illustration of vine pruning on page 75. Page 80 has a plan of a hop garden.

MASCALL'S BOOK was first published about 1569, but about a dozen reprints kept it going until 1656. This copy is the seventh issue recorded by Blanche Henrey (*British Botanical and Horticultural Literature before 1800*, 1975, volume I, page 232). Most of the first sixty pages are a translation of Davy Brossard's *L'Art & Maniere de semer, & faire pepinieres des sauvageaux*, published in several editions from 1543. Brossard was a Benedictine of the abbey of

St Victor, near Le Mans, a gardening monk who wrote from his own experience without calling on the directions of classical authors.

Mascall worked as clerk of the kitchen for Matthew Parker, Archbishop of Canterbury, but his own house, Plumpton Place, was near Lewes in Sussex. He is sometimes said to have introduced pippin apples into his orchard there, but he was not the first to bring these apples from France, as Henry VIII's fruit gardener brought grafts over much earlier in the sixteenth century. The 'Pipins' of Mascall's title-page refer to pips or seeds rather than a specific variety of apple, for the book begins with this fruit, talking about setting seeds and moving, improving, and multiplying the seedlings, before moving on to stone fruits and nuts. There are directions for rooting cuttings from trees and bush fruits, as well as quinces and mulberries. The whole range of grafting techniques is described, then the transplanting and the care of young trees and how to deal with pests and diseases. The last chapter of the translated section is a rag-bag, ranging from early fruit to keeping oaks and roses evergreen. 'Certaine Dutch practises' reported by Mascall include grafting and pruning vines, making wine, grafting several kinds of apple on one tree, watering trees in dry weather, and managing a hop garden.

The book is dedicated to Sir John Paulet (Lord St John) and a quatrain at the end of the 'Authours Conclusion of this Table' or list of contents gives the author's version of the Latin epigraph on the title-page:

> To God be praises on hie
> in all our worldly planting,
> And let us thanke the Romaines also,
> For the Art of Graffing.

The same poetic hand is shown in 'The Booke to the Reader', which jingles along like pantomine verse:

> The pleasure of this thing is great,
> The profit is not small,
> To such men as will practice it,
> In things meere naturall . . .
> Myne author does not write by gesse
> Practise made him excell.
> If thou wilt practise as he did,
> Thou maiest find out much more:
> He hath not found out all the truth,
> That nature hath in store.

# 6. AUSTEN, Ralph (d. 1676)

[engraved title-page: within a border of rules, below 'Profits' and 'Pleasures' shaking hands] A Treatise of Fruit-trees Shewing the manner of Grafting, Setting, Pruning, and Ordering of them in all respects: According to divers new and easy Rules of experience; gathered in ỹ space of Twenty yeares. Whereby the value of Lands may be much improved, in a short time, by small cost, and little labour. Also discovering some dangerous Errors, both in ỹ Theory and Practise of ỹ Art of Planting Fruit-trees. With the Alimentall and Physicall use of fruits. Together with The Spirituall use of an Orchard: Held forth in divers Similitudes betweene Naturall & Spirituall Fruit-trees: according to Scripture & Experiềce. By Ra: Austen. Prac-tiser in ỹ Art of Planting [vignette 10 x 11 cm. showing a fruit garden encircled by] A Garden inclosed is my sister my Spouse: Thy Plants are an Orchard of Pomegranates, with pleasant fruits: Cant: 4:12:13 [with tools in corners of the rectangle] Oxford printed for Tho: Robinson 1653. 4° 18 x 14cm. ¶–3¶⁴ A–M⁴ ★⁴ ★★⁴ P–T⁴ *i–xxiv* 1–29 32–97 *98* (i.e. 96) *i–xii* 1–32 35–41 *42* (i.e. 40 but no text is missing in either section) and an engraved title-page.

BINDING: Tan diced Russia leather; marbled edges.

PLATE: The title-page is signed by the engraver, John Goddard.

RALPH AUSTEN spent most of his life in Oxford, where he established a garden and nursery for fruit trees. He also explored the literary background of the subject, for Anthony à Wood reported that he was 'entred into the public library [the Bodleian], to the end that he might find materials for the composition of a book which he was then meditating', his *Treatise of Fruit-trees*. The results of his research are visible in the thickets of quotations, taken from biblical, classical, and contemporary sources and distributed through his text. The link between 'Profits' and 'Pleasures' offered by a productive garden, and illustrated at the top of the book's title-page, repeats a theme common since medieval times, when a garden was primarily a source of food and medicine and its possible beauty nothing more than a welcome by-product. As Austen says in his preface: 'This Art is a full store-House, out of which may be brought both Meat, Drink, and Mony, it is a rich Myne, without bounds or bottom, out of which we may digg Profits and Pleasures great, and many, and worthy the study, and labour of the most wise and Learned.' The book is dedicated to Samuel Hartlib, a friend of the poet John Milton, and another exponent of enlightened rural economy.

Starting with nurseries and grafting, Austen goes on to advise on the pruning and treatment of fruit, from apples and pears to figs, walnuts, and vines. Dishes and drinks made from various fruits are also described, with details of their medicinal properties. 'Peares are more nourishing then Apples,' so he says, but the drinks made from them seem equally good, for 'it will beggar a Physitian to live where Syder, and Perry, are of generall use.' A section on 'Errors discovered concerning the Art of Planting: first in the writings of some: secondly in the practice of others' recommends caution: 'Men that are taught must not resigne up their Reason to their Teachers, but judge of what's said.' Austen then goes on to deal with wrong directions aimed at impossible results, wrong causes cited to explain observed effects, and practical mistakes in the choice and

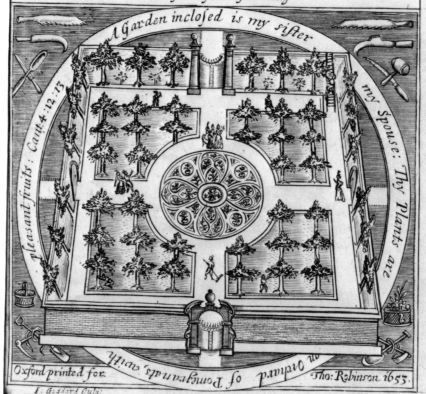

nurture of fruit trees. This section refers several times to Francis Bacon and his more rigorous attitude to received wisdom.

'The Spirituall Use of an Orchard', dedicated to the Reverend Doctor Langley, Master of Pembroke College Oxford, has its own title-page. As its name implies, it is more of a biblical anthology than a practical guide. A second edition of the *Treatise* in 1657 included the spiritual supplement, 'which being all divinity and nothing therein of the practice part of gardening, many therefore did refuse to buy it', according to the Oxford historian, Anthony à Wood. He may have been right, for a third edition in 1665, after Cromwell's Commonwealth had given way to the Restoration of King Charles II, abandoned spiritual orchards and concentrated on terrestrial ones alone.

## 7. DROPE, Francis (*c.* 1629–1671)

[within a ruled border] A Short and Sure Guid in the Practice Of Raising and Ordering of Fruit-Trees. Being the many years Recreation and Experience of Francis Drope, Bachelour in Divinity, late fellow of Magdalen College in Oxford. [rule] Oxford, Printed for Ric. Davis, An. Dom. 1672.
8° 15.5 x 9.5 cm. A⁶ B–H⁸ I⁴ *i–xii* 1–120.

BINDING: Half calf, grey marbled paper-covered sides. Armorial bookplate of Sir Thomas Neame (1885–1973), a fruit farmer from Kent. At the top of the title-page is an inscription with an illegible name crossed out and faintly replaced by 'George Snell——1720'.

AFTER the death of Francis Drope, a Canon of Lincoln Cathedral, his brother Edward published this little book of his observations on fruit trees. It is dedicated to Philip, Lord Wenman, Baron of Kilmainham, Viscount Tuam, 'presuming it may be serviceable for the preserving, and perfecting your new Orchard at Brackly', a village not far from Oxford in the neighbouring county of Northamptonshire. The village still has close links with Magdalen College, for the president of the college is one of the governors of the local Magdalen College School. Edward Drope also provided a preface to his brother's book: 'What he directs, is by his own Experience, which I take to be the best Instructer. Yet it was not his study (who was by profession a Divine) but his Recreation, an inoffensive delight he took in Planting.' As a Fellow of Magdalen College, Francis Drope must have spent a good many years living just across the High Street from the Oxford Botanic Garden, the oldest in Britain, which was established in 1621 on land owned by Magdalen. Another Fellow of Magdalen, William Browne, helped to compile the 1658 catalogue of the Garden's contents.

Drope's book gives advice on raising stocks from seed, establishing a nursery garden, and grafting and pruning older trees. His methods are gentle: 'Young Trees (like young cattle) do desire in their first years a tender education; which if not granted, they are hindred (or hide-

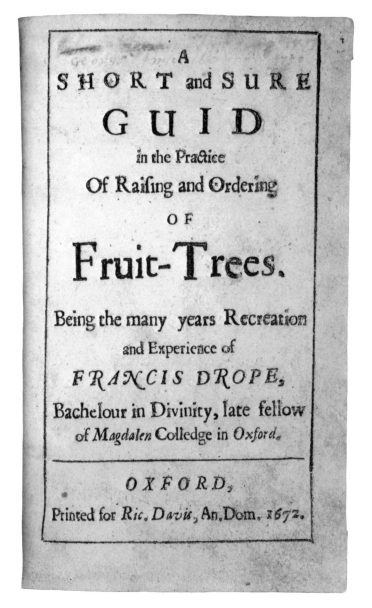

bound) in their growth and improvement.' In the words of E. A. Bunyard (*Journal of the Royal Horticultural Society*, 1915, volume 40, page 416) 'The fullest directions for raising stocks and, grafting trees are given in a style which is full of charm and quaintness. The grafting and budding of trees entirely occupy the writer, and the instructions throughout are of a very sound and practical order.'

# 8. COTTON, Charles (1630–1687)

The Planters Manual: being Instructions for The Raising, Planting, and Cultivating all sorts of Fruit-Trees, whether Stone-fruits or Pepin-fruits, with their Natures and Seasons. Very useful for such as are Curious in Planting and Grafting. [rule] By Charles Cotton Esq; [rule] London, Printed for Henry Brome, at the Gun in St. Pauls Churchyard, 1675.

8° 15 x 10 cm. A⁴ B–K⁸ *i–viii* 1–139 *140–144* and an engraved title-page.

BINDING: Modern green morocco, by Marcus Crahan.

PLATES: The frontispiece shows a series of rural occupations, from tree-planting to hay-making and bee-keeping. It is signed by Frederik Hendrik van Hove, a Dutch engraver who worked in England for the greater part of his life. The lettering within a central cartouche reads: 'The Planters Manuell Bÿ Charles Cotton eqs.' Beneath the picture are the words 'London Printed for Henrÿ Brome 1675'.

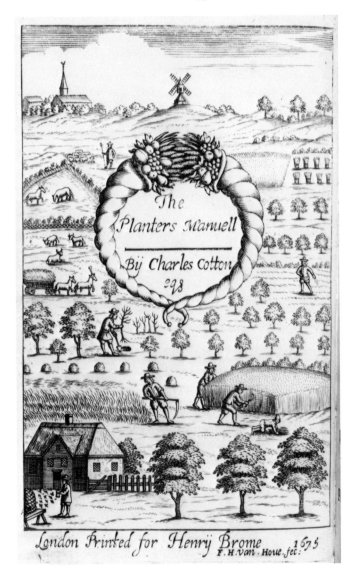

The engraved frontispiece, signed by F. H. van Hove

23

CHARLES COTTON is probably best known as the friend of Izaak Walton, the author of *The Compleat Angler*, but in his own right he was a minor poet and a translator from French, of Montaigne's essays, among other books. Although he did not acknowledge the fact in the book itself, *The Planters Manual* is a translation of *Instructions pour les Arbres fruictiers*, by M.R.T.P.D.S.M. (later identified as Monsieur R. Triquel or Triquet, Prieur de Saint Marc), first published in Paris in 1653 (see page 25). Cotton's preface 'to the reader' explains the production of the *Manual*:

> Though this little Treatise of Fruit-Trees was only written for the private Satisfaction of a very worthy Gentleman, who is exceedingly curious in the choice of his Fruits, and has great Judgment in Planting; yet having heard that Gentleman say it had given him the greatest Satisfaction of any Bauble he had seen of this kind, I began to think it might not be altogether unuseful to the Publick also, and therefore sent it to the Press . . . Seeing that (for ought I ever heard) Fruit-Trees are no Contrabanded Commodity betwixt the Nations, I cannot conceive but that it is worth the curiosity, pains and cost to furnish our selves from thence [that is, France] with those of the greatest excellency, both for Beauty and Flavour; nor why we should not as well better our selves by them this way, as altogether be debauch'd by their effeminate manners, luxurious kickshaws, and fantastick fashions, by which we are already sufficiently Frenchified, and more than in the opinion of the wiser sort of men, is consistent either with the constitution, or indeed the honour of the English Nation.

This ill-tempered advice was already being followed by many gardeners, like John Evelyn and Thomas Hanmer, who were buying fruit trees and other plants from nurseries in France or Holland. The book's most important directions are probably those about espaliers, which were still such a novelty in England that the translator inserted a definition of the term in a note: 'An Espallier is a Hedg-row of Fruit-trees set pretty near to one another, so that their boughs and branches are interlaced and interwoven into one another, and in that posture supported by a frame of Wood.' This French fashion of growing fruit was enthusiastically adopted on the other side of the English Channel, encouraged a little later by the translations of La Quintinie published in London in the 1690s (see pages 11–14). The French preference for pears, above all other fruit, is also reflected in the amount of space devoted to them in the book, for 'There are of Pears more different sorts, that deserve to be cultivated, than of any other fruit.' The varieties recommended, to be eaten raw or baked, are arranged month by month from June through to May, with nurserymen's names given for the rarer kinds.

The last four pages of this copy of *The Planters Manual* contain 'A Catalogue of some Books, Printed for, and sold by H. Brome, since the dreadful Fire of London, to 1675', that is, since 1666, when Henry Brome's stock of books was presumably destroyed in the great fire.

Instructions pour les Arbres fruitiers. Dernier edition. Reveuë & corrigée par l'Autheur. [vignette 3 x 3 cm. of crowned clasped hands holding a medallion bearing the initials CDS] A Paris, Chez Charles de Sercy, au Palais, au sixiéme Pillier de la Grand' Salle, vis-à-vis la montée de la Cour des Aydes, à la Bonne-Foy Couronnée. [rule 4 cm.] M. DC. LXXVI.

12° 15 x 8. 5 cm.  A–H in alternate 8s and 4s I⁶(–I6) *i–iv* 1–101 *102*.

BINDING: Bound with Jean Merlet *L'Abrege des bons Fruits*, 1675 (see page 26).

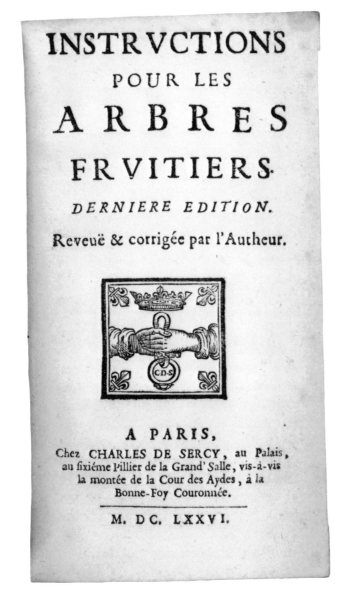

Title-page

THE FIRST EDITION of this manual was published in 1653, with the author identified only by the initials M.R.T.P.D.S.M. These were later elucidated in a *privilège* or licence for the book as Monsieur Robert Triquel (or Triquet), Prieur de Saint Marc. Later editions from Paris and The Hague also used the author's initials, but Charles de Sercy removed the most obvious sign of the book's writer in his 1676 edition, just as he suppressed similar indications in several other gardening books he reprinted. In this case he kept the preface 'Le Libraire au Lecteur' from Antoine Bertier, the book's first publisher, claiming that the manuscript was found among the papers of François Vautier, the King's physician, after his death:

> Apres la mort de M^r Vautier, premier Medecin du Roy, & un des plus curieux du Royaume, on a trouvé au nombre de ses Livres qu'il cherissoit le plus, ce Manuscrit, qui traite de la façon & facilité de bien planter, cultiver, tenir, & entretenir toutes sortes d'Arbres en Espaliers, contr'Espaliers, Hayes d'apuy, Buissons, Arbres de haute tige, ou en plein vent, & toutes sortes de Pepinieres; que les plus Curieux en ces sortes de Plants [*sic*] ont jugé que tous ceux qui avoient écrit de ces matieres n'avoient point recontré un si fort raisonnement, ny traité si nettement de tout ce qui se peut souhaiter pour la conservation des Arbres & des fruits: du temps de les cueillir pour les bien conserver; de la distinction des Saisons dans lesquelles ils meurissent; & quand il est à propos de les cueillir & manger. C'est pourquoy voyant l'approbation de tous les plus Sçavans; & desirant servir le Public, & contenter des personnes Illustres qui m'ont convié de le mettre sous la Presse, je l'ay facilement accordé.

This lofty pedigree may have helped to attract similar connoisseurs to the book's practical directions, a select list of varieties, and a complete calendar of pears recommending appropriate kinds for each month. These directions for the discriminating fruit-gardener were the basis of Charles Cotton's *Planters Manual* (1675: see page 23).

## 10. [MERLET, Jean (*fl.* 1654–1675)]

L'Abrege des bons Fruits, avec la maniere de les connoistre, & de cultiver les Arbres. Reveu & augmenté par l'Autheur, de plusieurs excellens & nouveaux Fruits. Divisé par Chapitres, selon les Especes. [vignette 3 x 3 cm. of crowned, clasped hands holding a medallion with the initials CDS] A Paris, Chez Charles de Sercy, au Palais, au Sixiéme Pillier de la Grande Salle, vis-à-vis la Montée de la Cour des Aydes, à la Bonne-Foy couronneé. [rule 5.5 cm.] M. DC. LXXV. Avec Privilege du Roy.

12° 15 x 8.5 cm. A–O in alternate 8s and 4s P⁶ *1–8* 9–177 *178–180.*

BINDING: Contemporary vellum. Armorial bookplate of Sir Thomas Neame (1885–1973), a fruit farmer from Kent. With which is bound two other books published by Charles de Sercy, Triquel's *Instructions pour les Arbres fruitiers* (see page 25) and Saint Etienne's *Instruction pour connoistre les bons fruits* (see page 28).

THE FIRST EDITION of Merlet's book was published in 1667, the second in 1675, and the third in 1690, all three by Charles de Sercy, who issued a flock of little gardening books in a format which gives them a strong family resemblance. A fourth edition was published much later, in 1740, so Merlet's book kept its value to gardeners. Its purpose, as described in the preface, included keeping up to date with new varieties:

> Ce petit Ouvrage, que j'ay reveu & augmenté dans cette deuxiéme Edition, de plusieurs Fruits excellens & curieux, découverts depuis ces dernieres années, qui contribuëront à l'embellissement de vos Jardins, & a la satisfaction particuliere de ceux qui les cultivent . . .

Once again, pears are the most popular fruit, filling seventy pages, but there are apples, plums, figs, strawberries, raspberries, gooseberries, cherries, apricots, peaches, vines, and nuts as well.

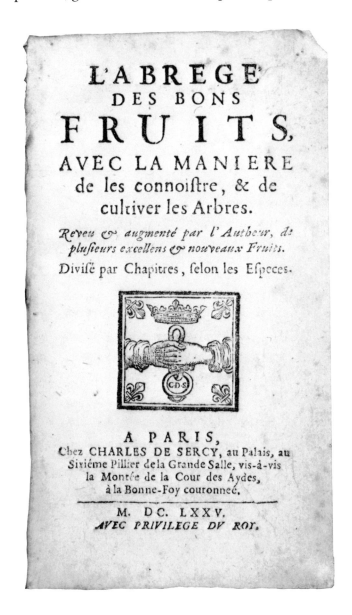

JEAN MERLET
*L'Abrege des bons Fruits*
second edition 1675
Title-page

## II. SAINT ETIENNE, Dom Claude

Nouvelle Instruction pour connoistre les bons fruits, selon les mois de l'année. Avec une Methode facile pour la connoissance des Arbres fruitiers, & la façon de les cultiver. Par Dom Claude S. Etienne' Religieux Feüillant. [vignette 3.5 x 3.5 cm. of crowned, clasped hands holding a medallion with the initials CDS] A Paris, Chez Charles de Sercy, au sixiéme Pillier de la Grand'Salle du Palais, vis-à-vis la montée de la Cour des Aydes, à la Bonne-Foy couronnée. [rule 4 cm.] M. DC. LXXVIII. Avec Privilege du Roy. 12° 15 x 8.5 cm. a⁴(±a1) A–R in alternate 8s and 4s *i–viii* 1–179 190–218 (i.e. 180–208).

BINDING: Bound with Jean Merlet *L'Abrege des bons Fruits* 1675 (see page 26).

Title-page

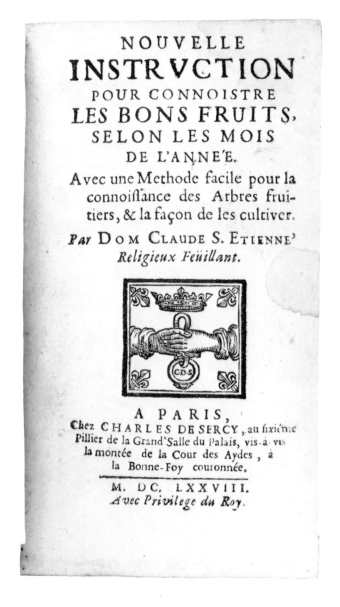

$S$AINT-ETIENNE'S BOOK first appeared in 1670, and this edition is the same text with a new title-page, giving the author's name in full, instead of initials alone. The publisher dedicated it to André le Nôtre, who is still the most famous French garden designer:

A Monsieur Le Notre, Controlleur General des Bastimens de France, & Intendant des Iardins de Sa Majesté.

Monsieur,

Encore qu'il ne soit pas permis ordinairement de faire des offrandes du bien d'autruy, je croy que l'interest du Public me fera pardonner mon larcin, & vous fera recevoir agreablement mon Present. C'est le travail d'un bon Pere Feüillent, qui imitant la vertu des anciens Anachorettes, a employé les heures qui n'estoient pas destinées dans son Ordre aux exercises de la Pieté, à travailler au Iardin, & à y élever de diferens Arbres. Vour verrez, Monsieur, qu'il a esté tres-curieux à les rechercher, & tres-intelligent à les connoistre & à les cultiver: Mais comme vous estes le plus connoissant des Hommes en cette Science, aussi bien qu'en beaucoup d'autres; & comme je sçay que vous honorez les Feüillens de vostre amitié; j'ay crû que vous me feriez obtenir pardon du larcin que j'ay fait à ce bon Religieux, & que vous auriez agreable le Present que je vous en faits.

The gardening monk—a Cistercian—began his book with a short section of general advice on planting and cultivating trees before plunging into a huge, month-by-month catalogue of pears, carefully distinguished as 'tres-bon', 'fort bon(ne)', 'excellent(e)', or 'telle quelle'. There are much shorter lists of plums, peaches, and apples, as well as an alphabetical index of the pear varieties, supplemented by a few extra ones of uncertain timing and a selection made for a patterned planting of dwarf trees.

## 12. LAWSON, William (*c.*1553–1635)

A New Orchard & Garden: or, The best way for Planting, Graffing, & to make any Ground good for a Rich Orchard: Particularly in the North, and Generally for the Whole Common-wealth, as in Nature, Reason, Situation, and all Probability, may and doth appear. With the Country House-wifes Garden for Herbs of Common use. Their Virtues, Seasons, Profits, Ornaments, Variety of Knots, Models for Trees, and Plots, for the best Ordering of Grounds and Walks. As also The Husbandry of Bees, with their several Uses and Annoyances: All being the Experience of Forty and eight Years Labour, And now the Sixth time corrected, and much Enlarged, By William Lawson. Whereunto is newly added the Art of Propagating Plants, with the true Ordering of all manner of Fruits, in their Gathering, Carrying home, and Preservation.

[vignette of tree-planting 7 x 10 cm. within a border of double rules, with a motto in English up the left side and Latin up the right] Skil and Pains, bring fruitful gains. Nemo sibi natus. London, Printed for George Sawbridge, at the Sign of the Bible on Ludgate-Hill. 1676.
4° 19.5 x 14 cm. A–L⁴ *i–vi* 1–82.

BINDING: Half calf, marbled paper sides. Inscribed by William Huddleston on the back of the title-page (see below), with several other notes in the text.

PLATES: The woodcut on the title-page is repeated on page 25. Several others showing garden plans, patterns for knot gardens, pruning or grafting tools, 'The perfect form of a Fruit-Tree', and a cross-section of a beehive are scattered through the text.

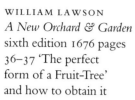

WILLIAM LAWSON
*A New Orchard & Garden*
sixth edition 1676 pages
36–37 'The perfect
form of a Fruit-Tree'
and how to obtain it

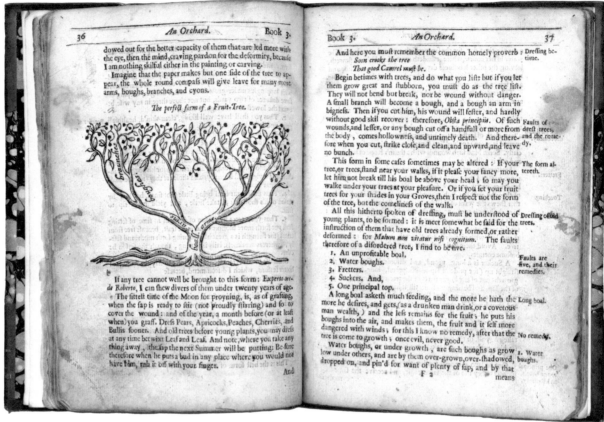

WILLIAM LAWSON'S *New Orchard and Garden* was first published in 1618, together with *The Country House-wifes Garden*, which was the first book in English specifically designed for female gardeners. A second edition in 1623 was also issued in the same year as part of Gervase Markham's *A Way to get Wealth*, and during the next seventy years appeared over and over again in subsequent editions of this favourite compilation. William Huddleston's note on the back of the title-page of this copy confirms its status as part of the Markham collection, for it reads, in part: 'Caled Gravis Markams Masterpeece. Wm Huddlstons Booke God give him Grase on it to Look. Not to Looke But understand for Learning is Better than houses is Better.' (The last two words, which echo those a little earlier, should read 'and Land' to complete the rhyme.) The 1623 second edition included for the first time a section on the art of propagating plants, contributed by Simon Harward. Although the title-page of this copy still mentions this section of the book, it is not among the contents.

Lawson had a garden near Teesmouth, in Yorkshire, so his book gave advice to gardeners in the colder north of England. His book is dedicated to Sir Henry Bellasis, or Belasyse (d. 1624), a baronet who lived at Newborough (now called Boroughbridge) and was interested in fruit trees. The author may have been describing his own garden, in the days when an orchard was

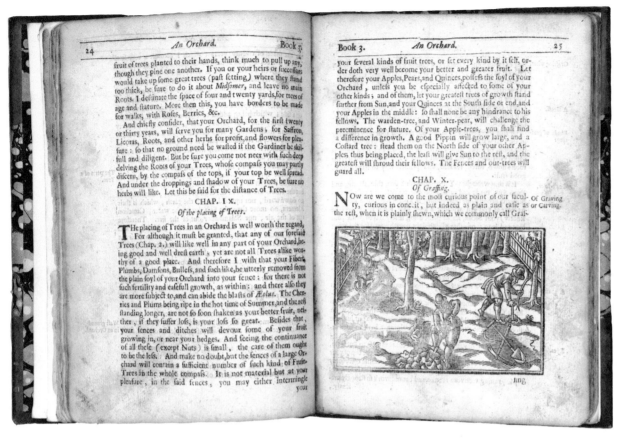

WILLIAM LAWSON
*A New Orchard & Garden*
sixth edition 1676 pages
24–25 Planning an orchard and planting trees

planted with herbs and flowers among its fruit trees, and the decorative functions of a garden were not separated from the purely useful ones. Certainly the book is based on his own long experience, and manages without the support of the quotations from classical writers so often called upon in this period to reinforce horticultural advice. Within a strong fence space must be made for walks among the trees and knots, so that 'the eye must be pleased with the form.' Good plants must be chosen and carefully settled in positions that suit them. Grafting, pruning, and other attentions must not be neglected, for 'the best form of a fruit tree cannot but both adorn and delight.' Pests and diseases must be dealt with, to preserve the paradise of 'a Garden, an Orchard of Trees and Herbs, full of pleasure, and nothing there but delights', among them sweet-smelling flowers in borders or beds, perhaps in the corners a mount or two, covered with fruit, and 'some Antick works' or other ornaments, with 'Store of Bees in a warm and dry Bee-house'. 'A Vine overshadowing a seat, is very comely, though her Grapes with us ripen slowly.'

*The Country House-wifes Garden*, according to its separate title-page (printed on page 57 of this copy) provided 'Rules for Herbs and Seeds of common Use, with their Times and Seasons when to Set and Sowe them. Together With the Husbandry of Bees, Published with Secrets very necessary for every House-wife: As also divers new Knots for Gardens', backed up by a quotation from Genesis: 'I have given unto you every Herb, and every Tree, that shall be to you for meat.'

## 13. LANGFORD, T. (*fl.*1681–1696)

[within a border of double rules] Plain and full instructions To raise all sorts of Fruit-trees That prosper in England; In that Method and Order, that every thing must be done in, to give all the advantage, may be, to every Tree as it is rising from its Seed, till it come to its full growth. Together With all necessary directions about those several ways of making Plantations, either of Wall-Fruit, or Dwarf-trees in Gardens, or large Standard-trees in Orchards or Fields. Touching which last, because it's so vast an Improvement of Land, all the profitable and practical ways are here directed to with all exactness. And In the last place the best directions are given for making liquors of the several sorts of Fruit. [rule] By T. Langford, Gent.

[rule] London, Printed by J. M. for Rich Chiswel at the Rose and Crown in S$^t$ Paul's Church-Yard, 1681. 8° 17.5 x 11 cm. A$^8$ a$^2$ B–C$^8$(C7+1) D–K$^8$ L$^6$ *i–xx* 1–148 (including eight pages listing 'Books Printed for and sold by Richard Chiswel') and 2 engravings.

BINDING: Brown calf, rebacked and repaired.

PLATES: Both are unsigned. The first, inserted after page 30, with an unnumbered leaf of explanation, shows various methods of grafting, the second, inserted opposite page 74, shows tools and the preferred layout of an orchard.

LANGFORD'S BOOK was given the best of starts by a letter from John Evelyn to its publisher, printed after the author's address to his readers, and saying:

I have read the *Treatise of Fruit-trees, &c*, which you lately put into my hand, and find the intire Mystery so generously discover'd from its very Rudiments, to its full perfection; that (with the ingenious and experienced Author) as I know of nothing extant which exceeds it, so nor do I of anything which needs be added to it. The Gentleman will by this free communication much oblige the whole Nation, and therefore needs not the suffrage of

Your Humble Servant,
J. Evelyn.

The author's own preface is pretty brisk. 'I have been long acquainted with raising Fruit-trees, and I think have left out nothing conducible to this end, that is any where else to be met with, and have added much more . . . The manner of expression I have used is plain, I have abstained carefully from all hard words, as judging it to much more purpose to be understood by a Plow-man, than commended by a Scholar.' From nurseries to seedlings and grafting, wall fruit and dwarf trees to plans of orchards and 'the annoyances about Fruit-trees', Langford gives clear directions. Then a chapter is devoted to vines, figs, quinces, medlars, walnuts, other nuts, and soft fruit (though no strawberries) before another recommends preferred varieties, and the last one talks about how to gather and store fruit, or make 'several sorts of liquors' from various kinds.

74

## The Practical Planter.

## CHAP. X.

### Of Planting an Orchard.

*Choice of ground.*

SECT. 1. So far as it lyeth in a Mans power to choose a plot of ground for his *Orchard*, he ought to do it with respect to these advantages.

It should lye conveniently near him, declining and lying open towards the *South, South-East,* or *South-West,* and defended from the *North, North-East,* and *North-West* winds by buildings, woods, or higher grounds; the land should rather incline to *dryness* than *moisture,* without *Springs;* the *Soil deep,* and a *fat* Earth, not a *stiff cold Clay,* or *binding Gravel,* nor a *light sandy* or *eskie hollow Earth:* Yet with good Husbandry, if it run not into the extreams of any of these, *Fruit-trees* may prosper reasonable well in it.

But the natural *Soil* for an *Orchard* is more to be respected than a *Garden,* for the *Garden-Fruit-trees,* and what else groweth there, rooteth little deeper than it may easily be *manured;* but *Pear-trees* and *Apple-trees* in *Orchards* should grow to be large Trees, and therefore send forth
roots

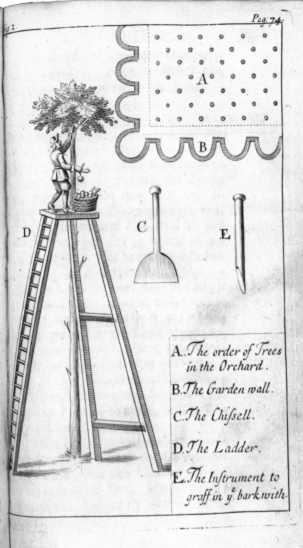

Pag: 74.

A. The order of Trees in the Orchard.

B. The Garden wall.

C. The Chisell.

D. The Ladder.

E. The Instrument to graff in y.̃ bark with.

T. LANGFORD
*Plain and Full Instructions to raise all sorts of Fruit-trees* 1681 page 74 and facing plate Planning and planting an orchard

A second, enlarged edition, published in 1696, was dedicated by Langford to his 'honoured master', Sir Samuel Grimston (1643–1700), who lived at Gorhambury in Hertfordshire, and was Member of Parliament for St Albans. The 1696 additions to Langford's book included a section on green-houses and their plants, and 'a catalogue of choice fruits, . . . greens and blossoming shrubs: to be had at Brompton park', the famous nursery garden run by George London and Henry Wise.

## 14. 'A LOVER OF PLANTING'

[within a border of double rules] The Compleat Planter & Cyderist. Together with the Art of Pruning Fruit-Trees. [rule] In two books. [rule]  I. Containing plain Directions for the propagating all manner of Fruit-Trees, and the most approved Ways and Methods yet known, for the making and ordering of Cyder, and other English Wines.   II. The Art of Pruning, or Lopping Fruit-Trees. With an Explanation of some Words which Gardeners make use of in speaking of Trees. With the Use of the Fruits of Trees for preserving us in Health, or for curing us when we are Sick. [rule] By a Lover of Planting. [rule] London, Printed for Thomas Bassett at the George near St. Dunstan's Church in Fleet-street. 1690.

8º 19 x 11 cm.  A⁸(±A1) B–R⁸ S⁴ i–xvi 1–256 *257–264*.

*With which is bound:*

[within a border of double rules] The Art of Pruning Fruit-Trees, with an Explanation Of some Words which Gardiners make use of in speaking of Trees. And a Tract Of the Use of the Fruits of Trees, For preserving us in Health, or for Curing us when we are Sick. [rule] Translated from the French Original, set forth the last Year by a Physician of Rochelle. [rule] London, Printed for Tho. Bassett, at the George near St. Dunstans Church in Fleet-street, 1685.

8º 19 x 11 cm.  A⁴ B–H⁸ i–viii 1–104 *105–112* (the last six pages containing 'A Catalogue of some books Printed for and to be sold by Thomas Bassett').

BINDING:  Contemporary panelled calf, rebacked. A pencil note on the front pastedown reads 'To send for Mulberry trees & Asparagus seed'. Armorial bookplate of the Earl of Harrington.

THE PREFACE to *The Compleat Planter* is dated 24 May 1683 and the book was first published in 1685, the same year as *The Art of Pruning Fruit-Trees*. The books were published together in a joint edition in 1690.

*The Compleat Planter*'s preface acknowledges 'the late Authors' John Evelyn, Ralph Austen, John Rea, Charles Cotton, and Leonard Meager, 'and above all, the ingenious Mr. Langford' (see page 32). The author continues: 'Out of them all . . . I cull'd such Rules and Observations, as with the addition of my one Experience, a more compendious and compleat Work thereof might be Compiled, which would save the Planter much Expense and Trouble in buying, and reading so many as have thereon writ.'

The book discusses not only cider but also perry, currant wine, cherry wine or brandy, gooseberry brandy, metheglin or hydromel, mead, and birch wine, made from the sap of birches. Two woodcut figures show a pruning tool (page 27) and a cider barrel (page 214).

*The Art of Pruning Fruit-Trees* is a translation of *L'Art de tailler les arbres fruitiers* (Paris, 1683) by Nicolas Venette, a physician of La Rochelle. The translator left the table of contents at the end of the book, in the French manner, and an English version of 'The Approbation of the Colledge-Royal of Physicians at Rochelle' dated '8th of March. 1683' is also given.

The author went to some trouble to make his directions understood. Woodcut figures in the text show just where to cut the trees, as described in the preface: 'I have caus'd seven Figures to be Grav'd which I judg'd necessary for the understanding of what I say.' The preface also claims: 'I have writ it after so popular a manner that the most Illiterate Gardiners might com-

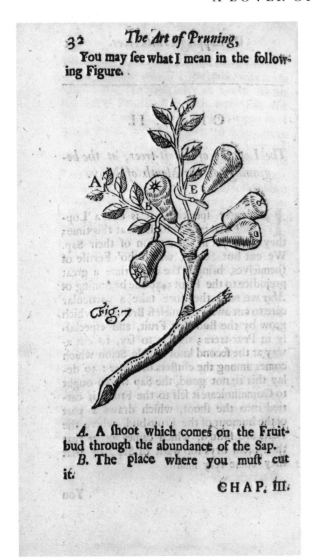

You may see what I mean in the following Figure.

*Fig. 7*

*A.* A shoot which comes on the Fruit-bud through the abundance of the Sap.

*B.* The place where you must cut it.

CHAP. III.

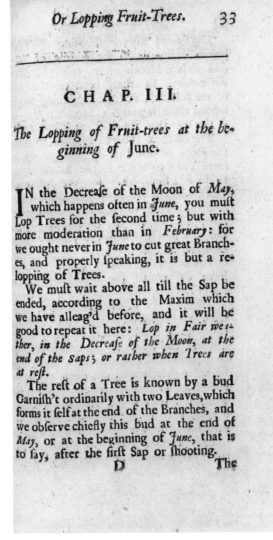

## CHAP. III.

*The Lopping of Fruit-trees at the beginning of* June.

IN the Decrease of the Moon of *May,* which happens often in *June,* you must Lop Trees for the second time; but with more moderation than in *February:* for we ought never in *June* to cut great Branches, and properly speaking, it is but a re-lopping of Trees.

We must wait above all till the Sap be ended, according to the Maxim which we have alleag'd before, and it will be good to repeat it here: *Lop in Fair weather, in the Decrease of the Moon, at the end of the Saps; or rather when Trees are at rest.*

The rest of a Tree is known by a bud Garnish't ordinarily with two Leaves, which forms it self at the end of the Branches, and we observe chiefly this bud at the end of *May,* or at the beginning of *June,* that is to say, after the first Sap or shooting.

D            The

NICOLAS VENETTE
*The Art of Pruning Fruit-Trees* 1685 pages 32–33
May pruning on a pear branch

prehend what I would say.' Illiterate or otherwise, gardeners were recommended to discriminate carefully, according to the fruit, the variety, and the season, before attacking their trees.

## 15. [FATIO DE DUILLIER, Nicholas (1664–1753)]

[within a border of double rules] Fruit-Walls Improved, By Inclining them to the Horizon: or, A Way to build Walls for Fruit-Trees; Whereby they may receive more Sun Shine, and Heat, than ordinary. [rule] By a Member of the Royal Society. [rule; vignette 4 x 4 cm. showing, within a border of double rules, a circle enclosing the sun shining on the earth, surrounded by another circle with the motto *Ultro ex his fontibus havri.* ('Drink from this fountain if you will.') T. L. (seven stars) V. S.] London: Printed by R. Everingham; and are to be sold by John

N. FATIO DE DUILLIER
*Fruit-Walls Improved*
1699 Frontispiece,
signed by Simon
Gribelin

Taylor, at the Sign of the Ship, in St. Paul's Church-Yard. MDCXCIX.

4° 25.5 x 19 cm. π² a⁴ b² c–d⁴ A⁴ C–R⁴ *i–iiiii–xxviii xxix–xxx* 1–128 and a frontispiece and 2 folding engraved plates.

*With which is bound:*

Nicolas Fatii Duillierii, R.S.S. Lineæ brevissimi descensus investigatio geometrica duplex. Cui addita est investigatio geometrica solidi rotundi, in quod minima fiat resistentia. [vignette 2.5 x 2.5 cm. of three rows of printers' flowers] Londini: Typis R. Everingham: Prostant apud Johannem Taylor, ad Insigne Navis, in Cæmeterio Divi Pauli, M DC XC IX.

4° A–C⁴ *1–2* 3–24 and 1 folding engraved plate.

BINDING: Red morocco with gilt decoration; all edges gilt. At the top of the spine are the letters 'a.s.' and at the foot 'F.951.' Armorial bookplate of William Arthur Cavendish-Bentinck, sixth Duke of Portland (1857–1943). Large-paper copy.

PLATES: The frontispiece and the first folding plate are signed S. Gribelin, the second folding plate and the mathematical one S. G., so all four were the work of Simon Gribelin (1661–1733), a French Huguenot engraver who settled in London in 1680. Within a border of leaves, the frontispiece shows Hermes and Athena. She is holding a bunch of grapes from the vine spread on a sloping wall in the background. The first folding plate shows a series of fruit walls, the second diagrams illustrating their construction. Engraved vignettes on pages iii and 1 are also signed by Gribelin, and the capitals M on page iii and A on page 1, as well as the tail-piece on page 128, are also his work.

NICHOLAS FATIO DE DUILLIER was born in Basle and educated in Geneva before moving on to Paris, The Hague, and eventually London, where he was elected a Fellow of the Royal Society in 1688. He was also a friend of Sir Isaac Newton, another F.R.S. Later in his life he lived at Worcester, in a region still noted for fruit-growing, where he died. His book on fruit walls describes a new kind of sloping terrace to help the cultivation of espalier fruits. This invention did not impress John Laurence, the country clergyman who published several books on fruit-growing about twenty years later (see page 44), for he thought the theory was not supported by practical trials. This is a wry comment, as *Fruit Walls* carries the imprimatur of the Royal Society, which was associated with the promotion of science tested by experiment and observation. Stephen Switzer also doubted the value of this idea (see page 55).

The book was dedicated to the Marquess of Tavistock, that is, Wriothesley Russell (1680–1711), Fatio's former pupil, who succeeded his father to become the second Duke of Bedford in 1700. 'While your Lordship fits Your Self, in Your Travels, to follow the Footsteps of so many glorious Ancestors, I prepare for You, in the Culture of Fruits, a Diversion to those great Occupations, which Your Birth will hereafter bring upon Your Lordship. I was walking with Your Lordship, when I first thought of this Way, to make our Gardens yield better Fruits.' The author's preface explains his 'mixture of Gardening and Geometry', thoughtfully telling readers unacquainted with mathematics that 'I have all along set, in the Margin, some Commas, over against such Places, as any one, not skilled in the Mathematicks, may freely avoid.' For the rest, it should be understood by 'any Lovers, of Gardening; even Ladies themselves not excepted.' Some basic advice about fruit is also recommended: 'Let the Rules and Directions given by Mounsieur La Quintinye be supposed here, as the main Foundation of our Hopes, in raising Fruit Trees.' These directions were by now available in English (see pages 11–14).

Above the directions to the book-binder on page xxx there is an 'advertisement' mentioning 'the Latin Mathematical Treatise, which will be bound at the end of some Copies of the present Discourse,' as in the Oak Spring copy.

Fatio's main studies were concerned with mathematics and astronomy, although his whole-hearted support of the Protestant religion was also a major factor in his life. This should be seen against the background of the persecution of the reformed faith in France and the exodus of Huguenots from that country, especially after Louis XIV's revocation of the Edict of Nantes in 1685. Fatio's fervour in the cause of the so-called 'Cévennes prophets' is said to have prompted Anthony Ashley Cooper, the third Earl of Shaftesbury, John Locke's pupil, to compose his 'Letter concerning Enthusiasm' in 1707. Fatio's zeal even led him to undertake a journey to Asia, in an effort to convert its inhabitants to Christianity.

N. FATIO DE DUILLIER
*Fruit-Walls Improved*
1699 page 118

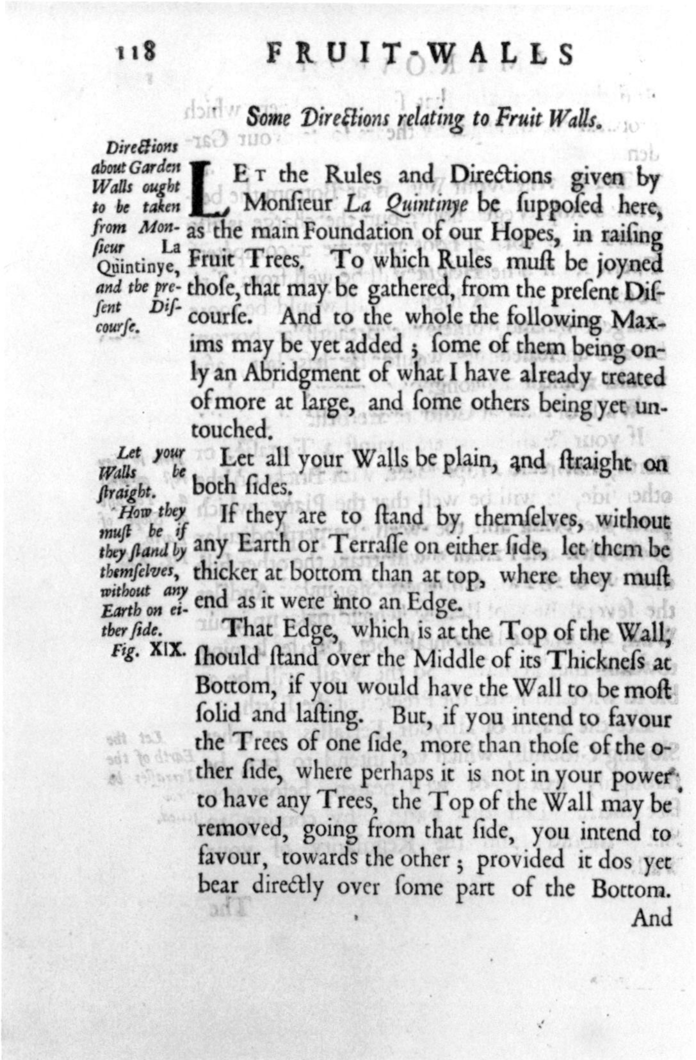

## FRUIT-WALLS

118

*Some Directions relating to Fruit Walls.*

*Directions about Garden Walls ought to be taken from Monsieur La Quintinye, and the present Discourse.*

LET the Rules and Directions given by Monsieur *La Quintinye* be suppofed here, as the main Foundation of our Hopes, in raifing Fruit Trees. To which Rules muft be joyned thofe, that may be gathered, from the prefent Difcourfe. And to the whole the following Maxims may be yet added; fome of them being only an Abridgment of what I have already treated of more at large, and fome others being yet untouched.

*Let your Walls be ftraight.*

Let all your Walls be plain, and ftraight on both fides.

*How they muft be if they ftand by themfelves, without any Earth on either fide.*

*Fig. XIX.*

If they are to ftand by themfelves, without any Earth or Terraffe on either fide, let them be thicker at bottom than at top, where they muft end as it were into an Edge.

That Edge, which is at the Top of the Wall, fhould ftand over the Middle of its Thicknefs at Bottom, if you would have the Wall to be moft folid and lafting. But, if you intend to favour the Trees of one fide, more than thofe of the other fide, where perhaps it is not in your power to have any Trees, the Top of the Wall may be removed, going from that fide, you intend to favour, towards the other; provided it dos yet bear directly over fome part of the Bottom.

And

38

# FRUIT IN FRANCE & BRITAIN

II  *The Early Eighteenth Century*

# 16. LIGER, Louis (1658–1717)

Culture parfaite des Jardins fruitiers & Potagers: avec Des Dissertations sur la taille des arbres. Par le Sieur Louis Liger. Nouvelle edition, Revûe, corrigée, & augmentée de plusieurs nouvelles Expériences. [printers' flowers, 1 x 1 cm.] A Paris, Chez Damien Beugnié, dans la grande Sale du Palais, au Pilier des Consultations, au Lion d'Or, [rule 6 cm.] M. DCCXIV. Avec Privilege du Roy.

12° 15.5 x 9.5 cm. ã⁸ A–2Z in alternate 8s and 4s 3A–3B⁴ 3C² i–xvi 1–569 570–572 including several woodcut diagrams.

BINDING: Contemporary calf; bookplate of Arthur Hugh Smith Barry, of Marbury Hall, Cheshire.

B. Ne croift-il point de branches chifonnes fur les figuiers ainfi que fur les autres arbres fruitiers?

M. J. Ouy, & pour lors n'eftant capables que d'apporter de la confufion par tout où elles naiffent, on obferve de les retrancher entierement.

B. Les figuiers ne donnent-ils pas auffi de faux bois?

M. J. Sans doute, & on le reconnoift facilement aux yeux qui y paroiffent, & qui font pour l'ordinaire plats, & éloignez les uns des autres; & lorfque fur un figuier telles branches s'offrent à nos yeux, les veritables regles de la taille veulent qu'on les racourciffe de beaucoup, pour les obliger dans la fuite de produire d'autres branches propres à porter du fruit.

### E X E M P L E.

*Dans un figuier en efpalier.*

A, Figuier en efpalier. B, branches de l'année précedente mal aouftées, & dont les extrémitez paroiffent noires, & qu'il faut couper. C, endroit où il faut cou-

per ces branches. D, branches de faux bois. E, endroit où l'on doit les tailler. F, branches chifonnes. G, où les retrancher. H, bonnes branches laiffées entieres.

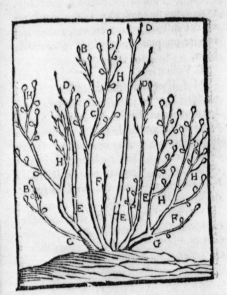

B. Toutes les obfervations que vous

LOUIS LIGER
*Culture . . . des Jardins fruitiers* second edition
1714 pages 526–27
An espalier fig tree

LOUIS LIGER, sieur d'Auxerre, wrote many books on husbandry, gardening, and rural economy in general, with several more on related subjects like hunting, fishing, and horses. The first edition of his *Culture parfaite des Jardins fruitiers* was published in 1702. Several changes and additions were made in the second edition, with the pattern of question and answer refined to a dialogue between Maistre Jacques, a knowledgeable gardener, and his son Bertran. Liger's reasons for the alterations are given in his preface (page *iii*):

> Voice une seconde Edition de ce Livre, qu'on n'espere pas etre moins bien reçûe du Public que la premiere, tant par les augmentations considerables qu'on y a faites, que par le nouvel ordre des matieres qu'on y a établie. On a crû qu'un entretien familier d'un homme bien entendu dans le jardinage, y plairoit mieux que de simples demandes & réponses; en effet, on sent dans ce stile quelque chose de moins sec que dans le premier: c'est un Pere qui instruit son Fils; tout y est naturel.

The first part of the book deals with basic subjects like soil and planning before turning to kitchen gardens. The second part is on nursery gardens, and the third on fruit trees and their pruning, with one chapter (XIX) 'De certaines connoissances nécessaires aux Inspecteurs & Directeurs des Jardins fruitiers & potagers des Maisons Royales, & de ce qu'ils doivent observer pour bien s'acquitter de leur employ', which seems to reflect the work of La Quintinie, who occupied just such a position in charge of the fruit and kitchen gardens of Louis XIV. Liger's book ends with a section on fig trees.

## 17. LAURENCE, John (1668–1732)

[within a border of double rules] The Clergy-Man's Recreation: Shewing the Pleasure and Profit Of the Art of Gardening. [rule] Quære agite ô proprios generatim discite Cultus, Agricolæ, fructusque feros mollite colendo. Virg. Georg. ['Then let the Learned Gard'ner mark with care The Kinds of Stocks, and what those Kinds will bear'—*Georgics* II translated by John Dryden, 1697; rule] By John Lawrence, A.M. Rector of Yelvertoft in Northamptonshire, and sometime Fellow of Clare-Hall in Cambridge. [rule] The Fifth Edition [double rule] London: Printed for Bernard Lintott, between the Temple Gates in Fleet-street, 1717.
8° 19.5 x 12 cm. A–F⁸ *i–xii 1* 2–84 including an engraved frontispiece.

BINDING: Contemporary panelled calf; with which is bound *The Gentleman's Recreation*, second edition, 1717,

*The Lady's Recreation*, by 'Charles Evelyn', 1717, and *The Fruit-Garden Kalendar*, 1718.

PLATE: The frontispiece, signed by the engraver Simon Gribelin, shows fruit trees planted along walls round a courtyard full of fountains and a parterre. It is similar to one by the same engraver used in James Gardiner's translation from Latin of René Rapin's poem *Of Gardens* (1706).

. . . By John Lawrence, AM. Rector of Bishops Weremouth. [rule] The Sixth Edition. [double rule] London: Printed for Bernard Lintot, at the Cross-keys, between the Temple Gates in Fleet-Street, 1726.
8° 19.5 x 12 cm. A⁸(A2+χ1.2, 2χ1) B–F⁸ [2] *i* ii–vi [8] *1* 2–84 including an engraved portrait frontispiece.

BINDING: Contemporary panelled calf, rebacked; with

which is bound *The Gentleman's Recreation*, third edition, 1723, and *The Fruit-Garden Kalendar*, 1718. The name Boycott is inscribed on the fly-leaf.

PLATE: This edition, the sixth, was the first with the portrait frontispiece signed by the engraver George Vertue and showing the author above an array of fruit.

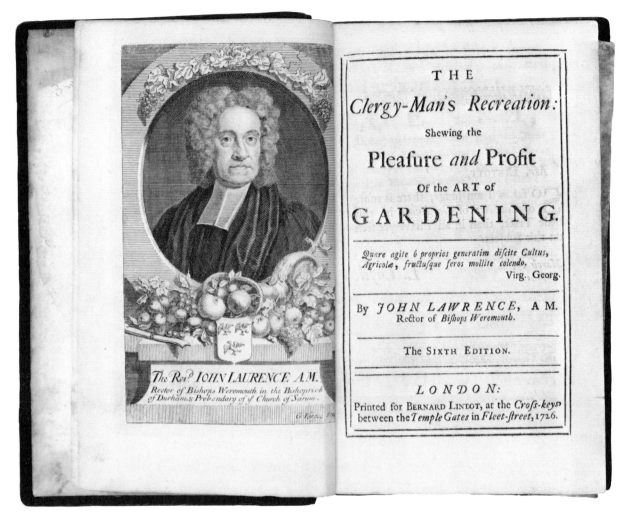

Portrait frontispiece signed by the engraver, George Vertue, and title-page

JOHN LAURENCE (who preferred this spelling of his name) was the son of a country clergyman. Following his father's pattern of life, he became rector of Yelvertoft, North-amptonshire, not far from Rugby, in 1700. He moved there from Cambridge, where he had been a Fellow of Clare Hall (now Clare College). Once settled at Yelvertoft he took to gardening, especially the cultivation of fruit trees, which had the advantage of producing both flowers and food. The first of his trio of books on the subject, *The Clergy-Man's Recreation*, appeared in 1714, and was so popular that it ran through five editions in three years, with a sixth in 1726, as well as forming part of several collections of the author's own or other works. It was based firmly on his own achievement in reclaiming a garden 'quite over-run with Couch or Twitch-grass,

Nettles and Goose-berry Bushes; and, which was a great deal worse, upon a wet white Clay, lying within half a Foot of the Surface' (preface). To those who thought clergymen might spend their time more usefully he explained, also in his preface:

> that the Diversions and Amusements of a Garden, with moderate Exercise, are not only most delightful to those that love them, but most wholsom to those that use them. . . . Most of the Time that I can spare from the necessary Care and Business of a large Parish, and from my other Studies, is spent in my Garden, and making Observations towards the farther Improvement thereof. For I thank God this sort of Diversion has tended very much to the Ease and Quiet of my own Mind.

He tackled the difficult patch at Yelvertoft as soon as possible, building a nine-foot brick wall and planting fruit trees along it. By the time he published his advice for other gardeners he was able to recommend pruning trees against walls (preferably brick ones) for horizontal growth, keeping the strong shoots and cutting out all the weak ones. A nursery of young trees was an almost essential adjunct to any garden, especially if evergreen hedges were wanted. Yew was Laurence's favourite plant for these: 'To make one in love with these Hedges, you need only take a walk either in Paradise or the Physick-Gardens at Oxford, where you are presented with all that Art and Nature can do to make these things most agreeable to the Eye.' The Oxford Botanic Garden is still on the same site, but without its yew hedges.

The choice of trees was important too: 'It is thought adviseable not to perplex a Lover of Fruit with an unnecessary number and variety of Sorts, when he has room only for a few good ones of each Kind. He that has room, and would encrease his collection, may have recourse to Monsieur Quintinye, or to the Abridgement by Mr. London and Wise, and he will quickly have his Curiosity satisfied.'

The sixth edition has an advertisement on page 84, saying 'Mr Laurence . . . has here laid down such Rules and Observations, founded upon his own Experience, as may be of great advantage to the Improvement of Fruit-Trees.' The author lacked patience with theorists whose ideas did not work in practice, for on page 46 he reproved Fatio de Duillier thus: 'To so little Purpose is it for Men of Theory to philosophize about these Matters, without having had some Experience and Knowledge in the Practice. . . . As an ingenious Author has done, who has wrote a Book in Quarto, to shew in a Mathematical Way the great Advantage of Slope-Walls.' So much for *Fruit-Walls Improved* (see page 37): Laurence admitted that sloping walls allowed more sun to reach the fruit, but the effect of the extra warmth was cancelled out by the retention of more rain, dew, or frost. His own experiment on transmitting variegation in jasmine, reported on page 65 of his book, attracted the attention of other botanists, including Richard Bradley, who reprinted it. In retrospect this experiment has been seen as an early record of a virus being passed on by grafting.

A dedication to Henry Grey, Duke of Kent (1671–1740) was added to some copies of the fifth and sixth editions of *The Clergy-Man's Recreation*, usually removed from copies of *The Fruit-Garden Kalendar* bound with them. The estate of this courtier and 'great Lover and Encourager of vegetable Nature' was near Brackley, not far from Yelvertoft. Laurence dedicated his *Fruit-Garden Kalendar* to him, but this dedication was often transferred to copies of *The Clergy-Man's Recreation* at the start of collections of Laurence's books in the same binding. All editions of *The Clergy-Man's Recreation* were also supplied with a note from Robert Lumley Lloyd (d. 1730), the rector of St Paul's, Covent Garden, who had a famous garden at Cheam in Surrey. Bernard Lintot, the publisher, to whom the note was addressed, inserted it on the back of the title-page in all editions, reasonably enough, for it said, in its entirety: 'So far as I am Judge, there is more of the Art of Gardening in this little Tract, then in all I have yet seen on this Subject.'

The little book was so successful that Laurence and Lintot supplemented it with two more on the same subject, *The Gentleman's Recreation* (see below) and *The Fruit-Garden Kalendar* (see page 47). After writing these three books, Laurence moved in 1721 to the richer parish of Bishops Wearmouth, near Durham, where he set to work on the improvement of a cold and exposed garden. In 1726 he published a larger book, *A New System of Agriculture*, over half of which is concerned with gardening rather than husbandry.

# 18. LAURENCE, John (1668–1732)

[within a border of double rules] The Gentleman's Recreation: or the Second Part of the Art of Gardening Improved. Containing several New Experiments and Curious Observations relating to Fruit-Trees: Particularly a New Method of building Walls with Horizontal Shelters. [rule] Illustrated with Copper Plates. [rule] —— Si quid novisti rectius istis, Candidus imperti; si non, his utere mecum. Hor. ['If you know something better than these precepts, pass it on. If not, join me in following these.' Horace *Epistularum* I: rule] By John Laurence, M.A. Rector of Yelvertoft in Northamptonshire. [rule] To which is added by way of Appendix, A new and familiar way to find a most exact Meridian Line by the Pole-Star: whereby Gentlemen may know the true Bearings of their Houses and Garden Walls, and regulate their Clocks and Watches, &c. By Edward Laurence, Brother to the Author of this Book. [rule] The Second Edition. [rule] London: Printed for Bernard Lintott between the Temple-Gates in Fleetstreet. 1717.

8° 19.5 x 12 cm. A⁸ a² B–H⁸ I² *i–xx* 1 2–115 *116* including an engraved frontispiece, plus 3 folding engravings.

BINDING: Bound with *The Clergy-Man's Recreation*, fifth edition, 1717.

PLATES: Both the frontispiece of a fruit garden and the three folding plates (two of fruit-garden plans, with the trees named, the third of a tree against a wall) are unsigned.

. . . By John Laurence, M.A. Rector of Bishops-Weremouth in the Bishoprick of Durham, and Prebendary of the Church of Sarum . . . The Third Edition. [rule] London; Printed for Bernard Lintot, between the Temple-Gates in Fleetstreet. 1723.

Collation as second edition, 1717, except for the addition of a fourth folding plate holding a diagram to illustrate Edward Laurence's directions. The unsigned headpiece on page 1 of the second edition was replaced by one signed 'F.H.' for Francis Hoffman, in the third. Hoffman's decoration was also used in Robert Furber's *Catalogue* of 1727, and his work appears again in Furber's *Short Introduction to Gardening* (see page 66).

BINDING: Bound with *The Clergy-Man's Recreation*, sixth edition, 1726.

JOHN LAURENCE
*The Gentleman's Recreation* second edition
1717 Frontispiece and title-page

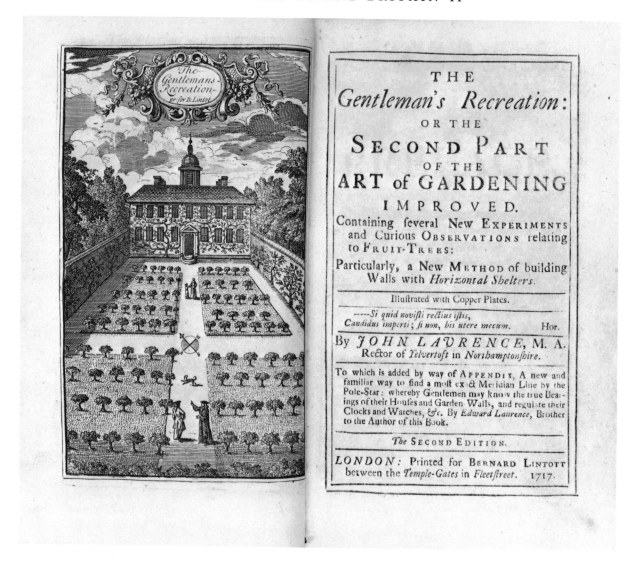

BUILDING ON the success of *The Clergy-Man's Recreation*, Laurence published *The Gentleman's Recreation* two years later, in 1716, with a second edition in 1717 and a third in 1723. In this book he concentrated on reasons for the failure of fruit trees and proposed remedies ranging from moving the garden, through better cultivation and pruning, to adding 'horizontal shelters' to fruit walls. 'The Design of the following Treatise is to put Gentlemen into a Method of having the most and the best of all sorts of Fruit, and that in the easiest, the cheapest and most expeditious ways' (page 7), allowing each tree enough room on a wall not more than eight or nine feet high. Samuel Collins was sufficiently provoked by this book to burst into print with *Paradise Retriev'd* (1717: see page 51).

An appendix to *The Gentleman's Recreation* contains a letter from Edward Laurence, a

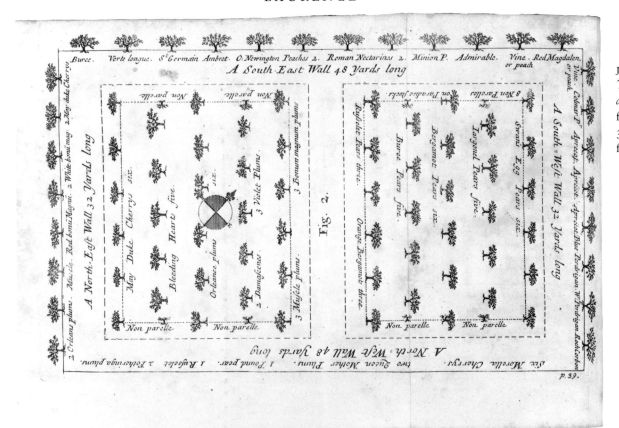

A South East Wall 48 Yards long

Fig. 2.

P. 39.

JOHN LAURENCE
*The Gentleman's Recreation* second edition 1717 folding plate facing page 39 A plan of a fruit garden

surveyor and John's brother, with directions for finding a meridian line. The last page of the book holds an advertisement for Edward's professional services, from drawing maps and measuring timber to teaching accounting 'and all other useful Parts of the Mathematicks'.

## 19. LAURENCE, John (1668–1732)

[within a border of double rules] The Fruit-Garden Kalendar: or, A Summary of the Art of Managing the Fruit-Garden. Teaching in order of Time what is to be done therein every Month in the Year. Containing several new and plain Directions, more particularly relating to the Vine. [rule] . . . . Redit Horticolæ labor actus in Orbem; Atque acer curas venientem extendit in Annum, Per sequitur Vitem attondens, fingitque putando. Vir. Geor. lib. 2. ['Much labour is requir'd in Trees, to tame Their wild disorder, and in ranks reclaim'—translated by John Dryden, 1697; rule] To which is added, An Appendix of

Page 123 Vignette of insect pests hatching on the leaves of a pear tree

47

the Usefulness of the Barometer; with some short Directions how to make a right Judgment of the Weather. [rule] By John Laurence, M.A. Rector of Yelvertoft, in Northamptonshire. [rule] London: Printed for Bernard Lintot, at the Cross Keys, between the Temple Gates, in Fleetstreet. 1718.
8° 19.5 x 11.5 cm. *A*⁸ B–K⁸ L⁴ [4] *i* ii–vi i–v *vi* 1–149 *150–152* and an unsigned folding frontispiece, showing a tree with bushes beneath, all carefully pruned.

BINDING: Bound with *The Clergy-Man's Recreation*, fifth edition, 1717, *The Gentleman's Recreation*, second edition, 1717, and *The Lady's Recreation*, by 'Charles Evelyn', 1717. A second copy, lacking the dedication, is bound with *The Clergy-Man's Recreation*, sixth edition, 1726, and *The Gentleman's Recreation*, third edition, 1723.

JOHN LAURENCE
*The Fruit-Garden Kalendar* 1718 folding plate facing title-page Removing weak branches from a pear tree (figure 1); vines trained as cordons (figure 2)

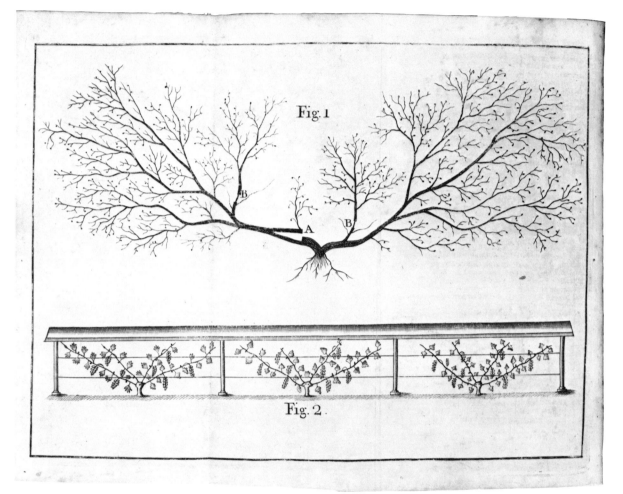

THE THIRD of Laurence's fruit books, *The Fruit-Garden Kalendar*, was written 'To make my Two former Treatises of Gardening compleat, and if possible more intelligible' (preface, page i). He had allowed himself to be prevailed upon 'because (so far as I can observe) most of our modern Authors in this way, have done little else but transcribe from Evelyn, Quintiney, and Woolridge; and therefore have been generally so unfortunate, as to insert their Errors and Mistakes, as well as their useful Rules.' Later in the preface (page iii) he went on: 'Indeed it seems to me no small Reproach to the English Nation, that we suffer so many French Books of Gardening to be obtruded upon us, containing Rules calculated for another Climate, and which tend to lead us into many Errors.'

The *Kalendar* virtually replaced the parts of Evelyn's *Kalendarium Hortense* relating to fruit, dealing with each kind, except apples, month by month. At this time apples were always grown as standards, needing less specialized attention than wall fruit. Grapes were particularly well cared for, as at Belvoir Castle in Lincolnshire, where the Duke of Rutland heated the sloping walls on which they grew from Lady Day to Michaelmas, 'whereby he is rewarded with the largest Grapes, and even the best Frontignacs in July' (page 22). A little later the Belvoir grapes were protected by glazed houses, on the advice of Stephen Switzer.

An exchange of letters with Richard Bradley about a blight caused by insects on pear trees occupies pages 121 to 131, while an appendix 'Of the Usefulness of the Barometer, with some short Directions how to make a right Judgment of the Weather' completes the book. Lintot filled every blank space with advertisements for his other publications, one list at the end of the preface, another before the appendix (including poems by Mr Pope and Mr Gay), and a third filling the last three pages.

Laurence and Bradley were also associated in support of Stephen Switzer's *The Practical Fruit-Gardener* (see page 53), 'revised and recommended by the Rev.d Mr. Laurence and Mr. Bradley' and first published in 1724, though it is not clear how much help they gave Switzer, beyond providing the short notes of commendation printed in the book.

In the first of the Oak Spring copies of *The Fruit-Garden Kalendar* the dedication to Henry Grey, Duke of Kent (see pages 44–45) is in its proper place; in the second it has been removed and inserted in *The Clergy-Man's Recreation*, sixth edition, 1726, which begins the volume.

# 20. 'EVELYN, Charles' (*fl.* 1717)

[within a border of double rules] The Lady's Recreation: or, The Third and Last Part Of the Art of Gardening Improv'd. Containing,   I. The Flower-Garden; shewing the best Ways of propagating all Sorts of Flowers, Flower-Trees, and Shrubs; with exact Directions for their Preservation and Culture in all Particulars.   II. The most commodious Methods of erecting Conservatories, Green-Houses, and Orangeries; with the Culture and Management of Exoticks, Fine-Greens, Ever-Greens, &c.   III. The Nature of Plantations in Avenues, Walks, Wildernesses, &c. with Directions for the Raising, Pruning, and Disposing of all lofty Vegetables.   IV. Mr. John Evelyn's Kalendarium Hortense, methodically reduc'd: Interspers'd with many useful Additions. [rule] By Charles Evelyn, Esq; [rule] To which are added, Some curious Observations concerning Variegated Greens, by the Reverend Mr. Laurence. [rule] London: Printed for J. Roberts, near the Oxford-Arms in Warwick-Lane, 1717. Price 2s. stitch'd.

8° in half-sheets 19.5 x 12 cm. a⁴ (−a3) b⁴ B−2B⁴ 2C⁴ [2] i−iv *v−xii* (gathering b forming the contents list bound before the frontispiece) *1* 2−200 and an engraved frontispiece.

BINDING: Bound with John Laurence *The Clergy-Man's Recreation*, fifth edition, 1717.

PLATES: The frontispiece of a walled garden is signed by the engraver Elisha Kirkall (*c*.1682–1742), whose work is found in many other botanical books too. He was also involved in some of the earliest colour-printing in England.

'CHARLES EVELYN'
*The Lady's Recreation*
1717 Frontispiece, engraved by Elisha Kirkall, and title-page

'CHARLES EVELYN', an unidentified author, used the name of John Evelyn and echoed the titles of John Laurence's books, *The Clergy-Man's Recreation* and *The Gentleman's Recreation*, in an attempt to sell his own. Laurence, in the preface to his *Fruit-Garden Kalendar* (page ii) wrote: 'The Book called the *Lady's Recreation* could not be published by my Approbation, because it was never seen by me, till it was in Print: Besides, I have Reason to think it was an Artifice of the Booksellers to impose upon the World, under the borrowed Name of Evelyn.'

As J.S.L. Gilmour has said (in *Huntia*, 1965, volume 2, page 121): 'This is all the more likely in view of the fact that the publisher was the notorious Edmund Curll! I can find no other trace of Charles Evelyn, and no doubt Curll invented him under a famous surname, cashed in on the word "Recreation" made popular by Laurence, and corresponded with Laurence under the invented name [to elicit his observations on variegated plants]. Who wrote the book will probably never be known.' The attempt to share Laurence's popularity appears to have had some success, as *The Lady's Recreation* had two more editions in 1718 and 1719 and is often found in the same binding as editions of the Laurence books. There were both London and Dublin versions in which collections of the books were even given a joint title-page.

The *Kalendarium Hortense*, which 'Charles Evelyn' claimed was a revised version of the one first published by John Evelyn in 1664, bears no relation to the earlier almanac, except in its arrangement month by month.

## 21. COLLINS, Samuel (*fl.* 1717)

[within a border of double rules] Paradise Retriev'd: [rule] Plainly and Fully Demonstrating The Most Beautiful, Durable, and Beneficial Method of Managing and Improving Fruit-Trees Against Walls, or in Hedges, Contrary to Mr. Lawrence, and Others upon gardening. Together with a Treatise on Mellons and Cucumbers. [rule] By Samuel Collins Esq; of Archester in Northampton-shire. [rule] —Satis est servare Repertum. Claudian. [*De Consolatu Stilichonis* II. 'It is greater to preserve what is already known'; rule] London: Printed for John Collins, Seedsman, over-against the May-Pole in the Strand; And sold by him, and R. Burleigh, in Amen-Corner. M. DCC. XVII.

4° 18.5 x 12 cm. A⁴ ⋆a² A–N⁴ O²(–O2) [2] i–v *vi–x 1–5* 6–106 and 2 unsigned, folding engravings showing 'Pears on an Espalier' and 'A Wall of Peaches and Nectarines'.

BINDING: Chemical calf, rebacked.

SAMUEL COLLINS, possibly a relation of John Collins, the seedsman who published his book, was so annoyed by John Laurence's books, especially *The Gentleman's Recreation* (first published in 1716: see page 45), that he put his own methods of growing fruit into print, though without achieving a similar success. As he said in his preface (page iv): 'The only Motive that induced me to write on this Subject, I must own, was the Sight I had of Mr. Lawrence and his Garden, after reading of his Book: I hope since that Reverend good Man has *preached* the Nobility, Gentry, and Clergy, into an Approbation of it, this may not come too late to Entertain them with Reasons, tho' of a different Practice.'

Collins thought Laurence suggested too much cutting affecting large branches of pears and plums and that the 'shelters' he recommended were absolutely useless in producing better fruit. 'I personally satisfied this Reverend Gentleman, That his Horizontal Tiles were purely Chimerical' (page 71). He also claimed that Laurence had confessed that he hadn't tried this method of protecting fruit until after his book had asserted its usefulness.

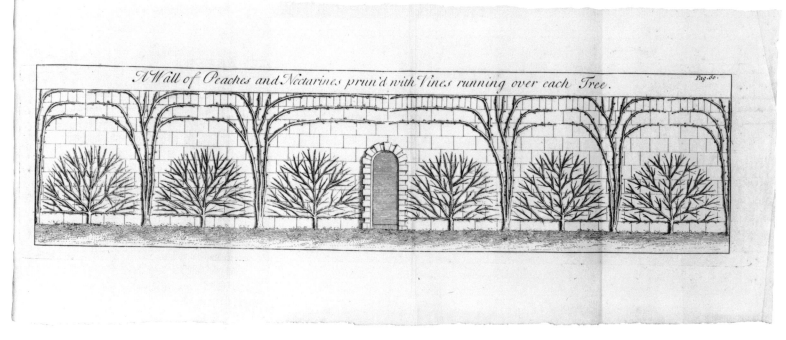

A Wall of Peaches and Nectarines prun'd with Vines running over each Tree.

*Pag.60.*

SAMUEL COLLINS
*Paradise Retriev'd* 1717
folding plate between
pages 60 and 61 'A Wall
of Peaches and Nec-
tarines prun'd with
Vines . . .'

A sequel to the argument was produced by Bernard Lintot, Laurence's publisher, who issued an anonymous pamphlet in 1717 entitled *A Letter from a Gentleman in the Country to his Friend in Town: concerning two books lately published by Mr. Bradley, and Mr. Collins, treating of Planting and Gardening.* Bradley's *New Improvements of Planting and Gardening*, which included some of Laurence's work, was praised in a single paragraph, while the rest of the booklet's thirty-four pages was used to rebuke Collins. He should 'have been contented to have told the world of a successful way he had of managing fruit-trees, and producing plenty, without condemning by whole-sale other methods, which have been found to be as successful as his own: as there are often-times two or three ways to a place, all of them equally safe and good.'

Collins was prepared to publish his disagreements with other authorities too, for example, regarding melons and cucumbers (pages 97–98): 'In order to set the fruit, it is the usual Practice of Gardeners, (even men so famous as Quintiney, and the worthy Mr. Evelyn) to cut off the Vines, a Joint or two beyond the fruit, and the reason they give for it is this, That the Sap has the less to feed, and consequently the fruit the larger . . . . Instead of stopping the strongest Vines, I take off half the weak ones, which suck more nourishment from the Root.'

The Practical Fruit-Gardener. Being the Newest and Best Method of Raising, Planting and Pruning All Sorts of Fruit-Trees, Agreeably to the Experience and Practice Of the most Eminent Gardeners and Nurserymen. [rule] By Stephen Switzer. [rule] Revised and recommended by the Reverend Mr. Laurence and Mr. Bradley. [rule] The Second Edition, To which are added three New Plans, and other large Additions. [rule] Honos erit huic quoque Pomo. Virg. Georg. II. ['Honour will be given to the apple too'; rule] London: Printed for Thomas Woodward at the Half-Moon over against St. Dunstan's Church in Fleet-Street. MDCCXXXI.
8° 20 x 12 cm. A⁸ b⁸ B–2A⁸ 2B⁸ *i–xxxii 1–363 364–376* and 6 folding plans.

BINDING: Contemporary calf. Bookplate of Joseph E. Young pasted over the armorial one of the Earls of Hopetoun. (J. C. Loudon, writing in 1822, thought that the garden of Hopetoun House, South Queensferry, near Edinburgh, still showed signs of Switzer's influence.)

PLATES: The first, second, and fourth, showing plans of fruit or kitchen gardens and following pages 30, 316, and 330, are signed by 'J. Clark', probably John Clark, who engraved plates in some of Richard Bradley's books about this time. The three plates added to this edition, following pages 326, 344, and 354, are not signed. They show the plan of a glass house, a 'Fruit Garden with Cross Walls,' and a 'Hollow Wall for forcing Fruit.'

STEPHEN SWITZER was trained as a gardener by George London and Henry Wise at their Brompton Park nursery in London, the leading one of its time. He may have worked for them at Blenheim too, though his main influence on gardens in both England and Scotland was probably via his thorough account of garden history and design, *The Nobleman's, Gentleman's, and Gardener's Recreation*, first published in 1715. The first edition of the *Fruit-Gardener* appeared in 1724, with a dedication to Charles Boyle, 4th Earl of Orrery (1674–1731), for whom Switzer had worked at his estate of Marston, in Somerset. There he was given the use of Lord Orrery's library when he was writing the book on hydraulics that he published in 1729. The *Fruit-Gardener* was so well received that a companion to it, *The Practical Kitchen Gardener*, appeared in 1727, followed by a second edition of the fruit book in 1731. Switzer's later career as a seedsman in London, where he had a shop in Westminster and gardens at Millbank and Vauxhall, led to more books, among them one on vegetables and another, *The Practical Husbandman and Planter*, which was issued in monthly parts in 1733 and 1734.

For Switzer 'A well contriv'd Fruit-Garden is an Epitome of Paradise it self, where the Mind of Man is in its highest Raptures, and where the Souls of the Virtuous enjoy the utmost Pleasures they are susceptible of in this sublunary State' (page 3) for 'A Fruit and Kitchen-Garden that has a proper Extent, may be as Beautiful as useful' (page 30). The book gives clear directions for the organization of this perfect garden, from choosing its site, raising the trees, grafting and pruning them, and giving each fruit the right treatment. Protective walls, sometimes heated, and other ways of forcing (or 'accelerating') fruit are also described, in a section that was enlarged in the second edition of the book.

The publisher, Thomas Woodward, prefaced the book with recommendations from two

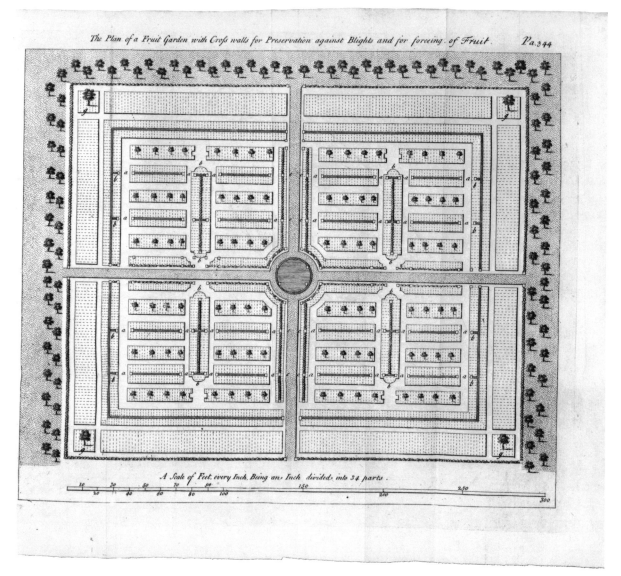

*The Plan of a Fruit Garden with Cross walls for Preservation against Blights and for forceing of Fruit.*   Pa.344

STEPHEN SWITZER
*The Practical Fruit-Gardener* second edition
1731 folding plate
facing page 344
'The Plan of a Fruit
Garden . . .'

*A Scale of Feet, every Inch, Being an Inch divided into 34 parts.*

of his other authors, John Laurence (see pages 42–49) and Richard Bradley, a prolific writer on gardening, botany, and agriculture, and the first (though unsatisfactory) professor of botany at Cambridge. Bradley found Switzer's book 'The most useful Book that I have seen of this Kind; it being founded on practical Rules,' while Laurence thought that 'It contains a great many curious Discoveries and Rules of Practice, with which nothing but long Experience and accurate Observation could furnish him.' The observations recorded include several on Laurence's own advice on the protection of fruit trees:

> Mr. Laurence's horizontal Shelters have naturally led Gentlemen to other inventions for the Security of their Fruit-Trees . . . The sloping Shelters now us'd by several ingenious Planters . . . will I doubt not, be very successful to this Purpose.

Mr. Laurence's Contrivance of horizontal Shelters has indeed amus'd the World pretty much, since that small Treatise of Gardening and managing of Fruit-Trees has been publish'd . . . but . . . he rather upon further Trials and Experience advis'd his Friends to put pieces of Wood in their Walls, and lay Boards thereon at such times as the Tree required it.

Laurence's innovations were praised in the preface and on pages 291–92, but later in the book (pages 314–15 and 318–19) another bright idea, suggested by Fatio de Duillier (see page 37), was firmly dismissed:

Experience has taught (and that in a sloping Wall, I think, of the Author's own directing) that though the Sun may act with more Vigour in its solstitial Capacity on a sloping than on a perpendicular Wall, yet it is as deficient in its Performances in the Morning; and by the Authors own Arguments, as well as the Observation of almost every Body that has made any Observation at all, that Dews are expell'd at least an Hour in the Morning sooner from a perpendicular Wall than from a sloping one; so that what is gain'd at one time is lost [at] another . . . We are surely inform'd by the Observation and Experience of the Gardeners at *Belvoir Castle* . . . that those Walls after all their Expence, were useless till assisted by artificial Heat . . . The first building of these sloping Walls at Belvoir was . . . at the Instigation, and I believe by the Direction of the Author of a Treatise in large Quarto, of *Fruit-Walls improv'd*. That Gentleman being at that Time Tutor to the then Marquis of *Tavistock*, afterwards Duke of *Bedford*, to whom it was dedicated: But notwithstanding the plausible shew made by that Theorist, by which one would have thought that that accelerating would be more certainly perform'd; yet the Gardeners found it did not do when reduc'd to Practice, how well soever it appear'd in the Theory.

At Belvoir the Duke of Rutland eventually heated his fruit wall by piping warm air through a brick tunnel beneath it, an early example of this technique.

## 23. LANGLEY, Batty (1696–1751)

Pomona: or, The Fruit-Garden Illustrated. Containing Sure Methods for Improving all the Best Kinds of Fruits Now Extant in England. Calculated from Great Variety of Experiments made in all Kinds of Soil and Aspects. Wherein The Manner of Raising Young Stocks, Grafting, Inoculating, Planting, &c. are clearly and fully demonstrated. With Directions. [double vertical rule 4 cm. with Directions I–III on left, IV–VI on right] I. For Pruning; wherein the Reasons, Manner, and Consequences thereof are clearly demonstrated. II. For Nailing; wherein the true Distances that the Branches of Fruit-Trees are to be laid upon the Walls, are set forth: Being a most important and useful Discovery, unknown to Gardeners in general. III. For Preserving their Blossoms from the Injuries of Frosts, Winds, &c. IV. Rules for the Thinning of their young-set Fruits, so as to leave no more than Nature can strongly support, and ripen in the greatest Perfection. V. For Preserving and Ordering Young Fruits, from their Blossom to the Time of their Maturity. VI. To give them their true Taste and Colour when fully grown, Season of Ripening, Manner of Gathering, Preserving, &c. [rule] Likewise several Practical Observations on the Imbibing Power and Perspirations of Fruit-Trees; the several Effects of Heat and Moisture tending to

# POMONA:

## OR, THE

## *Fruit-Garden Illuftrated.*

Containing SURE METHODS for Improving all the

# Beft Kinds of FRUITS

Now EXTANT in

# ENGLAND.

### CALCULATED FROM

## Great Variety of EXPERIMENTS made in all Kinds of SOILS and ASPECTS.

### WHEREIN

The Manner of *Raifing* YOUNG STOCKS, *Grafting, Inoculating, Planting, &c.* are clearly and fully demonftrated.

### With DIRECTIONS,

I. For PRUNING ; wherein the *Reafons, Manner,* and *Confequences* thereof are clearly demonftrated.
II. For NAILING ; wherein the *true Diftances* that the Branches of FRUIT-TREES are to be laid upon the Walls, are fet forth : Being a moft important and ufeful Difcovery, unknown to Gardeners in general.
III. For PRESERVING their Bloffoms from the *Injuries* of *Frofts, Winds,* &c.

IV. RULES for the THINNING of their *young-fet Fruits,* fo as to leave no more than Nature can ftrongly fupport, and ripen in the greateft Perfection.
V. For *Preferving* and *Ordering* YOUNG FRUITS, from their *Bloffom* to the Time of their *Maturity.*
VI. To give them their *true Tafte* and *Colour* when fully grown, Seafon of *Ripening,* Manner of *Gathering, Preferving,* &c.

Likewife feveral Practical OBSERVATIONS on the *Imbibing Power* and *Perfpirations* of FRUIT-TREES ; the feveral Effects of *Heat* and *Moifture* tending to the *Growth* and *Maturity* of FRUITS.

To which is added,
A Curious ACCOUNT of the Moft Valuable CYDER-FRUITS of DEVONSHIRE.

The Whole Illuftrated with above Three Hundred DRAWINGS of the feveral FRUITS, Curioufly Engraven on Seventy-nine large Folio Plates.

## By *BATTY LANGLEY* of TWICKENHAM.

### LONDON:

Printed for G. STRAHAN in *Cornhill* ; R. GOSLING, W. MEARS, F. CLAY, D. BROWNE, B. MOTTE, and L. GILLIVER, near *Temple-bar* ; J. STAGG in *Weftminfter-Hall* ; J. OSBORN, at *Gray's-Inn Gate* ; and C. DAVIS in *Pater-Nofter-Row.* M.DCC.XXIX.

the Growth and Maturity of Fruits. [rule] To which is added, A Curious Account of the Most Valuable Cyder-Fruits of Devonshire. [rule] The Whole Illustrated with above Three Hundred Drawings of the several Fruits, Curiously Engraven on Seventy-nine large Folio Plates. [rule] By Batty Langley of Twickenham. [rule] London: Printed for G. Strahan in Cornhill; R. Gosling, W. Mears, F. Clay, D. Browne, B. Motte, and L. Gilliver, near Temple-bar; J. Stagg in Westminster-Hall; J. Osborn, at Gray's-Inn Gate; and C. Davis in Pater-Noster-Row. M. DCC. XXIX.

2° 39.5 x 25 cm. a–d² B–2P² 2Q²(–2Q2) *i–ii* iii–xviii *1* 2–150 and 68 engravings.

BINDING: Dark brown calf, rebacked. Signature of John Wilkes, M.P. (1727–1797) on front pastedown.

PLATES: 79 etchings printed on 68 leaves, the numbering sometimes in Roman, sometimes in Arabic figures. The double plates LVIII and LVIIII have been exchanged with numbers XLVIII and XLIX in this copy. Four engravers did most of the work: Jan van der Gucht, Thomas Bowles, William Henry or Peter Toms, and John Carwitham. James Smith contributed two and B. Cole a single one. The original drawings were made by the author.

BATTY LANGLEY
*Pomona* 1729 page iii A band of decoration linking the book with the workshop of Samuel Richardson, novelist and printer

BATTY LANGLEY, the son of a gardener in Twickenham, added architecture to the knowledge of plants he probably acquired from his father, and he published books on the design of both houses and gardens. His work as a surveyor offered advice on landscape gardening and a willingness to organize the planting of gardens, as well as their decoration with fountains or buildings of his own, somewhat Gothic, design. The preface of *Pomona* (page vii) suggests mixing fruit trees with others:

> Since that Fruit-Trees are known to be beautiful as well as profitable, 'tis therefore that I advise the Planting of them with Forest-Trees, in Wildernesses, and other Rural Parts of Gardens, that their various agreeable Mixtures of Leaves and Fruits, may not only delightfully entertain the Eyes of the Beholders, as they pass thro' the several Meanders thereof, but their Taste also.

Proposals for the publication of *Pomona* were issued as a broadsheet on 10 May 1727 and again in the *Monthly Catalogue* for August of the same year, inviting subscriptions to 'an accurate and complete system of all the best kinds of fruit . . . extant in England'. The text described in the prospectus, giving 'an explanation of their culture in English and French', had dwindled to English only by the time the book was published in October 1728, a little ahead of the date on the title-page. The book records contemporary named varieties of fruit, and is the first to illustrate them, with etchings taken from the author's own drawings, which he made with great care, using tracings of the outlines of leaves or bisected fruits. There are instructions and illustrations for pruning too, an operation of supreme importance, as the preface (pages xi–xii) makes clear:

> I humbly conceive that . . . Pruning is the direct Business of the Head Gardener himself . . . For one experienc'd Pruner will perform more Work in one Season, than any Nobleman or Gentleman's

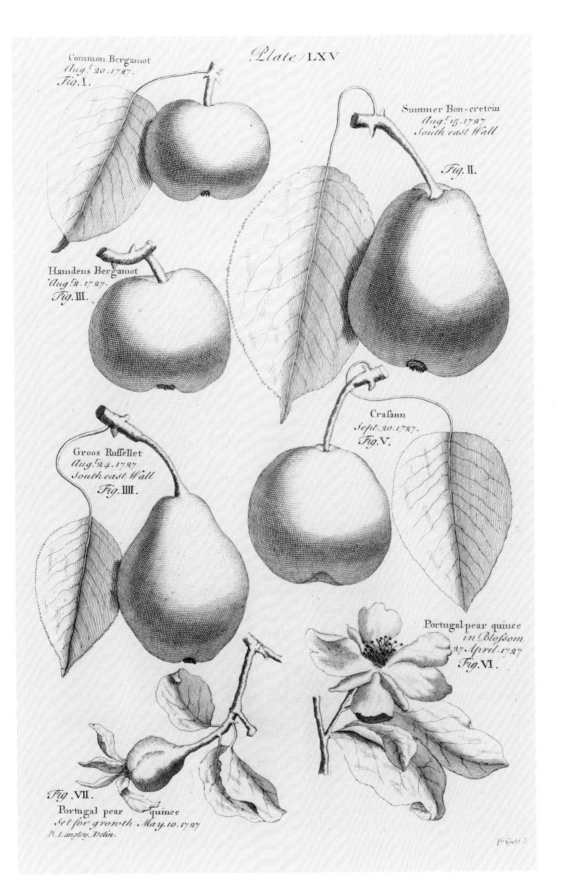

Common Bergamot
Aug. 20. 1727.
Fig. I.

Summer Bon-cretein
Aug. 15. 1727.
South east Wall
Fig. II.

Handens Bergamot
Aug. 2. 1727.
Fig. III.

Groos Ruſſellet
Aug. 24. 1727.
South east Wall
Fig. IIII.

Craſann
Sept. 20. 1727.
Fig. V.

Portugal pear quince
in Bloſſom
27 April. 1727
Fig. VI.

Fig. VII.
Portugal pear    quince
Set for growth May. 10. 1727
B. Langley. Delin.

Plate LXV

J.o Gucht f.

BATTY LANGLEY
*Pomona* 1729  plate LXV
Pears and quinces,
drawn by the author
and engraved by Jan
van der Gucht

Table can require: and therefore when unskilful People (as aforesaid) are employ'd in such Works, . . . the Gentleman whom they serve, is certain of being greatly injur'd, and very often his Trees are totally ruin'd thereby.

Each figure is dated, and the engravers included Jan van der Gucht (son of Michael), Thomas Bowles, and John Carwitham. The author was well able to choose his craftsmen, for his brother Thomas was an architectural engraver, who helped him in several of his publishing projects and also in a school for architectural draughtsmen. Langley was obviously well informed about nurserymen too, especially those in or near Twickenham, some of whom may have provided specimens for him to draw.

An 'Account of the most valuable cyder-fruits of Devonshire', by Hugh Stafford, of Pynes, near Exeter, is included on pages 135 to 150, and the book is dedicated to Queen Sophia, the wife of George I. Blanche Henrey, drawing on the study of Samuel Richardson by William M. Sole, has shown that the ornaments used at the beginnings and ends of chapters in *Pomona* identify this handsome book as one of the products of the novelist's printing-shop.

John Wilkes, a former owner of this copy, is best remembered for his troubled parliamentary career as the Member of Parliament for Aylesbury, and later Middlesex. In April 1775 he led a protest against the British government's treatment of its North American colonies, though this was not the only one of his activities that led him to be described as 'a friend to liberty' on his memorial tablet in the Grosvenor Chapel in London. Between his public battles he cultivated interests in French and Italian literature and painting, and he published some of his own writing. After he left Parliament in 1790 his last years were spent at his house in Sandown, on the Isle of Wight. In the British Library (Add. MS. 30893) there is a catalogue of the sale of the books found there after his death. Langley's *Pomona* is not among those listed, but several other gardening books are there: William Mason's *English Garden* (1782), the abridgement of Philip Miller's *Gardeners Dictionary* (1771), William Hanbury's *Complete Body of Planting and Gardening* (1770–71), Alexander Hunter's edition of Evelyn's *Silva* (1786), and Thomas Johnson's revision of Gerard's *Herball* (1636). *Pomona* would have fitted well enough into this company.

## 24. HITT, Thomas (d. 1770)

A Treatise of Fruit-Trees. By Thomas Hitt, Gardener to the Right Honourable Lord Robert Manners, at Bloxholme, in Lincolnshire. [vignette 2.75 x 2 cm.] London: Printed for the Author; And Sold by T. Osborne, in Gray's-Inn. MDCCLV.

8° 19.5 x 11 cm. A⁴ B–2B⁸ 2C⁴ a⁴ *i–iii* iv–viii *1* 2–392 *393–400* and 7 folding engravings of garden plans and pruning diagrams.

BINDING: Contemporary calf.

PLATES: All seven are engraved by Thomas Jefferys. They are attached to the outer margins of pages 20, 34, 96, 154, 188, 212, 228, in accordance with the 'Directions for the fixing of the Plates' printed on the last page.

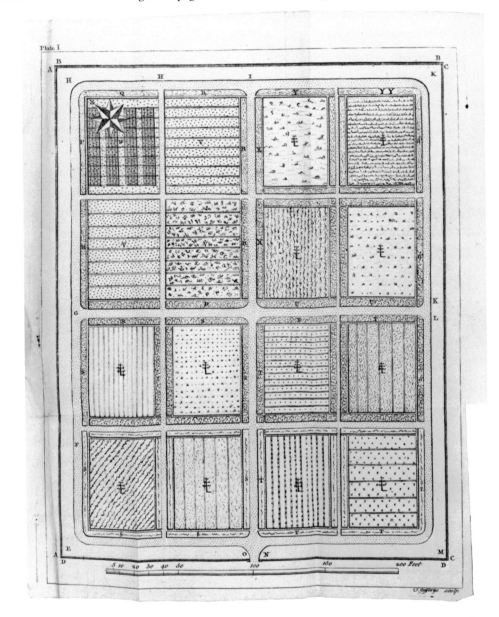

THOMAS HITT
*A Treatise of Fruit-Trees* 1755 plate 1 A design for a fruit garden, engraved by Thomas Jefferys

AFTER HIS TRAINING at Belvoir Castle, home of the dukes of Rutland, Thomas Hitt was gardener to Lord Robert Manners, a member of the same family, at Bloxholm, Lincolnshire, before moving south to Kent. He became a nurseryman at Bromley, specializing in fruit trees in a county still famous for its fruit crops. His early training seems to have led him towards this interest, for in the preface to his book (page v) he says:

61

At Belvoir-Castle, there was in the time of my apprenticeship at that place, a greater number of good sorts than those I have mentioned; the greatest part of them having been sent from abroad by the right honourable the earl of Stair to his late grace the Duke of Rutland, and improved by his present grace, by adding other new and good sorts, when they were to be met with.

His book, which ran into three London editions and a Dublin one within fifteen years, included directions for the packing and safe transport of trees from their nurseries 'to places remote from whence they are raised'. Hitt recommended large hampers, especially for carefully shaped espaliers, though he had to admit that trees sent off in more usual and less lavish wrappings of straw and matting had survived and flourished.

The book was aimed at less experienced gardeners. To quote the preface again (page viii): 'Several practitioners . . . despise books, and take a pleasure in rendering them useless to others; but there are many young men who love to read for the sake of improvement, and to such, I hope this work will be serviceable.'

## 25. LA RIVIERE, — de, and DU MOULIN, —

Méthode pour bien cultiver les arbres a fruit, et pour élever des treilles. Par les Sieurs de la Riviere & du Moulin. [rule 6 cm.] Nouvelle édition. [rule 6 cm.; decoration 2 x 2.5 cm.] A Paris, Chez Des Ventes de la Doué, Libraire, rue S. Jacques, vis-à-vis le College de Louis-le-Grand. [decorated double rule 5 cm.] M. DCC. LXX. Avec Approbation & Privilége du Roi.

12° 15.5 x 9.5 cm. a⁶ A–2C in alternate 8s and 4s 2D⁶
i–xii 1 2–319 320–324 and 2 folding engravings.

BINDING: Half vellum, marbled paper sides; all edges red. Armorial bookplate of Sir Thomas Neame (1885–1973), a fruit farmer from Kent.

PLATES: Opposite page 155 is an unsigned engraving of a ladder on a triangular frame, and opposite page 305 another showing the pruning of a vine trained against a wall.

EARLIER EDITIONS of this book were published in Utrecht in 1738 and 1739. The authors offer the fruits of their long experience, as they say in the 'Avertissement':

Les deux Auteurs de cette Méthode ne se sont étudiés pendant plus de vingt ans, qu'à rechercher les causes, & qu'à donner de justes raisons de tout ce qu'ils voyoient arriver aux Arbres qu'ils cultivoient par plaisir . . . Ces deux Auteurs se sont persuadés qu'ils ne déplairoient pas au Public, s'ils enseignoient d'une maniere claire, courte & aisée à mettre en pratique tout ce que l'expérience de tant d'années leur a fait connoître être nécessaire pour bien cultiver les Arbres à fruit.

They begin with the soil, nursery gardens, all kinds of grafting, planting and transplanting, trellis, espaliers, and pruning. Their folding ladder is described and illustrated before a section on dwarf trees and bush fruits. Warning is given of possible diseases, as well as requirements for an ideal fruit house (page 230):

# MÉTHODE

POUR

BIEN CULTIVER

LES

# ARBRES A FRUIT,

ET POUR ÉLEVER

DES TREILLES.

*Par les Sieurs* DE LA RIVIERE
*&* DU MOULIN.

NOUVELLE ÉDITION.

A PARIS,

Chez DES VENTES DE LA DOUÉ,
Libraire, rue S. Jacques, vis-à-vis
le College de Louis-le-Grand.

M. DCC. LXX.

*Avec Approbation & Privilége du Roi.*

Comme la fin qu'on se propose en cultivant les Arbres, n'est pas seulement le plaisir de les voir chargés de beaux & bons Fruits: mais qu'on cherche sur-tout de les conserver jusqu'à leur parfaite maturité, afin d'en goûter toute la bonté & l'agrément: il faut penser d'abord à faire construire une bonne Fruiterie pour loger ses Fruits quand on les cueillera.

Oak shelves are best, or very dry pine, for if it is not dry enough it will give the fruit a bad taste. To give the fruit its proper colour before it is picked, some of the leaves around it should be snipped off to let in extra light. Fruit must be picked and put away gently, with plums resting on vine or nettle leaves.

The authors' favourite kinds of pears, apples, and plums are recommended, and the book ends with directions for the management of vines and how to train them on walls.

63

# 26. FURBER, Robert (c. 1674–1756)

[Twelve Plates with Figures of Fruit, engraved from designs by Pieter Casteels. London, 1732.]
Broadsheets. 58 x 47 cm.

BINDING: Bound with Furber's *Twelve Months of Flowers* in quarter calf, with contemporary patterned paper boards. Armorial bookplate of Henry Grey, Duke of Kent (1671–1740), George I's courtier, on front cover, and that of his descendant, Thomas Philip, second Earl de Grey (1781–1859), of Wrest Park, Bedfordshire, on front pastedown, repeating the family coat of arms, with its pair of lively dragons.

PLATES: All twelve of the hand-coloured engravings are based on paintings by Pieter Casteels (1684–1749) who came from Antwerp to settle in London in 1708. He also painted the flower-pieces used in Furber's *Twelve Months of Flowers*, a year or two earlier. Henry Fletcher, who engraved the flowers, did seven of the fruit plates too, while of the remaining five James Smith engraved February and November, G. vander Gucht January, John Clark April, and C. Du Bosc August. The plates are dated January to December 1732 in cartouches beneath the fruit. In the centre of the top parts of the uncoloured frames the signs of the zodiac are also enclosed in small cartouches.

ROBERT FURBER's nursery garden, near Hyde Park gate in Kensington, was well established by 1724, when a list of his trees and shrubs grown out of doors was printed in Philip Miller's *Gardeners and Florists Dictionary*. Furber's own catalogues, among the earliest issued as pamphlets, also began to appear in the 1720s, though the grandest of them, the double series of *Twelve Months of Flowers* and *Twelve Plates with Figures of Fruit*, were first published a little later, from 1730 to 1732. In the preface to his 1727 catalogue, Furber wrote:

> I have for many Years . . . been collecting, propagating, and improving great Variety of the most curious and valuable Trees, Plants, Fruit-Trees, &c. both Foreign and Domestick . . . I have added a Catalogue of great Variety of Fruit-Trees, which I have for several Years been collecting, and have them all for sale, which I can warrant to answer so well their Names, as also their Colour and Shape . . . I have placed their Names in the order their Fruits ripen successively, and the time of their keeping to perfect Maturity through the several Seasons of the Year; allowing the difference of Seasons and Situations, which alters the Colours, Shape, Goodness, and time of Ripening, as the Soil and Summer prove.

The fruit illustrated in the twelve pieces, arranged on or around bowls, dishes, or baskets, ranges from the apples and pears of January and February to the cherries, currants, mulberries, plums, peaches, strawberries, and other soft fruit of June. Over 350 varieties are shown, each one numbered in reference to the names printed below each picture. By the name of each variety is a letter S, D, E, or W, for standard, dwarf, espalier, or wall, and indicating its habit of growth or most productive method of treatment. So decorative a catalogue should have encouraged Furber's customers to increase their orders for his fruit. He described the fruit plates and their preparation in his preface to *A Short Introduction to Gardening* (see page 66), which brings together plant lists to accompany them.

## 27. FURBER, Robert (*c.*1674–1756)

A Short Introduction to Gardening; or, A Guide to Gentlemen and Ladies, in Furnishing their Gardens. Being several Useful Catalogues of Fruits and Flowers. By Robert Furber, of Kensington. [two tail-pieces side by side, 2 x 7 cm.] London: Printed by H. Woodfall, without Temple-Bar. MDCCXXXIII.

4° 17.5 x 10.5 cm. A⁴ a⁴ B–L⁴ M² *i–iii* iv–vii *viii–xviii* 1–12 [2] 13–24 [2] 25–30 [2] 31–36 [2] 37 [3] 38–49 [2] 50–68 *69* and 2 engravings.

BINDING: Half red leather, marbled paper sides. Armorial bookplates of Charles Harman Payne (*fl.*1890–1922), the horticultural bibliographer, and Sir Thomas Neame (1885–1973), a fruit farmer from Kent.

PLATES: The dedication plate faces the title-page. Within a cartouche surrounded by fruit, flowers, and a couple of muscular putti is an inscription: 'To his Royal Highness Prince William Duke of Cumberland, Their Royal Highnesses Princes Mary and Princes Louisa The Nobility, Clergy, Gentry and other Subscribers; this Work is Humbly Dedicated, with all Respect by Their most Obedient Humble Servant, Robert Furber, of Kensington.' The other plate, facing the start of 'The Subscribers Names', is headed 'Subscribers' and contains the names of the three royal patrons, the Duke of Cumberland's surrounded by a trophy of arms, the two Princesses' each within a wreath of flowers. Although the plates are not signed, they seem to be the work of Francis Hoffman, who was associated with some of Furber's other publications, including his 1727 catalogue. The woodcut head- and tailpieces in the preface and lists also look like his work, which is found in several books and newspapers of the 1720s too. In 1706 Hoffman published an edition of *The Pilgrim's Progress* in verse.

FURBER's little book, a great rarity, has a misleading title, for it is essentially a supplement to the large plates of fruit and flowers he had just published to illustrate his nursery stock in a most dramatic way: (see page 65). The subscribers' list here is longer than the one printed with the *Twelve Months of Flowers* a couple of years earlier, though some names appear in both, like Peter Collinson and Christopher Gray, two eager importers of American plants. Among the additions are the Duke of Bedford's gardener, Lewis Kennedy, the garden designer Charles Bridgeman, and 'Mr. Bowles, Printseller, 50 Sets' and 'Mr. Bird, Frame-maker, 25 Sets'.

The first half of the book is devoted to fruit, including 'A List of Several Uncommon Sorts of Fruit contain'd in the Twelve Pieces', that is, his fruit plates, and some preparatory definitions of 'certain *Terms* used in speaking of *Fruits*, . . . We say of *Fruits*, that they are

Of a grateful Taste or Flavour, of a fragrant or fine Smell.
*Aromatic* or *Spicy*, of a warm or spicy Taste or Smell.
*Musky*, or of a rich spicy perfumed Taste or Smell.
*Vinous*, or of a wine-like Taste or Smell.
*Odoriferous*, musked or perfumed.
*Sharp* or *sour*, or of a biting Taste.
Of the *Flesh* or *Pulp* we say, it is
*Soft, buttery, melting,* or *sweet.*

And the list goes on, ending with '*Mealy,* when dry or over-ripe'. Below this guide to the appropriate vocabulary is the comment that 'It has been observed that such Fruits, as grow on

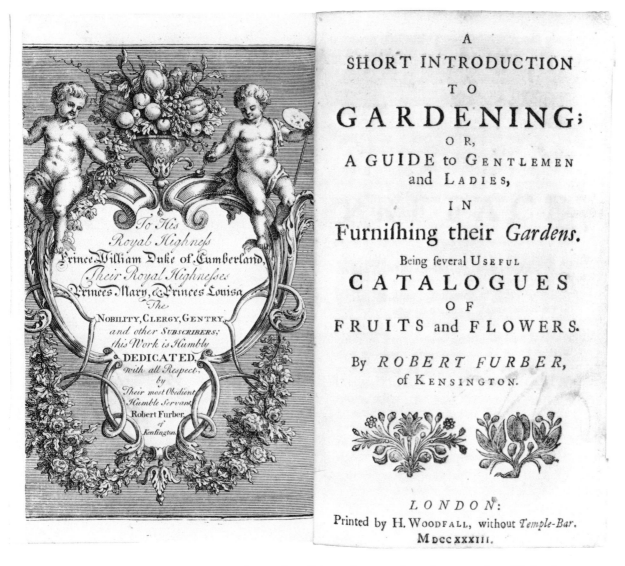

ROBERT FURBER
*A Short Introduction to Gardening* 1733 Dedication plate, possibly the work of Francis Hoffman, and title-page

*Dwarfs* or *Espaliers*, are better tasted, and will keep longer than those against Walls; but are not so large and beautiful.'

Furber's own description of this little book in his preface sums it up with proper pride:

Having at length, by my own unwearied Application, and the kind Assistance of many Gentlemen and Gardeners, compleated my Collection of the various Kinds and different Sorts of Fruits produced in this Kingdom; and having, according to my Proposals, disposed them in monthly Order on twelve Copper-Plates, coloured from the Oil-Paintings, after the real Fruits: Now in order to render this Work still farther useful, I take the liberty of presenting this little Book to my Subscribers; hoping they will accept it as a Mark of my Gratitude for their Favours, and of my sincere Desire to render the whole Design, as useful and pleasant as possible. It contains several Catalogues of Fruit disposed in such a manner as to shew at one View all that a curious Enquirer can be desirous of knowing [that is, standard, dwarf, or espalier; aspect required; season]. . . By these Catalogues Gentlemen will be assisted in furnishing their Gardens and their Tables with the greatest Variety, and the best of Fruits, without being liable to such a Disappointment as usually follows an injudicious or random Choice . . .

Gardening is the Employment Providence has allotted me; and it happily falls out to be a Business the most suitable of all others to my Genius and Inclination. I have spent many Years in collecting, cultivating and improving all the different Kinds of Trees, Plants, Fruits, and Flowers, that I could possibly obtain; and in doing this, have spared neither Cost nor Pains.

With intent to make the Love of Gardening more general, and the understanding of it more easy, I have from time to time published Catalogues, containing large Variety of Trees, Plants, Fruits, and Flowers, both Foreign and Domestic, cultivated by me for Sale. Nothing more need here be said of the Monthly Flower-Pieces, which I published some time ago, as they have been so generally approved, but it may not be amiss to give some little account of the Fruit-Pieces which this Book accompanies.

In making this Collection, I have been generously supplied with Choice of the finest Fruits, and Increase of the same, as well as greatly assisted in comparing and naming them, by a great many, both of Gentlemen and Gardeners, who are not only good Judges of the Culture, but exquisitely nice in distinguishing the Flavour, and most minute Difference of the several Sorts of Fruits; and no Name has been inserted at the Bottom of the Plates, or in the following Catalogues, but by their unanimous Opinion and Consent. — But after all, I don't pretend, that either the Plates or Catalogues contain every individual Species of the Fruits, which may be found among us: new Sorts are frequently produced, and will, perhaps, be so long as the World endures; nor can they be increased, dispersed, and known immediately: I may however venture to affirm, that I have collected a greater Variety than has yet been brought together, and few I hope will be found wanting. — As for the Designing, Engraving, and Colouring, I shall say no more, but that I have taken the utmost Care to have them performed in the best manner, by the most able Hands.

ROBERT FURBER
*A Short Introduction to Gardening* 1733 page *ix*
Head-piece to list of subscribers

# FRUIT IN FRANCE & BRITAIN

III  *Duhamel and After*

# 28. DUHAMEL DU MONCEAU, Henri Louis (1700–1782)

Traité des Arbres fruitiers; contenant leur Figure, leur Description, leur Culture, &c. Par M. Duhamel du Monceau, de l'Académie Royale des Sciences; de la Société Royale de Londres; des Académies de Petersbourg, de Palerme, & de l'Institut de Bologne; Honoraire de la Société d'Edimbourg, & de l'Académie de Marine; Associé à plusieurs Sociétés d'Agriculture; Inspecteur Général de la Marine. Tome Premier. [vignette of fruit blossom 6.5 x 3 cm.] A Paris, Chez [bracket] Saillant, Libraire, rue Saint-Jean de Beauvais. Desaint, Libraire, rue de Foin. [double rule, upper one heavier, 11.5 cm.] M. DCC. LXVIII. Avec Approbation et Privilège du Roi.

4° 33.5 x 24.5 cm. π² A–2T⁴ 2V²(–2V2) [4] *i* ii–xxix *xxx–xxxii 1* 2–338 and a frontispiece and 62 coloured engravings.

. . . Tome Second . . .
π² A–2M⁴ [4] *1* 2–280 and 118 coloured engravings.

BINDING: Contemporary red morocco, gilt arms and spine, bound for the royal librarian, Jérome Frédéric Bignon. Bookplate of Arpad Plesch (1890–1974); the book was bought at the sale of his library at Sotheby's in London on 16 June 1975.

PLATES: The frontispiece was drawn by Jacques de Sève and engraved by N. de Launay. It shows an orchard scene with fruit being picked. The fruit plates, with twigs and flowers as well, were the work of Claude Aubriet (*c.* 1665–1742), Ma(g)deleine Basseporte (1701–1780), his pupil, and René Le Berryais (1722–1807), with a large team of engravers transferring their drawings, among them Catherine and Elisabeth Haussard, L. A. Herisset, and B. L. Henriquez signing the greatest number. The colouring of this copy matches the splendour of the binding.

*For the description of two other remarkable copies of this book see pages 72–81.*

DUHAMEL DU MONCEAU was born in Paris and studied law at Orléans before attending classes in the natural sciences at the Jardin du Roi, later the Jardin des Plantes. After that his career was both varied and full. As the *Dictionnaire de Biographie française* (1970) describes him, 'd'une activité prodigieuse, doué d'une merveilleuse mémoire, ayant autant de facilité pour la parole que pour la plume, homme de plein air aussi bien qu'homme de cabinet, il se consacra aux activités les plus diverses,' among them meteorology and metallurgy. He became a member of the Académie des Sciences as a chemist in 1728, before being re-labelled a botanist two years later, in which capacity, on the Académie's instructions, he carried out studies of saffron and the anatomy of pear trees. His appointment in 1731 as Inspecteur général de la Marine prompted a treatise on rope-making, but he also continued working on plant physiology and agriculture. In this field he was one of the outstanding botanists of the eighteenth century. The volumes of his *Traité complet des Bois et des Forêts* were published from 1755 to 1767. His knowledge of trees was based on practical experience, for on his estates at Vrigny and Monceau (Loiret) and his brother's at Denainvilliers he established botanic gardens for the culture of trees, shrubs, and new exotics. He was also one of the French gardeners who encouraged the planting of potatoes in their country.

From trees in general Duhamel turned his attention to fruit trees in particular, though not before his *Art de faire les tapis façon de Turquie* (1766) had introduced the label *tapis de la Savonnerie* for French carpets showing oriental influence, some of which were manufactured in a former soap factory at Chaillot—hence Savonnerie. The text of the *Traité des Arbres fruitiers* has contributions from both Duhamel's brother and the Abbé Le Berryais, who also made so many illustrations for it (see page 91). Both these helpers made observations relevant to Duhamel's attempts to distinguish botanical species from garden varieties of fruit, using all the relevant characters.

The first volume begins with directions on grafting and pruning before starting on descriptions of particular fruits and specific varieties of them—almonds, apricots, a barberry, cherries, quinces, figs, strawberries, gooseberries, apples, medlars, and a mulberry. The lion's share of the second volume is taken up by pears, with peaches, plums, grapes, and a raspberry.

As well as the octavo edition (see page 81) in French, the book was translated into German and published in Nuremberg in 1775–83, and an enlarged edition by Poiteau and Turpin was published from 1807 to 1835, 'augmentée d'un grand nombre d'espèces de fruits obtenus des progrès de la culture' (see page 89). Two undated collections of about 150 appropriate plates and text from the *Nouveau Duhamel* (see pages 82–87) were also issued as 'new editions' of the *Traité des Arbres fruitiers*.

H. L. DUHAMEL
*Traité des Arbres fruitiers*
1768 volume I
Inscription on free
endpaper, recording
Jeanne Parrocel's work

THERE ARE two other remarkable copies of the *Traité des Arbres fruitiers* in the Oak Spring Garden Library, and it seems that there is also an unexpected relationship between them.

The first, large (36 x 27 cm.) and uncut, its plates specially printed without numbers, borders, or artists' names, was obviously intended for the exceptional treatment it received. Each fruit, blossom, and leaf was painted in gouache by Jeanne Françoise Parrocel (1734–1829), one of a large dynasty of painters. She specialized in flowers and animals, and for this commission she waited till she had seen each ripe fruit before painting it, signing nearly all the plates 'Je Parrocel pinxit'. A note in the first volume reads: 'Cet ouvrage à été peint sur nature avec tout le soin imaginable, il a fallu bien du temps, du talent et de l'argent pour le conduire a sa perfection.' That seems to sum it up quite well, for the result of her work is a marvel. The collector who commissioned it may have been Jean-Baptiste Paris de Meyzieu, who died in 1778, leaving his books to Paris d'Illens, who sold them in London on 26 March 1791. The sale catalogue describes the elder Paris as 'a Gentleman . . . Not less conspicuous for his Taste in distinguishing, than for his Zeal in acquiring, whatever, of this Kind, was most perfect, curious, or scarce.' It then went into raptures about this book, lot 102:

'Tis impossible to give an idea of the execution of this book without seeing it; each plate is a bold masterly painting done with perfect exactness. No figure was painted but when opportunity offered

72

of having the fruit and blossom in perfection, so that it was the work of many years . . . The labour and difficulty of the execution being thus explained, 'tis for connoisseurs to decide upon the merits of it.

It was bought by Thomas Payne on behalf of the 2nd Duke of Newcastle for £147, one of the highest prices in the sale. Its new owner added his coat of arms to the green vellum sides of the bindings, which have red morocco spines. Each volume also bears the bookplate of Hermann Marx. On 2 July 1979 the book was sold again, at Sotheby's in London, this time by the Linnean Society.

H. L. DUHAMEL
*Traité des Arbres fruitiers*
1768 The Duke of
Newcastle's copy:
vellum bindings
with his coat
of arms

H. L. DUHAMEL
*Traité des Arbres fruitiers*
1768 volume 1 plate
facing page 184 Cerise
de Hollande, drawn by
Magdeleine Basseporte,
engraved by E. Haus-
sard, and painted by
Jeanne Parrocel

Cerise de Hollande.

Magd. Basseporte del.        E.the Haussard Sculp.

*Cerise de Hollande.*

H. L. DUHAMEL
*Traité des Arbres fruitiers*
1768 volume I plate X
at page 200 Cerise de
Hollande, drawn by
Magdeleine Basseporte
and engraved by
E. Haussard

H. L. DUHAMEL
*Traité des Arbres fruitiers*
1768 volume I plate
facing page 212 Figue
Violette, drawn by
René Le Berryais,
engraved by P. L.
Cor, and painted by
Jeanne Parrocel

J. Parrocel Painnée              *Figue Violette.*

THE THIRD COPY at Oak Spring was bought in 1956, without a record of its provenance. It is bound in four volumes, with the frontispiece and plates uncoloured, but a watercolour of each plate is bound in after the printed version. These were described as 'originals', but they are certainly not the drawings from which the plates were engraved, by Aubriet, Basseporte, or Le Berryais. Several of the sheets of paper on which they were painted have a very English Whatman watermark, though no date.

The bindings also helped to link this copy with London. They are red morocco, inlaid with strips of dark green round the borders of the sides. Elaborate gold tooling also forms bands round the sides and down the spine. Many components of the decoration—vases, palmettes,

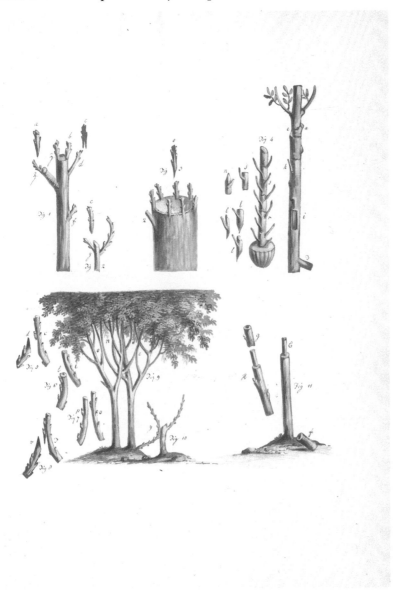

H. L. DUHAMEL
*Traité des Arbres fruitiers*
1768 volume 1 plate
facing page 32
Grafting methods:
watercolour copy,
probably by
John Harris

H. L. DUHAMEL
*Traité des Arbres fruitiers*
1768 volume II plate II
at page 218 Figue Vio-
lette, drawn by René Le
Berryais and engraved
by P. L. Cor

*Figue Violette.*

H. L. DUHAMEL
*Traité des Arbres fruitiers*
1768 volume II plate II
at page 218 Figue Vio-
lette: watercolour copy,
probably by John Harris

H. L. DUHAMEL
*Traité des Arbres fruitiers*
1768 The copy with
extra watercolours
Volume 1 The binding
by Christian Samuel
Kalthoeber

mermaids, key-pattern borders—are identical to those used by Christian Samuel Kalthoeber, a Prussian bookbinder who worked in London from about 1782 to 1817, on a copy of William Caslon's *Specimen of Printing Types* (1785) from the library of King George III, now in the British Library.

When the watercolours in this copy are compared with Jeanne Parrocel's paintings there are similarities which can be explained only by assuming that the other artist, probably John Harris, was following her example. The first cherry plate, 'Guignes', at page 200, has in its lower right-hand leaf a hole which was added by Parrocel to the printed outline and copied by Harris; the strawberry plates at page 262 follow her example too, even to the colours she used for the ribbons tying the bunches of stalks together; but perhaps the most convincing evidence is a split fig, 'Figue Violette', at page 208. The uncoloured printed plate leaves the fruit whole, but Parrocel painted it with the typical splitting of a ripe fig, copied in every detail by Harris. These coincidences, and several other less striking ones, make it appear likely that Harris was commissioned to copy the Parrocel paintings once the book containing her work was in England, that is, after 1791. The faint signature 'J. Harris' or 'J. Harris pinxt' appears on a few of the watercolours. It seems likely that this refers to John Harris the elder (d. 1834, R.A. 1797–1814) a painter, watercolourist, and engraver who engraved the plates of J. E. Smith's and John Abbot's *Insects of Georgia . . . and the Plants on which they feed* (London, 1797). The happy chance of these two special copies of the *Traité des Arbres fruitiers* finding their way to the same library has made it possible to elucidate their relationship.

## 29. DUHAMEL DU MONCEAU, Henri Louis (1700–1782)

Traite des Arbres fruitiers, contenant leur figure, leur description, leur culture, &c. Par M. Du Hamel Du Monceau, De l'Académie Royale des Sciences; de la Société Royale de Londres; des Académies de Pétersbourg, de Palerme & de l'Institut de Bologne; Honoraire de la Société d'Edimbourg, & de l'Académie de Marine; Associé à plusieurs Sociétés d'Agriculture; Inspecteur général de la Marine. Tome premier. [vignette 3 x 3.5 cm.] A Paris, Chez Desaint, Libraire, rue de Foin. [double rule, upper one heavier, 6.5 cm.] M. DCC. LXXXII.
8° 20.5 x 12 cm. $\pi^2$ A–V$^8$ *i–iv 1* 2–320 and 34 engravings.

. . . Tome second . . .

$\pi^2(-\pi2)$ A–X$^8$ *i–ii 1* 2–296 299–338 (i.e. 336, as no text is missing) and 79 engravings.

. . . Tome troisieme . . .
$\pi^2(-\pi2)$ A–O$^8$ P$^4$ Q$^8$ R$^6$ *i–ii 1* 2–260 and 63 engravings.

Volume 1 page 181
Head-piece for the description of the almond

BINDING: Contemporary speckled calf, gilt spine, marbled edges. Each volume signed 'Germain Boissier' on fly-leaf.

PLATES: Miniature, unsigned versions, occasionally reversed, of those in the quarto edition of the *Traité des Arbres fruitiers* (see page 71).

H. L. DUHAMEL
*Traité des Arbres fruitiers*
octavo edition 1782
volume I plate facing
page 160 Pruning:
how to shape
trees

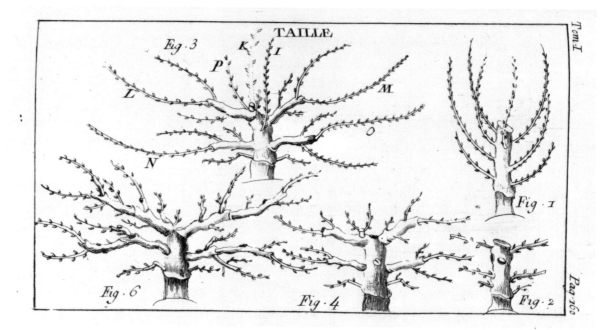

THIS pocket-sized edition of the *Traité des Arbres fruitiers*, with small, uncoloured illustrations, was published fourteen years after the first one, and a similar edition was issued in Brussels in the same year. The more humble format makes the octavo version look like the eighteenth-century equivalent of a modern paperback edition, designed to appeal to readers unable to afford the grander quarto but no less eager to read Duhamel's book.

## 30. DUHAMEL DU MONCEAU, Henri Louis (1700–1782)

[engraved title-page] Traité des Arbres et Arbustes que l'on cultive en France en pleine terre Par Duhamel Seconde Édition considérablement augmentée. [vignette 18.5 x 18.5 cm. of Agriculture personified in a grove beside a stream] A Paris, Chez Didot aîné, au Louvre; Michel, Rue des Francs-Bourgeois au Marais Nᵒ 699; et Lamy, Quai des Augustins Nᵒ 26.

2ᵒ 49.5 x 32 cm. $\pi^2(\pi 2+1)$ 1–20² 20*bis*² 20*ter*²(–20*ter*2) 21–66² 67² (The last gathering is not signed 69, as stated

in the Hunt Botanical Library *Catalogue of Redoutéana* (1963, page 50); this figure is a page reference to the text from an index entry.) *i–ii 1* 2–4 *1* 2–80 77*bis–*80*bis* 77*ter–*78*ter 81* 82–264 *i* ii–iv and 60 coloured plates.

Traité des Arbres et Arbustes que l'on cultive en France, Par Duhamel. Nouvelle Édition, augmentée de plus de moitié pour le nombre des Espèces, distribuée d'après un ordre plus méthodique, suivant l'état actuel de la Botanique et de l'Agriculture; Avec des figures, d'après les dessins de P.-J. Redouté, Peintre du Muséum d'Histoire Naturelle, et de la classe des Sciences Physiques et Mathématiques de l'Institut, Membre de la Société d'Histoire Naturelle de Paris. Dedié a sa Majesté l'Impératrice Reine. [rule 7.5 cm.] . . . Nobis placeant antè omnia sylvæ. [Virgil *Eclogues* II: 'The gods, to live in woods, have left the skies', translated by John Dryden, 1697; rule 7.5 cm.] Tome second. [monogram of E and M 5.5 x 5 cm.] A Paris, Chez Étienne Michel, Éditeur, rue des Francs-Bourgeois, n°. 6, au Marais. [wavy line 3.5 cm.] 1804.

π²(π2+1 as ★) 1–61² a²(–a2) b² *i–vi 1 2*–244 *i* ii–v *vi* and 72 coloured plates (plates 30 and 31 reversed; plate 40 labelled p. 140 instead of p. 137).

. . . Tome troisième. . . . 1806
π² 1–58² 59²(–59:2) a² *i–iv 1* 2–234 *i* ii–iv and 60 coloured plates.

. . . Tome quatrième. . . . 1809
π² 1–2² 3²(–3:2) 3*bis*² 4*bis*² 4–60² (leaf 2 in gatherings 35–40, 49–60 signed with ★) 61² *i–iv 1* 2–10 9*bis*–14*bis* 11–240 *1* 2–4 and 68 coloured plates (plate 22 wrongly renumbered by hand 23; plate 23 wrongly printed 22).

Nouveau Duhamel, ou Traité des Arbres et Arbustes que l'on cultive en France, Rédigé par G.-L.-A. Loiseleur Deslongchamps, Doct.-Méd. de la Faculté de Paris, et Membre de plusieurs Sociétés savantes, nationales et étrangères; Avec des figures d'après les dessins de MM. P.-J. Redouté et P. Bessa. Dédié a Sa Majesté l'Impératrice Joséphine. [wavy line 8 cm.] . . . Nobis placeant ante omnia sylvæ. [wavy line 8 cm.] Tome cinquième. [monogram of M and B, 5.5 x 5 cm.] A Paris, Chez [bracket 1.5 cm.] Étienne Michel, Éditeur, rue de Turenne, n°. 42, au Marais; Et Arthus-Bertrand, Libraire-Éditeur, rue Hautefeuille, n°. 23. [wavy line 2.5 cm.] 1812. π² 1–16² 17²(17:2+1) (leaf 2 in gatherings 14–16 signed with ★, in gathering 17 with 17) 18–82² 83² *i–iv 1* 2–330 *1* 2–4 and 83 coloured plates and 2 uncoloured ones.

. . . J.L.A. Loiseleur-Deslongchamps . . . [dedication omitted; 'Virg.' added at the end of the quotation] . . . Tome sixième . . . Étienne Michel, Éditeur, rue Saint-Louis, n°. 42, au Marais; . . . 1815.
π² 1–9²(9:2+1 signed as 9★) 10–67² 68² *i–iv 1* 2–36 35*bis*–36*bis* 37 38–266 *1* 2–6 (page 120 wrongly numbered 200) and 81 coloured plates.

Nouveau Duhamel, ou Traité des Arbres et Arbustes que l'on cultive en France, Rédigé par J.L.A. Loiseleur-Deslongchamps, Doct.-Med. de la Faculté de Paris, et

Membre de plusieurs Sociétés savantes, nationales et étrangères; et Étienne Michel, Éditeur, Associé libre et correspondant de l'Académie Royale de Marseille; de la Société Académique d'Aix (Bouches-du-Rhône), et de la Société d'Émulation de Rouen. Avec des figures d'après les dessins de MM. P. J. Redouté et P. Bessa. [wavy line 6.5 cm.] . . . Nobis placeant ante omnia sylvæ Virg. [wavy line 6.5 cm.] Tome septième. [monogram of M and B, 5.5 x 5 cm.] A Paris, Chez [bracket 1.5 cm.] Étienne Michel, Éditeur, rue Saint-Louis, n°. 42, au Marais; Et Arthus Bertrand, Libraire, rue Hautefeuille, n°. 23. [wavy line 2.5 cm.] 1819.
π² 1–63² 64² 65² *i–iv 1* 2–252 *1* 2–7 *8* and 72 coloured plates.

BINDING: A large-paper copy. Volumes I to IV bound in red morocco with silk liners, gilt borders and spine, all edges gilt, the Austrian double eagle in gilt in the centre of the back and front covers. These four bindings were the work of A. P. Bradel. His ticket in volume II reads: 'Relié par Bradel l'Aîné Relieur de la Bibliothèque Imp^le Neveu et Succ^r de Derome le Jeune Rue S^t Jacques N° 105 Hotel de la Couture A Paris'. Volumes V to VII were bound to match, presumably in Vienna, where a smaller coat of arms was used on the sides. 'F.I.' crowned in a circle on the verso of the half-titles, with 'Fid[ei] C[ommis]' below, recording the library's period in trust. The fly-leaf of volume I bears the bookplate of Arpad Plesch (1890–1974), for this copy was bought at the Plesch sale at Sotheby's in London on 16 June 1975. At the bottom of the last leaf in each volume is a stamp reading 'Aus der National-Bibliothek in Wien als Doublette ausgeschieden am 15.1.49', showing when the Austrian National Library discarded this historic duplicate, which began as the gift of Napoleon to his father-in-law, the Emperor Francis I.

PLATES: This copy contains an engraved title-page, 2 uncoloured, unsigned plates (numbers 33 and 34 in volume V, showing olive presses) and 496 stipple engravings, printed in colour and finished by hand, 306 from drawings by Pierre Joseph Redouté (1759–1840) and 190 from those of Pancrace Bessa (1772–1846). Since the Hunt Botanical Library published *A Catalogue of Redoutéana* in 1963, including Ian MacPhail's descriptions of the *Nouveau Duhamel* (item 14, pages 49–52) which is said to contain prints of 463 drawings by Redouté and 33 by Bessa, these mistaken figures have been repeated elsewhere. They are found, for instance, in the catalogues of both the Plesch sale (1975) and the de Belder sale (1987), though Claus Nissen, in *Die botanische Buchillustration* (1951, item 549)

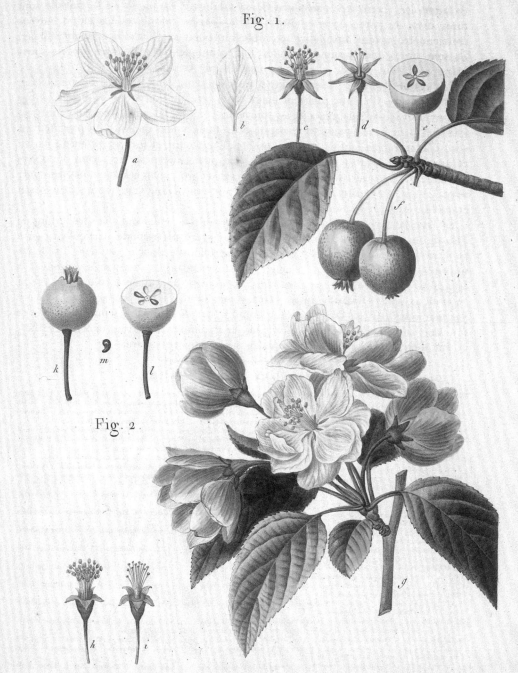

H. L. DUHAMEL *Traité des Arbres et Arbustes (Nouveau Duhamel)* volume VI 1815 plate 42 Crabapples, drawn by Pancrace Bessa and engraved by Dubreuil

T. 6. Nº 42.

Fig. 1.

Fig. 2

Fig. 1. MALUS hybrida.  POMMIER hybride.
Fig. 2. MALUS spectabilis.  POMMIER à bouquets.

P. Bessa pinx.  Dubreuil sculp.

gave figures which agree with the Oak Spring copy (formerly the Plesch one). The plates in this copy are distributed according to the following list:

Volume I:   1–60
Volume II:   1–66 66[*bis*] 67–71, that is, 72 plates in all
Volume III:   1–28 27*bis*–28*bis* 29–58, that is, 60 plates in all
Volume IV:   1*bis*–3*bis* 4–11 11*bis* 1–3 12–33 33*bis* 34–63, that is, 68 plates in all (though lacking number 47*bis*, which is recorded by Nissen)
Volume V:   1–72 72*bis* 73–84, that is, 85 plates in all, including numbers 33 and 34, which are uncoloured and unsigned
Volume VI:   1–74 74*bis* 75–80, that is, 81 plates in all
Volume VII: 1–72

Redouté drawings fill the first four volumes, except for a trio of date palms (plates 1–3 in volume IV) which are by Bessa, 'd'après les dessins originaux faits en Egypte par Redouté jeune', that is, Henri Joseph Redouté (1766–1852), who accompanied Napoleon's expedition to Egypt in 1799. The second set of date palms (plates 1*bis*–3*bis*) in the same volume are the elder Redouté's, based on specimens sent from the south of France by M. Martin of St Tropez, and the two sets distinguish between the more widespread date and the Egyptian one. A note in the index explains the confusion and its resolution.

Both artists appear in volume V, with 34 plates by Bessa (numbers 47, 51–62, 64–70, 72, 72*bis*, 73–84) and 49 by Redouté, as well as the two uncoloured, unsigned plates of olive presses (of which number 34 is a copy of the engraving facing page 72 in volume II of Duhamel's *Traité des Arbres* (1755)). The plates of the last two volumes are all Bessa's work. The *Nouveau Duhamel* contains some fine work by Redouté, the leading botanical artist in France during this period, but Bessa's work is often of equal quality, and he certainly deserves his proper share of the credit. Twenty-nine engravers were involved in transferring the original drawings (now in the Bibliothèque Nationale in Paris) to the printing plates, and many of them also worked with Redouté or Bessa on other books. One of the engravers, identified as 'la Cit^{ne} Rolet' or Citoyenne Rolet on plate 10 of volume I, returned to being 'M^{lle} Rolet' in later reissues, neatly indicating the decline of revolutionary enthusiasm in France.

The vignette on the title-page of volume I, drawn by Charles Percier and J. T. Thibaud, etched by Victor Pillement, and finished by F. D. Née, shows Agriculture personified as a young woman sitting beneath an oak, close to a figure of Nature and surrounded by tools, trees, and shrubs. Nearby is Pan, the guardian of forests, and the Sun, who gives life to Nature, with a fountain and a river flowing through a plain. As the explanation on the verso of the half-title says, 'On a voulu indiquer par cette réunion les principaux agents de la végétation.'

THE *Nouveau Duhamel*, named in homage to its predecessor, the *Traité des Arbres* (1755), was published in eighty-three parts forming seven volumes from 1800 to 1819. It was virtually a completely new book, expanded from the two volumes of the *Traité*. Its main editor was Etienne Michel, with other contributions from J. L. A. Loiseleur-Deslongchamps, C. F. Brisseau-Mirbel, J. L. M. Poiret, J. H. Jaume Saint-Hilaire, and Veillard. Poiret seems to have joined the team in the course of volume III, for he is thanked in an editorial note at the end of the index in that volume. A similar note at the end of the next volume welcomed 'M. Loiseleur des Lonchamps' as a new recruit to the group of botanists conducting the work. The posthumous help of René Le Berryais (1722–1807) is acknowledged on page 1 of volume V:

La cession que nous a faite M^{me}. Troussel-Dumanoir des manuscrits et dessins que feu M. Le Berriays, collaborateur du Duhamel, pour son *Traité des Arbres fruitiers*, avait destinés pour les Tomes trois et quatre de cet important ouvrage, nous facilitera beaucoup, lorsque dans nos livraisons, nous aurons a traiter des Arbres dans leur état Sauvage et Domestique . . . Nous saisirons toutes les occasions que se presenteront dans le cours de cet ouvrage, pour rendre a M. Le Berriays la portion de gloire et de reconnaissance que ses travaux lui assurent parmi les savans Agronomes qui ont illustré la France.

H. L. DUHAMEL *Traité des Arbres et Arbustes* (*Nouveau Duhamel*) volume VII 1819 plate 67 The grape Muscat rouge, drawn by Pancrace Bessa and engraved by Dubreuil

VITIS vinifera.   VIGNE cultivée. *var. Muscat rouge*

P. Bessa pinx.   Dubreuil sculp.

The illustrations of the *Nouveau Duhamel* were also transformed, with 306 plates by Redouté and 190 by Bessa, who concentrated on citrus fruit, apples, pears, conifers, roses, and oaks. The parts were published in three states, plain (9 francs each), coloured (18 francs), and coloured on large paper (30 francs), to form a total of 1000 copies. The grander ones were printed in colour and, at least the large-paper copies, finished by hand. The result was a beautiful book which was also the standard account of the trees of western Europe for several decades, an appropriate way of keeping alive the name of Duhamel. It was reissued in 1825 and again in or about 1852. Selections from it were also published as 'new editions' of Duhamel's *Traité des Arbres fruitiers* (see page 71) and Michel's *Traité du Citronier* (see page 202) is another extract.

Not everyone praised the *Nouveau Duhamel*. John Claudius Loudon, the best dendrologist of the next generation of gardeners, summed it up in the first volume (1838, page 189) of his *Arboretum*:

> A new edition of this work was commenced in the year 1800, and it was completed in seven volumes folio in 1819 . . . The published price of a royal folio copy was 124l. 10s., and of a common copy nearly 100l. . . . Both engravings and descriptions are of very unequal merit, and many of the former (at least in our copy, which is a large paper one) are altogether unworthy of the consequence attempted to be given to the work by large type, large paper, and other characteristics of the mode, now gone by in both France and England, of publishing for the few. As a proof of the truth of what we assert, large paper copies may now be purchased in London for between 30l. and 40l., and small paper copies for twenty guineas.

The Oak Spring copy, at least volumes I to IV, was given by Napoleon I to his father-in-law, the Emperor Francis I of Austria, when Napoleon married Marie-Louise, Archduchess of Austria, in 1810. This seems like a monumental piece of tactlessness, as volumes I to V were dedicated to Napoleon's first wife, Josephine, and all but volume I proclaimed this fact on their title-pages, even the one of volume V, which is dated 1812, three years after the divorce and two after Napoleon's remarriage. The dedication, inserted in volume II in this copy and signed by 'B. Mirbel', praised Josephine's taste for gardening:

> Madame,
> Daignez permettre que je publie sous vos auspices cette nouvelle édition du Traité des Arbres et Arbustes de Duhamel.
> Ce citoyen zélé aimoit passionément l'agriculture: il n'ignoroit pas qu'elle seule peut donner aux empires une puissance et un éclat durables. Pour prix de ses travaux Duhamel obtint l'estime de ses contemporains et de la postérité.
> Vous, Madame, . . . vous aussi, vous aimez l'agriculture; vous prenez plaisir a rassembler dans vos jardins les végétaux les plus rares, et déjà vous désignez les cantons de la France que vous voulez enrichir de ces productions étrangères . . .

A. POITEAU *Recueil des plus beaux fruits* 1846 plate 367  An early white peach, drawn by Poiteau and engraved by Bocourt

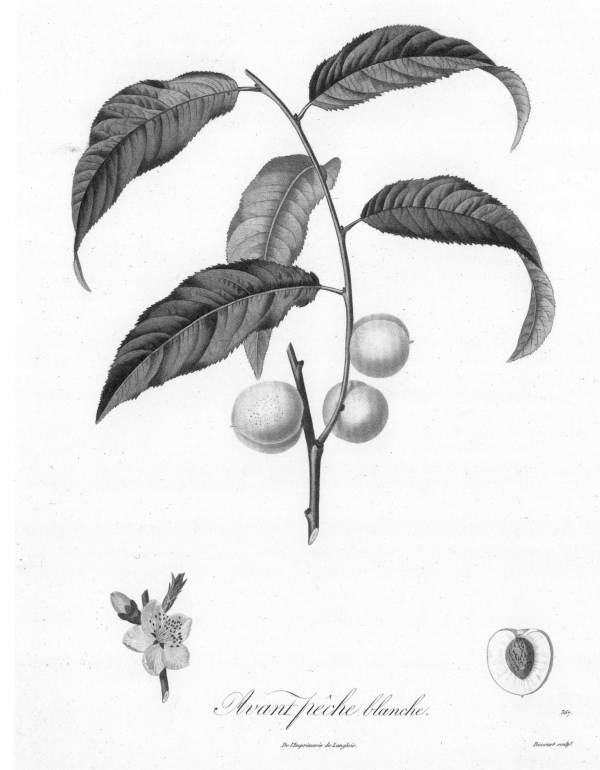

*Avant pêche blanche.*

367.

De l'Imprimerie de Langlois.

Bocourt sculp.

## 31. POITEAU, Antoine (1766–1854)

[Pomologie française. Recueil des plus beaux fruits cultivées en France. Paris, Langlois & Leclerc. 1846.]
2° 41 x 28.5 cm. 141 (of 423) coloured engravings with accompanying text, bound in three volumes with binder's titles as follows: Fruits à pépins (49 plates); Fruit à noyaux (49 plates); Fruits en baies et en chatons (43 plates).

BINDING: Quarter black leather, black and green marbled paper sides.

PLATES: All but one are printed in colour and signed 'De l'Imprimerie de Langlois'; some are retouched by hand. Poiteau was responsible for about half the plates in this selection, and Pierre Jean François Turpin (1775–1840) for the rest. 'Turpin pinxt' has been added in pencil to the bottom left-hand corner of all his plates, as the engraved name was removed after Turpin's death. Most of the engraving was done by Gabriel, Bocourt, and Bouquet, with occasional help from other members of the team working on the *Nouveau Duhamel* (see page 85).

FROM 1807 to 1835 a new edition of Duhamel's *Traité des Arbres fruitiers*, expanded by Poiteau and Turpin, was published in seventy-two parts with over four hundred new plates. Ten years later, after Turpin's death, it was reprinted with a new title under the name of Poiteau alone, and this selection of just over a quarter of the plates is taken from the reprint. The first volume contains apples, pears, quinces, medlars, an arbutus, a persimmon, and four citrus fruits; the second peaches, apricots, plums, cherries, an olive, and a cornus; and the third strawberries, raspberries, gooseberries, mulberries, almonds, hazels, a blackcurrant, a barberry, and a walnut.

Poiteau was trained as a botanist after an apprenticeship as a gardener in the Jardin des Plantes. After some years abroad, he worked with Turpin on the illustrations for several books, both belonging to the group associated with Redouté. Although Turpin was a botanist too, only Poiteau compiled the text of this collection of fruit.

## 32. [LE BERRYAIS, Louis René (1722–1807)]

Traité des Jardins, ou Le nouveau De La Quintinye, Contenant la Description et la Culture, l°. des Arbres Fruitiers; 2°. des Plantes Potagères; 3°. des Arbres, Abrisseaux, Fleurs, et Plantes d'Ornement. Par M. L. B★★★ [double rule] Première partie. Jardin fruitier. [double rule] Nouvelle édition. [vignette 1.5 x 3.5 cm.] A Avranches, Chez Le Court, Imprimeur-Libraire. [rule] M.DCC. LXXXV. Avec Approbation & Privilége du Roi.
8° 20 x 12 cm. π⁴ A–2D⁸ 2E² [10] *i* ii–xxiv *1* 2–410 *411–412*.

. . . Seconde partie. Jardin potager . . .
π² A–2C⁸ *i–iv 1* 2–416.

. . . Troisième partie. Jardin d'ornement . . .
π² A–2L⁸ 2M² *i–iv 1* 2–546 *547–548* and 12 unsigned, folding engravings.

. . . Contenant la Description & la Culture, 1°. des Arbres Fruitiers; 2°. des Plantes Potagères; 3°. des Arbres, Arbrisseaux, Fleurs & Plantes d'Ornement; 4°. des Arbres, Arbrisseaux & Plantes d'Orangerie, & de Serre-Chaude. Par M. L. B★★★. [double rule] Quatrième partie. Orangerie, Serre-Chaude. [double rule] Troisième édition. [ornament 1 x 1 cm.] A Paris, Chez Belin, Libraire, rue Saint-Jacques. A Caen, chez Manoury, l'aîné, Libraire, rue S. Pierre. A Avranches, chez Le Court, Imprimeur-Libraire.

L. R. LE BERRYAIS
*Traité des Jardins* new
edition 1785 volume 3
plate 1 Grafting fruit
trees

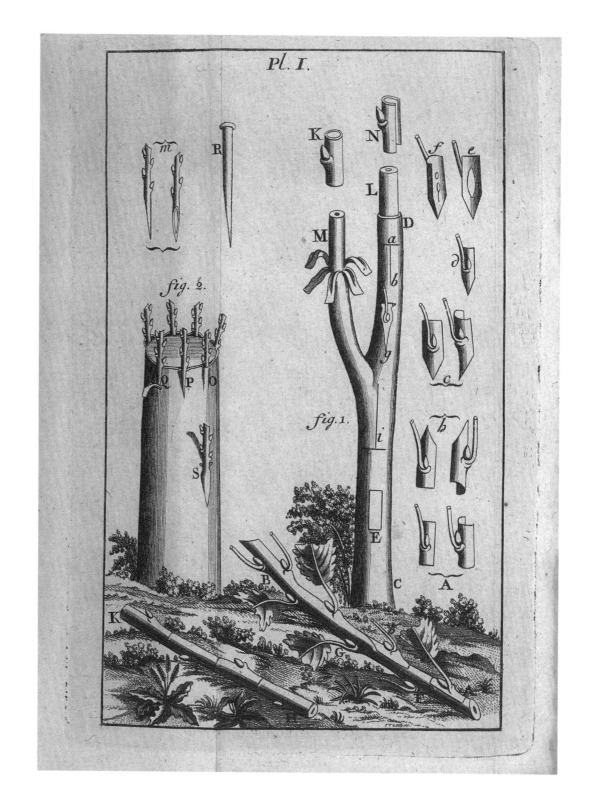

[rule] M. DCC. LXXXVIII. Avec Approbation & Privilége du Roi.
π² A–2H⁸ 2I⁴ 2K⁸ 2L² i–iv 1 2–523 524 and 15 unsigned, folding engravings.

BINDING: Contemporary speckled calf; all edges red. Volume IV contains a few pencilled annotations.

PLATES: The engravings are taken from the author's own drawings. Those bound at the end of volume III are numbered I–XI★, that is, there are twelve in all. The plates in the last volume, bound between pages 504 and 505, contain plans for the construction of orangeries and green-houses. Occasional woodcut tailpieces and decorations of printers' flowers are scattered through the text.

THE ABBÉ LE BERRYAIS spent most of his life in or near Avranches, latterly at Bois-Guérin, where his garden had a view over the bay and Mont St Michel. Here he grew and trained his own fruit trees and developed new varieties, among them the pear Louise Bonne and several cherries, some of which he presented to King Louis XV. His knowledge of fruit was called on in the help he gave to Duhamel du Monceau in the *Traité des Arbres fruitiers*, first published in 1768 (see page 71), for which he drew and coloured illustrations of many trees, as well as contributing descriptions. At Bois-Guérin he was generous with both seeds and grafts, teaching others how to deal with them in what was virtually a free school of gardening. With Duhamel, he was also among the band of enthusiasts who encouraged the cultivation of potatoes in France. During the disturbed years of the Revolution, Le Berryais lived in hiding in Rouen, but his skill and enthusiasm were recognized in 1800 by the award of a gold medal by the Société d'Agriculture in Paris.

The *Traité des Jardins*, first published anonymously in 1775, has nothing to do with La Quintinie but the use of his name, in itself an indication of a lasting reputation as a reliable authority. The first volume deals with the fruit garden and starts with a gardener's calendar, listing work to be done and produce in season each month. The second part, on the *potager* or kitchen garden, also has an 'Explication de quelques Termes de Botanique & de Jardinage' on pages 408 to 416. The third section is about *jardins d'ornement* and their trees, shrubs, and flowers, and the fourth on orangeries and heated green-houses, complete with plans and directions for the culture of tender exotic plants. Oranges and other citrus fruits in their out-door periods are given special attention in volume III too. The book was a great success and ran into three editions in not much more than a decade. There was also an abridged version in a small format, *Le petit La Quintinye*, first published in 1793 and reprinted several times.

Facing the title-pages of volumes II to IV of the *Traité* are advertisements for 'le Sieur Vilmorin-Andrieux, Marchand Grainier-Fleuriste & Botaniste du Roi, & Pépiniériste, Quay de la Mégisserie a Paris,' offering for sale 'Tous les Arbres, tant Fruitiers que d'Ornement; les Arbrisseaux & Arbustes; le Plant, les Oignons, les Bulbes, les Graines de toutes les Plantes Potagères, & de Parterre; les Arbres, Arbrisseaux & Plantes d'Orangerie, & de Serre-chaude, dont il est fait mention dans les quatre Parties de cet Ouvrage'. The great dynasty of Vilmorin nurserymen began in the eighteenth century, and the firm's Paris shop is still in the Quai de la Mégisserie. Le Berryais seems to have kept a close eye on the Vilmorin garden, for at the end of volume IV of the *Traité* there is a last-minute note: 'Ce volume étoit achevé d'imprimer lorsque j'ai trouvé dans le Jardin de M. Vilmorin plusieurs Plantes nouvelles, tant d'Orangerie que de Serre-chaude. J'ai cru devoir ajouter ici les plus intéressantes avec quelques autres que j'avois omises.' The additional list on pages 505 to 517 includes a new mimosa, tea plants, a double-flowered camellia, indigo, a white-flowered datura, and a rose apple, ending with a mention of the plants too new to have been given names: 'Je ne fais point mention de plusieurs belles plantes nouvelles de Serre-chaude, parce qu'elles ne sont pas encore nommées.'

The Abbé's later writings, which included additions to the *Traité des Arbres fruitiers* and a *Petite Pomone française*, as well as treatises on cider and perry, remained unpublished.

## 33. ABERCROMBIE, John (1726–1806)

The British Fruit-Gardener; and Art of Pruning: comprising, The most approved Methods of Planting and Raising every useful Fruit-Tree and Fruit-bearing-Shrub, whether for Walls, Espaliers, Standards, Half-Standards, or Dwarfs: The true successful Practice of Pruning, Training, Grafting, Budding, &c. so as to render them abundantly fruitful: and Full Directions concerning Soils, Situations, and Exposures. By John Abercrombie; of Tottenham-Court, Gardener: Author of Every Man his own Gardener, First published under the Name of Tho. Mawe. London: Printed for Lockyer Davis, in Holborn. MDCCLXXIX.

12° 18 x 12 cm. $A^4$ B–2X$^4$ 2Y$^2$ [2] *i* ii–iv *v–vi* 1 2–104, 104–119, 119–346 (i.e. 348).

BINDING: Brown calf.

JOHN ABERCROMBIE was the son of a market gardener near Edinburgh, where he was trained by his father before going south to work at Kew and other gardens. By the 1760s he had a nursery and market garden at Hackney, on the eastern side of London, and later he sold seeds and plants at Tottenham Court and Newington, not far away. His working life as a gardener has been overshadowed by the success of his books on gardening, especially *Every Man his own Gardener*, first published in 1767 under the name of Thomas Mawe. As a footnote in the preface of the *Fruit-Gardener* says, by 1779 'seven editions . . . have been printed. —This Work, from a diffidence in the writer, was first published as the production of "Thomas Mawe, Gardener to his Grace the Duke of Leeds, and other Gardeners:" it was however entirely written by the author of the following sheets.' By 1848 it had reached its twenty-fifth edition. Over twenty other books by Abercrombie include one on hot-houses and another on 'the garden mushroom', as well as *The Complete Wall-Tree Pruner* (1783) and *The Hot-House Gardener* (see page 261).

In the preface to the *Fruit-Gardener* he explains:

Numerous are the Treatises written on the present subject; few of them, however, have fairly resulted from *Practice*, and therefore it is little to be wondered, that they have been found erroneous and deficient, and liable to mislead in the most essential particulars . . . The favourable reception of a

THE

# Britiſh Fruit - Gardener ;

AND

## ART of PRUNING:

COMPRISING,

The moſt approved Methods of PLANTING
and RAISING every uſeful FRUIT-TREE
and FRUIT-BEARING-SHRUB, whether for
Walls, Eſpaliers, Standards, Half-Standards,
or Dwarfs :

The true ſuccefsful Practice of PRUNING,
TRAINING, GRAFTING, BUDDING, &c.
ſo as to render them abundantly fruitful :

AND

Full Directions concerning SOILS, SITUA-
TIONS, and EXPOSURES.

By JOHN ABERCROMBIE;

Of TOTTENHAM-COURT, Gardener :

AUTHOR OF

EVERY MAN HIS OWN GARDENER,

Firſt publiſhed under the Name of Tho. MAWE.

LONDON:

Printed for LOCKYER DAVIS, in Holborn.
MDCCLXXIX.

former Work has encouraged it's author to submit to the lovers of Gardening, this his Practice in the Culture of Fruit-trees. Indeed, even after some of the sheets were printed off, his idea of it's bulk had not extended beyond the limits of a pamphlet: he was not aware, that by printing merely from *Practice*, before he had planned his Treatise in Manuscript, he was liable (as it has now happened) to encrease his Pamphlet to a Volume.

The book is arranged in alphabetical chapters from almonds to walnuts, each one with details of varieties, propagation, and treatment. The last few chapters are general ones on grafting, situations and soils, planting, protection, and thinning.

## 34. PRESTON, Ralph (*fl.* 1785)

The Modern English Fruit-Gardener, and Practical Wall-Tree Pruner: explaining the improved methods of Propagating, Raising, Planting, Pruning, and Training all sorts of Fruit-Trees, for Walls, Espaliers, and Standards: With the Art of forcing early Fruits in Hot-Walls, Peach-Houses, Vineries, &c. Illustrated with Designs for Hot-Walls and Forcing-Houses. By Ralph Preston, Gardener at Chelsea. [vignette of a basket of grapes 2.5 x 3.5 cm.] London: Printed for John Fielding, (No. 23) Pater-Noster-row. 1785: (Entered at Stationers-Hall.)

12° 16.5 x 9 cm. A⁶ B–K¹² *i–v* vi–xii *1* 2–216 and a folding, engraved frontispiece.

BINDING: Quarter calf, marbled paper sides. Armorial bookplate of Sir Thomas Neame (1885–1973), a fruit farmer from Kent.

PLATES: The frontispiece, showing 'Designs for Hot Walls and Forcing-Houses, for Early Fruits' in six plans and sections, is signed by 'Preston & Dodd designers' and the engraver John Lodge.

The folding frontispiece with designs for hot-houses, drawn by 'Preston & Dodd' and engraved by John Lodge, and the title-page

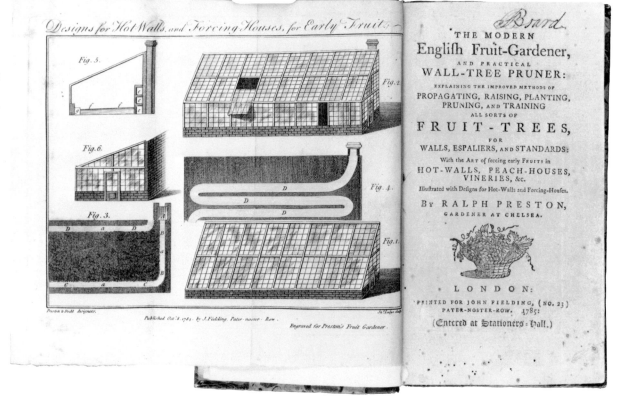

PRESTON'S MANUAL runs briskly through the processes of raising and training fruit trees in general, before treating each kind separately and then giving advice on methods of forcing early fruit, especially peaches, cherries, and grapes. The preface explains the author's intention, with the usual grumbles about rival books:

Though many treatises have recently appeared upon the culture of fruit-trees, none of them appear competent to convey that general information they promise. In some of them, many of the most valuable improvements are intirely omitted; in others, they are treated in a manner too superficial, to convey the necessary information to the unexperienced practitioner . . . Upon the whole, the author flatters himself, that he has not made any material omission on the subject he has undertaken, as he presumes, that a long and sedulous attention to this essential branch of gardening, and a regular series of experiments, has rendered him equal to the task he has undertaken to perform.

## 35. [HUERNE, Joseph van (*fl.* 1790–1831)]

Collection du Regne Vegetal, Arbres Forestiers et Fruitiers, leurs Fruits. &c. Donné par son grand-Père mons: J. van Huerne à Joseph de Pelichy le 9 avril 1831. [Bruges, 1790–1813].
Manuscript 60 x 48 cm. with 46 leaves containing 15 watercolours and gouaches of branches of trees or shrubs and 24 of fruit and foliage; the rest of the leaves are blank.

BINDING: Quarter tan calf, marbled boards.

FOUR ARTISTS have signed one or more of the watercolours: Pierre François Ledoulx (1730–1807) made 14 of them and several of the unsigned ones look very like his work; Jean Charles Verbrugge (1756–1831) made 5 and 'Mademoiselle Jeanne Verbrugghe', possibly his daughter, signed a drawing of a flowering bay twig; and Joseph François Ducq (1762–1829) painted and signed a drawing of an enormous cluster of fir cones. The rest are unsigned. Ledoulx and Verbrugge were both known as flower-painters in Bruges.

Most of the illustrations have notes in the same hand as the inscription on the title-page of the manuscript, presumably that of Joseph van Huerne. The trees, shrubs, and fruit painted by the artists may have been products of his own garden, for the most part, but the comments in the annotations record the writer's observations in other gardens too, like the one on page 12, implying a visit to the Chelsea Physic Garden or the nearby garden of the Royal Hospital in London: 'Le Cone plus grand detaché de la branche, vient d'un semblable arbre du Jardin Roÿal de Celséa, en Angleterre'.

The fruit, some accompanied by leaves and twigs, includes cherries, currants, plums, hazel nuts, medlars, peaches, pears, apples, grapes, figs, and a papaya (the last marked 'for the greenhouse'). There are several oddities among the pictures, bizarre fruits like the twin apples on page 33, labelled 'belle fleurs monstrueuses de l'année 1812'. At least one of the artists was a gardener too, for the note on page 16 records that the blackcurrant on this page was grown in the garden of J. C. Verbrugge, who painted the tiny plant, a single one of its flowers, and a single currant.

A similar album of flowers from the same source appears to have been dismantled and sold

J. C. VERBRUGGE
Cherries, blackcurrants, and a strawberry, a watercolour from page 16 of Joseph van Huerne's album *Collection du Règne végétal* (1790–1813)

*Regne Végétab.*

1. groseiller noir germé de la semence dans le jardin de mr j.c. verbrugghe (dont cette copie est de sa main) apres le mois de mai de l'année 1806. aijant eu a peine deux feuilles dans le cours de la dite année; ceci est, en tout, de grandeur naturelle tel qu'il fut le 4. mai 1807. portant iv. boutons et une Fleur Ouverte, dont une seule a donné un Fruit en maturité ici representé d'apres nature.

as separate watercolours. A copy of M. R. Besler's *Gazophylacium Rerum Naturalium* (1642), annotated and inscribed by J. van Huerne, is described in the Hunt Library catalogue (volume I (1958) number 238, pages 255–56).

## 36. PARRY, Sarah Matilda (*fl.* 1818–1850)

Fruits from the Gardens of Summer Hill. [1794–1828.] Scrap-book 53 x 36 cm. containing watercolours of fruit, mostly two or three on sheets 22 x 27 cm. which are mounted two to a page on 61 brown-paper leaves.

BINDING: Later half green leather, green cloth. Binder's title: 'Fruits grown at Summer Hill, Bath, by Caleb Hillier Parry'. Armorial bookplate of C. H. Parry (1755–1822). A leather label saying 'Sarah Matilda Parry' and a hand-written label 'Fruits from the Gardens of Summer Hill' are both presumably from an earlier binding. Signed 'Sarah Matilda Parry Dunannie Aug$^{st}$ 2nd 1850' on a tipped-in fly-leaf, followed by a pencil note 'Bought by me from a 2$^{nd}$ hand bookshop in Tunbridge Wells 16/4/ 1931. F.S.P. (i.e. Hall's)'. Sold to Oak Spring Garden Library by Harry W. Pratley, another bookseller of Tunbridge Wells, Kent, on 28 October 1966.

SARAH MATILDA PARRY was one of many children of Caleb Hillier Parry (1755–1822), a Cheltenham doctor. Another of his offspring was Rear-Admiral Sir William Edward Parry (1790–1855), the Arctic explorer who was the first to make his way through the North-West Passage. Dr Parry spent the last part of his life in Bath, moving from one spa town to another, where he built a large house called Summer Hill. With the large house went a large orchard, well stocked with all the usual fruits, which were recorded in their due seasons by Sarah Matilda Parry from 1818 to 1822. A few earlier drawings of apples and peaches are signed by Mary Parry and dated July 1794.

Over eighty different apples are illustrated, each with its name and the date of the portrait. Local anonymous varieties with labels like 'Fine Cyder Apple' or 'Aromatic Pippin' are represented among more familiar kinds like 'Ribstone Pippins' and 'Winter Pearmain', each apple given its exact colouring and markings, with any blemishes the chosen specimen may have had. On folio 18 an 'Unknown' and a 'Golden Harvey,' dated 17 and 23 September 1822 are annotated 'My dear father did not live to see the produce of either of these, being amongst the last he planted in Autumn of 1820.'

Apples are followed by pears, forty-two of them, with 'Crassane' and 'Winter Bergamot' of October 1819 captioned 'My dear Father approved these drawings more highly than any in the Collection.' After the pears come twenty cherries, a couple of apricots, eight green, red, or yellow gooseberries, twenty-five plums and a damson, sixteen peaches, six nectarines, two figs, and a medlar. The whole collection makes a splendid sampler of the kinds of fruit in cultivation early in the nineteenth century, thanks to the precision of the artist's style, though this became more sophisticated over the years, with careful shadows and the elegant curves of cherry stalks

SARAH MATILDA
PARRY *Fruits from the
Garden of Summer Hill*
1794–1820 plate 2 Un-
known and Brandy
Apple (November
1818)

Plate 99 Five plums
(September 1820)

SARAH MATILDA
PARRY *Fruits from the
Garden of Summer Hill*
1794–1820 plate 101
Damson (October
1820)

becoming more prominent. Her colouring seems marvellously accurate, even to the subtle variations among the russet apples or furry peaches.

A plan of the 'Upper Garden' dated September 1828 is mounted on the book's second leaf. It shows the location of the tree bearing each variety. A three-page index at the end of the book also gives the locations of the trees as well as the pictures of their products.

During Caleb Parry's life Summer Hill was visited by Wordsworth and other eminent friends, like Edward Jenner and other scientists. After his death the house was almost bought by William Beckford when he left Fonthill, but he eventually settled elsewhere in Bath. The house was demolished late in the nineteenth century.

## 37. FORSYTH, William (1737–1804)

A Treatise on the Culture and Management of Fruit-Trees; in which a new Method of Pruning and Training is fully described. To which is added, a new and improved Edition of "Observations on the Diseases, Defects, and Injuries, in all kind of Fruit and Forest Trees." With an Account of a particular Method of Cure, published by Order of Government. [double rule 3 cm., upper one heavier] By William Forsyth, F.A.S. and F.S.A. Gardener to His Majesty at Kensington and St. James's, Member of the Œconomical Society at St. Petersburg, &c. &c. [double rule 3 cm., lower one heavier] The Sixth Edition, corrected. With references to figures of the Fruits. [swelled rule 2.5 cm.] London: Printed for Longman, Hurst, Rees, Orme, and Brown, Paternoster-Row. And T. Cadell and W. Davies, Strand. 1818.

8° 21 x 12.5 cm. A⁸ a⁶ B–2H⁸ 2I²(–2I2) *i–iii* iv–xxvi *xxvii–xxviii 1* 2–481 *482* and a frontispiece portrait and 13 other engravings (all but V and XII folding).

BINDING: Tan calf, all edges gilt. Bookplate of Sir Robert Peel, of Drayton Manor, near Tamworth, Staffordshire, probably the first baronet (1750–1830), a manufacturer and a Member of Parliament, rather than his son (1788–1850), the better-known Liberal politician.

PLATES: The frontispiece is engraved by Freeman. The other 13 plates are all dated February 1st 1803, and numbers V, VIII, XI, and XII are signed by the artist G. Christie and the engraver H. Mutlow. They show pruning diagrams and tools.

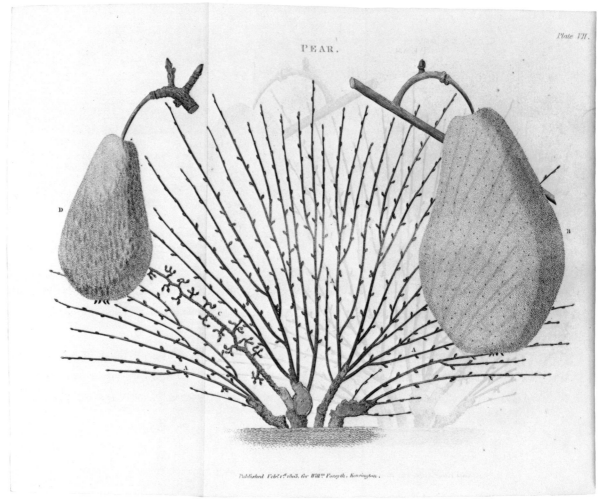

PEAR.

*Plate VII.*

Published Feb.y 1.st 1803, for Will.m Forsyth, Kensington.

WILLIAM FORSYTH
*A Treatise on the Culture and Management of Fruit-Trees* sixth edition 1818 plate VII 'An old decayed Pear-tree, with four stems, which was headed down, . . . and the young wood trained in the common way, or fan-fashion'

WILLIAM FORSYTH was one of that legion of Scottish gardeners who spent their working lives south of the border. His career began at the Chelsea Physic Garden and continued at Syon House, until he returned to Chelsea in 1771 to take over the care of the garden from Philip Miller, who had been in charge of it for nearly half a century. In 1774 Forsyth constructed one of the earliest English rock-gardens there, using a mixture of old stone from the Tower of London and lava brought back from Iceland by Sir Joseph Banks. Ten years later he took charge of the royal gardens at St James's and Kensington. His eminence in the gardening world made him one of the founder members of the Royal Horticultural Society on 7 March 1804, when John Wedgwood's proposal of 29 June 1801 at last led to an inaugural meeting in the house of Mr Hatchard, the bookseller, in Piccadilly. The current Hatchard's bookshop bears a tablet commemorating the occasion.

Forsyth's study of the growth of trees led to the production of a plaster alleged to produce new growth from diseased wood, a remedy adopted by the Admiralty in an effort to maintain its supply of oak for ships. Although Forsyth received the thanks of both houses of parliament and an official reward for the manufacture of this compound, it was later proved to be quite useless, after a prolonged argument among gardeners and scientists, conducted in part in the columns of the *Gentleman's Magazine*. The recipe for the plaster was published, with further information, in *Observations on the Diseases, Defects, and Injuries of Fruit and Forest Trees* (1791) and again in Forsyth's later book, *A Treatise on the Culture and Management of Fruit-Trees*, which first appeared in 1802. This *Treatise* ran through seven editions in twenty-two years, the first three in only two years, and two American adaptations of it were also published (see pages 147–151). Some of its readers thought the book greatly indebted to Thomas Hitt's *Treatise of Fruit-Trees*, first published in 1755 (see page 60), but E. A. Bunyard, in his 'Guide to the Literature of Pomology' (1915) explains the lack of originality of 'the voluble Forsyth' by saying that 'the details of culture had been well thrashed out by previous authors, and little room for innovations was left.' There is a certain charm in the author of *The Anatomy of Dessert* (1929) reproving one of his predecessors for volubility, for his own book contains a series of rhapsodies in highly flavoured prose, which is hard to avoid in distinguishing and describing the different tastes of many varieties of each fruit, from apples to strawberries.

## 38.  MAJOR, Joshua (*c.*1787–1866)

A Treatise on the Insects most prevalent on Fruit Trees, and Garden Produce, giving an account of the different states they pass through, the depredations they commit, and recipes for their destruction, including the recipes of various authors, with remarks on their utility; also, A Few Hints on the Causes and Treatment of Mildew and Canker on Fruit Trees and Cucumbers, &c. &c. &c. [rule 3.5 cm.] By Joshua Major, Landscape Gardener. [rule 3.5 cm.]

London: Longman, Rees, Orme, Brown, and Green, Paternoster-row; and John Baines & Co., and J. Y. Knight, Leeds. [rule 0.5 cm.] 1829.
8° 23 x 14 cm. $A^8$ B–$S^8$ $T^4$ $V^2$ *i–v* vi *vii* viii–xv *xvi* *9* 10–288 *299* 300–302 (i.e. *289* 290–292, as no text is missing).
BINDING: Original grey boards, green cloth spine, and label (price 10*s*.6*d*.). Bookplate of William M. Maude.

JOSHUA MAJOR was a landscape gardener at Knowsthorpe, near Leeds, who later wrote *The Theory and Practice of Landscape Gardening* (1852) and *The Ladies' Assistant in the Formation of their Flower Gardens* (1861). His *Treatise on Insects*, in spite of its title, concentrates on the plants and not the pests, for it is arranged according to the plants affected, starting with fruit trees. After the trees come several soft fruits and vegetables, a section on forcing houses, 'various trees and shrubs', and cucumbers. An appendix describes bellows and other instruments of attack, giving recipes for the sprays to be used.

The author's preface (page v) sets the scene:

Every one who has been engaged in Horticultural pursuits must be fully aware, from painful experience, that the Horticulturist has to struggle against almost innumerable enemies of the insect

JOSHUA MAJOR
*Insects . . . on Fruit Trees*
1829 Title-page

A

# TREATISE

ON THE

## INSECTS

MOST PREVALENT ON FRUIT TREES,

AND GARDEN PRODUCE,

GIVING

AN ACCOUNT OF THE DIFFERENT STATES THEY PASS THROUGH, THE
DEPREDATIONS THEY COMMIT, AND RECIPES FOR THEIR
DESTRUCTION, INCLUDING THE RECIPES OF VARIOUS
AUTHORS, WITH REMARKS ON THEIR UTILITY;

ALSO,

A FEW HINTS ON THE CAUSES AND TREATMENT

OF

### MILDEW AND CANKER

ON FRUIT TREES AND CUCUMBERS, &c. &c. &c.

BY JOSHUA MAJOR,

LANDSCAPE GARDENER.

LONDON:

LONGMAN, REES, ORME, BROWN, AND GREEN,
PATERNOSTER-ROW;
AND JOHN BAINES & CO., AND J. Y. KNIGHT, LEEDS.

1829.

race, by which all his exertions are frequently rendered abortive. The principal object which the author of this work proposed to himself was to give such information as would enable the Horticulturist to free himself from the most formidable of his insect enemies.

The list of subscribers on the last four pages contains a fine sample of the gardening world of the north of England, with a few southern names too. It begins with the Earl of Carlisle of Castle Howard. His gardener, Mr Thomas Law, ordered five copies and is listed later on, with T. and J. Backhouse, the nurserymen of York, Mr Lambec, 'Gardener at Sir George Sitwell's, Bart. Renishaw', and George Lane Fox of Bramham Park.

Pomona: being a selection of Choice Fruit. The whole carefully drawn from nature. [swelled rule 2.5 cm.] By Peter Henderson, author of The Seasons, or Flower Garden; and Treatise on Flower Painting. [double rule, upper one heavier, 11.5 cm.] Thy bounty shines in autumn unconfin'd, And spreads a common feast for all that lives. — Thomson. [that is, the autumn section of James Thomson's poem, *The Seasons*, first published in 1730; double

PETER HENDERSON
*Pomona* 1808 page 5
Observations on colouring fruit

OBSERVATIONS

ON

## COLOURING FRUIT.

IF a true knowledge of Nature gives pleasure, a faithful imitation of her works must necessarily produce a much greater. The great arts of Poetry and Painting, is to present us with the most perfect images of Nature, by collecting all her scattered beauties, and combining them together; which forms those perfect models, which so frequently give delight in both Poetry and Painting.

Although all the works of Nature, in their original formation, are perfect, yet there are some more pleasing than others, and should be selected for imitation. He may be said truly to live who is capable of enjoying the beauties of the creation. The admirer of Nature must at all times feel gratified by tracing her through the various changes in her vegetable production: let us mark the early buds in Spring, expand into leaves; next appears the flower, and so on in succession, until yellow Autumn, with loaded bough, presents us with a banquet of Nature's richest fruits.

" Here, as I steal along the sunny wall,
Where Autumn basks, with fruit-empurpled deep,
My pleasing theme continual prompts my thought;
Presents the downy peach; the shining plum;

rule, lower one heavier, 11.5 cm.] London: Published as the Act directs, by R. Ackermann, Repository of Arts, Strand. Printed by G. Hayden, Brydges Street, Covent Garden. [double rule, upper one heavier, 1 cm.] 1808. 2° 36 x 29 cm. $A^2 B^2 C^2$ $i–iv$ $1$ $2–7$ $8$ and 10 engravings.

BINDING: Grey paper wrappers, the front and spine modern, the mottled back, possibly part of the original

one, pasted to the later spine; blue-grey buckram case.

PLATES: Henderson's plates were coloured by hand, possibly by the artist himself. Six of them (numbers 1, 2, 5, 6, 9, and 10) are dated January 1 1809 and the other four (numbers 3, 4, 7, and 8) January 1 1808, so it seems possible that the collection was issued in 1809 rather than 1808.

PETER HENDERSON was responsible for about half the plates in Robert Thornton's *Temple of Flora* (1799–1807), that odd book combining showy flower pictures with theatrical scenic backgrounds, but he painted portraits of human subjects as well as flowers and fruit. His *Pomona* concentrates on soft fruit—grapes, plums, currants, cherries, with one nut, a couple of apples, and a pear added to plate 9, the first of two groups that form the last two plates.

## 40a.  BROOKSHAW, George (*fl.* 1804–1822)

Pomona Britannica; or, A Collection of the Most Esteemed Fruits at present cultivated in the country; together with the Blossoms and Leaves of such as are necessary to distinguish the various sorts from each other. Selected principally from the Royal Gardens at Hampton Court, and the remainder from the most celebrated gardens round London. Accurately drawn and coloured from Nature, with Full Descriptions of their various Qualities, Seasons, &c. By George Brookshaw, Esq. [swelled rule 5 cm.] London: Printed for the Author, by T. Bensley, Bolt Court, Fleet Street. Published by White, Cochrane, and Co. Fleet Street; E. Lloyd, Harley Street; and W. Lindsell, Corner of Wigmore Street. 1812.
1° 57 x 45 cm. $\pi^1 2\pi^1$ a–c$^1$ B–2H$^1$ 2I$^1$ [4] $i$ ii–v $vi$ 1 2–60 61–62 and 90 coloured plates.

BINDING: Contemporary Russia leather, blind-stamped border within gilt one on sides, rebacked; all edges gilt.

Bookplate of William Legge, 4th Earl of Dartmouth, with a label saying 'Patshull Case VIII', presumably referring to the library of Patshull House, near Wolverhampton, Staffordshire, the family seat.

PLATES: The aquatint plates with some stipple engraving were printed in colour and finished by hand. Only one of them (XLVIII, the Royal Muscadine grape) carries an engraver's name, that of H. Merke, though Nissen (*Die botanische Buchillustration*, page 124) also credits the artist's older brother, Richard Brookshaw, with some of the work, particularly the dark-coloured grounds. The numbering of the ninety plates, 1 to XCIII but lacking XXXIX, XLII, and XLVI, the Montserrat Pine, an unknown new pineapple from the Duke of York's garden, and the Striped Sugar-Loaf Pine, as suitable specimens were not available, is explained on page 32. The plates are dated from March 1804 to 1812.

BROOKSHAW'S *Pomona*, described in 1909 by S. T. Prideaux (*Aquatint Engraving*, page 295) as 'one of the finest colour-plate books in existence', is surely the only fruit book to rival the showy quality of the flowers in Thornton's *Temple of Flora* (1799–1807). It seems appropriate, considering its size and ostentation, that it should have been dedicated to 'His Royal Highness George, Prince Regent' (later George IV), who acquired that title only in 1811, the year before the book was completed. In 1812 the book cost 59 pounds 18 shillings, though

PLATE LXXI.
*White Candia*

GEORGE BROOKSHAW
*Pomona Britannica* folio
edition 1812 plate LXXI
White Candia Melon

Prideaux states that it was also issued in thirty parts, which would fit in with the dates on the plates and the author's statement at the beginning of the introduction that 'This work . . . has occupied nearly ten years constant attention and labour.' The plates show 256 varieties of fifteen fruits, beginning with strawberries and going on through soft fruit and stone fruit to pineapples, grapes, melons, nuts, figs, pears, and apples. Pineapples and grapes occupy almost as many plates as apples and pears, and peaches have rather more, for Brookshaw's descriptions were intended for gardeners well supplied with both greenhouses and the skilled hands needed to use them properly to produce fine fruit. Many of the plates show the fruit, sometimes with leaves and flowers, against the dark backgrounds that have come to be considered Brookshaw's trademark. The contrast they provide certainly adds a theatrical effect that makes these plates so popular as single decorative pictures from dismembered copies of the book.

The artist's studies of fruits were adapted for a second book, a quarto using the same title but published in a smaller format in 1816 and 1817 (see below), and a third time in an even smaller book, the octavo *Horticultural Repository*, which was issued posthumously in 1823. The anonymous writer of a preface to the *Repository* recorded Brookshaw's death the previous winter and mourned 'this able artist, and observing horticulturist', one of those 'persons of genius and of talent who labour for the pleasures and conveniences of their species; yet, who live almost unknown, and sink into the tomb unheard of and undistinguished'. The *Pomona* was intended to be an accurate record of the best available varieties of fruit and to encourage people to cultivate them. Brookshaw's introduction underlines the importance of the subject by recommending it to the infant Horticultural Society (founded in 1804): 'It should be the business of the Horticultural Society, to try experiments to improve the growth of fruit. How much soever the subject has been neglected, it is of sufficient importance to demand attention.' It also expresses the author's and artist's own hopes for his book's value: 'If any hints that have been given in the course of these sheets, should induce the lovers of fruit to make any discovery, or be the means of improving their gardens, the end will have been in a great measure answered for which this Work was executed.'

## 40b. BROOKSHAW, George (*fl.* 1804–1822)

Pomona Britannica, or A Collection of the Most Esteemed Fruits at present cultivated in Great Britain; selected principally from the Royal Gardens at Hampton Court, and the Remainder from the most celebrated Gardens round London. Accurately Drawn and Coloured from Nature. With full descriptions of their various qualities, seasons, &c. [swelled rule 3.5 cm.] by George Brookshaw, Esq. Vol. I. [swelled rule 4 cm.] London: Printed by Bensley and Son, Bolt Court, Fleet Street; for Longman, Hurst, Rees, Orme, and Brown, Paternoster Row; and John Lepard, 108, Strand. [rule 2 cm.] 1817.
4° 33.5 x 27 cm. *A*² B⁴ *C*² and 33 unsigned leaves *i–v* vi–xii *1* 2–4 and 66 unnumbered pages and 30 coloured plates.

GEORGE BROOKSHAW
*Pomona Britannica*
quarto edition 1817
volume I plate II
Raspberries

. . . Vol. II . . .

$\pi^2$ and 33 unsigned leaves 70 unnumbered pages and 30 colored plates.

BINDING: Diced Russia leather, blind-stamped border within gilt one on sides (similar to the Patshull copy of the larger *Pomona Britannica*: see page 104); marbled edges.

Label of the binder Benedict, N? 4 Mays Buildings, St Martins Lane, London.

PLATES: The sixty line and stipple engravings were partially printed in colour and finished by hand. Many are adaptations of plates in the larger edition.

THIS quarto edition of Brookshaw's huge *Pomona* began to be issued six years after the completion of its larger sibling, which it often echoes in both text and illustrations. A prospectus with the Oak Spring copy is dated 6 May 1816 and promised publication of the first part on 1 June, with the others following at the beginning of the next eleven months, each part containing five plates and the appropriate text. The parts were priced at 'One guinea each to Subscribers'.

There are no pineapples in this edition, which is probably an indication of the more modest gardeners Brookshaw hoped to attract with this less expensive edition. The plates illustrate 174 varieties of other fruits, about eighty less than the large *Pomona*, and the preface (page vi) uses the name of Sir Joseph Banks, President of the Royal Society and a founder member of the Horticultural Society, as a recommendation: 'When, long ago, I first communicated my plan to Sir Joseph Banks, he told me he was so deeply convinced of the necessity and great utility of the undertaking, that he had for twenty years been wishing to have such a work executed', that is, a practical book with 'clear, characteristic descriptions, and exact coloured delineations drawn from the best specimens to be found in nature, of the most select varieties of Garden-fruits'.

The last four pages in volume II contain a 'Table of Reference to the Gardens from which the most curious and rare specimens were obtained', from the royal ones of Hampton Court, Windsor, and Kensington Palace, to noble ones like Sion House, Strawberry Hill, Osterley, and Chiswick, and those of knowledgeable connoisseurs like 'Mr Maddox', that is, James Maddock the younger, the nurseryman of Walworth, Dr John Coakley Lettsom, of Grove Hill in Camberwell, and Sir Joseph Banks himself.

## 41. BROOKSHAW, George (*fl.* 1804–1822)

Groups of Fruits, accurately drawn and coloured after nature, with full directions for the young artist: designed as a companion to the treatises on flowers and birds. [double rule, upper one heavier, 4 cm.] By George Brookshaw, Esq. author of the Pomona Britannica, Treatise on Flower Painting, &c. [double rule, lower one heavier, 4 cm.] London: [double rule, lower one heavier, 2 cm.] Printed for William Stockdale, 181, Piccadilly; by Augustus Applegath and Henry Mitton, 24, Nelson-square, Great Surrey-street. [rule 1 cm.] 1817.

1° 36 x 26 cm. 20 unsigned and unnumbered leaves including 12 engravings, 6 coloured by hand.

BINDING: Half red leather, rebacked, new corners, contemporary marbled paper sides, the front one with a printed label, 'Fruits by Brookshaw'. Bookplate of Paul Mellon.

GEORGE BROOKSHAW
*Groups of Fruits* 1817
Apricots plain and
coloured

BOTANICAL drawing-books were popular during the eighteenth and early nineteenth centuries, as many amateur artists, especially female ones, were eager for instruction in the skill of painting flowers in particular. Many of these books were cheap and fairly slim, often with a handful of coloured plates facing or followed by uncoloured versions for the students to practise on. Brookshaw published a trio of these little books in 1817, one each on flowers, fruit, and birds, but the first issues are exceedingly rare. Even that determined botanical bibliographer, Blanche Henrey, had to admit to having seen 'only the second edition (1819) of each of these works' and a copy of the one on fruit in its 1817 issue, which formed lot 89 of the Arpad Plesch sale in 1975, was catalogued as 'the only recorded copy of the first edition'. There is at least one more copy in existence, in the Oak Spring Garden Library, which also contains 1817 editions of the rest of the trio, on flowers and birds.

The plates show cherries, apples, apricots, plums, pears, and redcurrants, with a leaf of text for each fruit. Brookshaw's general advice was quite brisk. 'In copying these groups of fruit, I recommend the student to attend more to the drawing and general freedom of the whole, than to a minute imitation of the exact turn or size of a leaf, or any other particular part.' The precision of his own work in both the large and small editions of *Pomona Britannica* makes it seem unlikely that he practised what he preached.

## 42. HOOKER, William (1779–1832)

Pomona Londinensis: containing coloured engravings of the most esteemed fruits cultivated in the British gardens, with a descriptive account of each variety. [swelled rule 1.5 cm.] Assisted in the descriptive part by the President and Members and Sanctioned by the Patronage of the Horticultural Society of London. [rule 2.5 cm.] Vol. I. [double rule, upper one heavier, 4.5 cm.] London: Printed by James Moyes, Greville Street, Hatton Garden. Published by the Author, 5, York Buildings, New Road, Marylebone; and sold by J. Harding, St. James's Street; J. and A. Arch, Cornhill; and Rodwell and Martin, Bond Street. [rule 1.5 cm.] 1818.

4° 33 x 24.5 cm. $\pi^4$ A–C$^4$ D$^2$ E$^4$ F$^2$ G$^4$ (G2+1) H$^2$ I$^2$(–I2) K$^4$ L$^4$(–L4) M$^4$ N$^2$ O$^2$(–O2) P$^4$ Q$^2$ R$^2$ (–R2) 104 unnumbered pages and 49 engravings, coloured by hand.

BINDING: Contemporary diced Russia leather, rebacked; by William Wesley & Son, 28 Essex Street, Strand, London. Bookplate of Moncure Biddle.

PLATES: The forty-nine aquatints were engraved and coloured by Hooker from his own drawings, which still survive in the Lindley Library of the Royal Horticultural Society. The large-paper copies are said to have even better finished plates, though the ones in the quarto are fine.

WILLIAM HOOKER was a pupil of Franz (or Francis) Bauer, the Austrian brought to Kew as its resident artist by Sir Joseph Banks. It is uncommon for a botanical artist to be able to write systematic descriptions of his subjects, but Hooker shared this ability with the French artist, Antoine Poiteau (see pages 89, 206). Several of Hooker's drawings, mostly of fruit, appeared in the first five volumes of the Horticultural Society's *Transactions* from 1815 to 1824. The originals, like the ones for his *Pomona*, were among the books and drawings sold by the society in a moment of financial crisis in 1859, but they were bought back in 1927. Hooker's *Paradisus Londinensis*, with over a hundred plates of plants growing in or near London, was published in parts from 1805 to 1808. He also illustrated Frederick Pursh's flora of North America, published in London in 1814.

*Pomona Londinensis* was issued in seven parts from 1813 to 1818, dedicated to the President (Thomas Andrew Knight, an authority on fruit: see page 214), Vice-Presidents, Honorary Members, and Fellows of the Horticultural Society:

The zeal with which Horticulture is now pursued in every part of this Empire, and in the neighbouring Countries on the Continent; the introduction of valuable acquisitions of new or hitherto unknown fruits, increased by the widely extending correspondence of the Horticultural Society of London, will be deemed a sufficient apology for the publication; and will, the Author trusts, ensure it a favourable reception.

The White Dutch Currant.

WILLIAM HOOKER
*Pomona Londinensis* 1818
plate XXXVI The White
Dutch Currant

The reception was not good enough to allow the *Pomona* to continue, for no more parts were published after the end of Volume I, which described thirteen apples, eight pears, seven plums, five peaches, four nectarines, four cherries, and one or two examples of several other fruits. Most of the plates show leaves and twigs as well as fruit, and several have cross-sections too. Hooker tried to choose the best varieties of his time, making frequent references to La Quintinie, Duhamel, and Switzer. Contemporary gardeners and nurserymen were also called on to provide both fruit and information, for example, plate XXXI, the Black Circassian Cherry, which 'was introduced into this country in the year 1794, by Mr. Hugh Ronalds, of Brentford, who imported it from Circassia. It has subsequently been extensively dispersed from his Nursery.' Ronalds's book of apples was published in 1831 (see page 216).

## 43. NOISETTE, Louis Claude (1772–1849)

Le Jardin fruitier, contenant L'histoire, la description, la culture et les usages des Arbres fruitiers, des Fraisiers, et des meilleurs espèces de Vignes qui se trouvent en Europe; les usages des Fruits sous le rapport de l'économie domestique et de la Médicine; des principes elementaires sur la manière d'élever les arbres, sur la Greffe, la Plantation, la Taille, et tout ce qui a rapport a la conduite d'un Jardin fruitier. Par L. Noisette, et rédigé d'après ses notes par L.-A. Gautier, Docteur en Médicine; Ouvrage orné de 90 planches représentant 220 espèces de fruits coloriés d'après nature. Premier volume. [ornament 2 x 10 cm. of two suns either side of an urn, with vine clusters] Paris, Audot, Libraire-Editeur, rue des Maçon-Sorbonne, Nº 11 [double rule 2.5 cm.] 1821.
4° 29 x 21.5 cm. $\pi^2$ a–m$^4$ *1* 2–95 *96* and 10 engravings, coloured by hand.

. . . Deuxième volume . . .
$\pi^2$ 1–22$^4$ *1* 2–176

. . . Troisième volume . . .
$\pi^2$ *i–iv* and 80 engravings, coloured by hand and numbered as in the 'Avis au relieur' on the last page of volume II: 1–9, 9*bis*, 10, 10*bis*, 11–52, 52*bis*, 55–77.

BINDING: Quarter red calf, blue mottled paper-covered boards.

Le Jardin fruitier, histoire et culture des arbres fruitiers, des ananas, melons et fraisiers; descriptions et usages des fruits. Manière de former et diriger une pépinière; par

Louis Noisette, botaniste-cultivateur, membre de plusieurs sociétés savantes françaises et étrangères, auteur du Manuel complet du jardinier. Seconde edition, Considérablement augmentée, et ornée de figures de tous les bons fruits connus, gravées sur de nouveaux dessins faits d'après nature; par P. Bessa, Peintre du Muséum d'histoire naturelle: Imprimées en couleurs et retouchées au pinceau par les coloristes de l'Herbier de l'Amateur. [decorated rule 3.5 cm.] Première partie. [decorated rule 3.5 cm.] Paris. Audot, Libraire-Éditeur, rue du Paon, 8, École de Médicine. 1839.
8° 23 x 14 cm. $\pi^4$ a$^2$(–a2) 1–5$^8$ 6$^8$(–6:8) *i–vii* viii–ix *x* 1 2–94 and 7 engravings (numbers IV and VII folding).

*With which is bound:*

. . . Deuxième partie . . . 1833.
1–17$^8$ 18–21$^4$ (22 missing) 23–27$^4$ 28$^6$ *1–7* 8–288 (22 blank pages) 297–348.

. . . Volume de Planches . . . 1839.
$\pi^2$ *i–iv* and 146 (of 152) engravings, printed in colour and finished by hand, numbered I–XLI, XLI*bis*, XLII–LXXVIII, LXXVIII*bis*, LXXIX–LXXX, LXXX*bis*, LXXXI–CXVI (CXVII–CXXII missing), CXXIII–CXLIX. Two of the plates, CXXVII and CXXIX are double ones, showing the grapes 'Raisin Poiteau' and 'Gros Gamet'.

BINDING: Quarter dark red leather, red leather-cloth sides. An 'Avis au relieur' on the last page of volume II gives instructions for binding as in this copy, that is, the

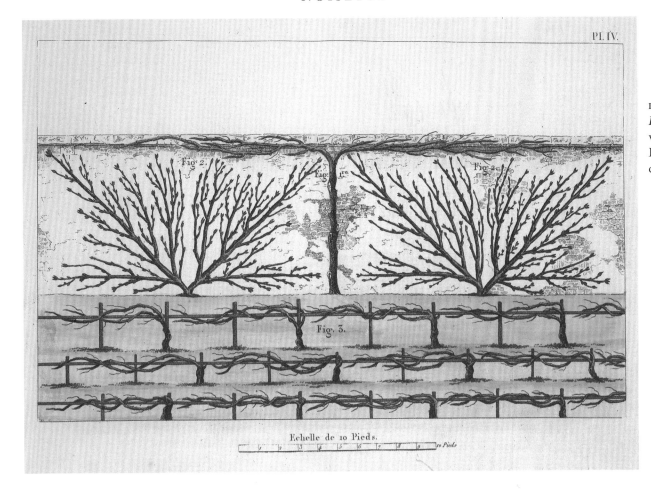

PL. IV.

LOUIS NOISETTE
*Le Jardin fruitier* 1821
volume I plate IV
Espaliers and
cordons

two sections of text, separated by the plates of processes and tools, in one volume, and the coloured fruit plates in a second.

PLATES: The unsigned fruit plates of the first edition of the *Jardin fruitier* are nearly all copied from those of the 1768 first edition of Duhamel's *Traité des Arbres fruitiers* (see page 71), which were based on drawings by René Le Berryais, Ma(g)deleine Basseporte, and Claude Aubriet. Only the quinces (plates 9 and 9*bis*), the nuts (plates 15 and 16), a few apples and pears, and most of the grape plates (60, 68–77) are not linked with Duhamel drawings. The adaptations, often reversed, and sometimes using only parts of the *Traité* pictures, are usually printed four to a plate in the Noisette book. Most of the *Jardin* plates bear no engraver's name either, but Theodor Susémihl signed most of the grapes (60–63 and 70–77), as well as the spreading espaliered tree on plate IV of the ten in volume I (repeated as plate II in the second edition) showing pruning methods and tools.

Although Nissen's *Die botanische Buchillustration* (1951) gives Pancrace Bessa the credit for the drawings reproduced in the first edition of the *Jardin fruitier*, it seems unlikely that he was responsible for adapting the *Traité* drawings, though the new grape plates look much more like his work. The illustrations of the second edition are undoubtedly by Bessa, who was also working on plates for the *Nouveau Duhamel* (see page 85) while the parts of the first edition of the *Jardin* being published. Once again grapes show the closest resemblances, though the *Nouveau Duhamel* ones have more foliage than those in the *Jardin fruitier*. The two editions of the Noisette book also share some of the same grapes, for instance, 'Muscat rouge' (plates 64 and CXXIII) and 'Raisin d'Alep/Morillon panaché' (plates 75 and CXXXI), confirming the impression that Bessa added the grapes to the first edition.

The same publisher, Audot, issued the first series of the *Herbier de l'Amateur* from 1812 to 1827, hence the announcement on the title-page of the second edition of the

*Jardin fruitier*, pointing out that the colouring had been done by the team responsible for the popular *Herbier*. The set of plates used as models by the colourists was sold by Sotheby's in London on 18 November 1975, with other books from the collection of Arpad Plesch. Five lithographs among the engraved plates were left uncoloured: four pears, numbers LXX, LXXI, LXXXVI, and LXXXVIII (the last one called 'La Quintinye') and an apple, number C, 'Josephine'.

Although the second edition of Noisette appears to have almost twice as many fruit plates as the first, 152 rather than 80, most of those in the first edition contain three or four fruits, with leaves and flowers, while nearly all in the second edition show single fruits with fewer trimmings, so that the difference in the number illustrated is less great than it seems.

LOUIS NOISETTE
*Le Jardin fruitier* 1821
volume I plate VII
Grafting tools and
methods

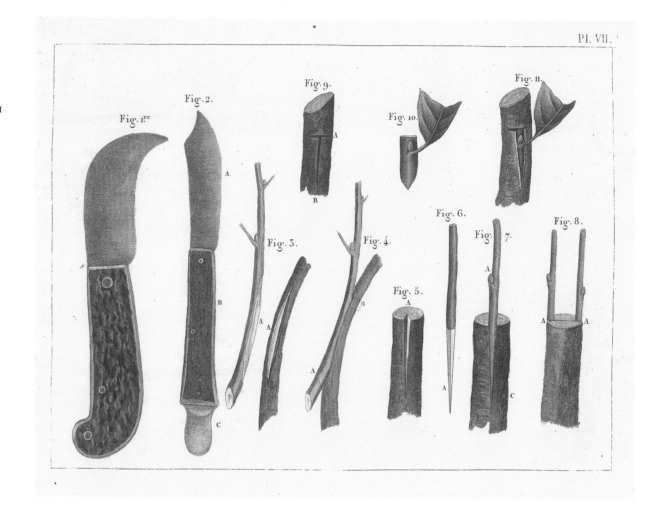

LOUIS NOISETTE was the son of a gardener and followed the same occupation in 1795, after his military service, when he took charge of the gardens and greenhouses of the Val de Grâce hospital in Paris. Three years later he was renting land for his own nursery garden in the Faubourg Saint-Jacques. Once his garden was established he travelled to Hungary with Prince Esterhazy, furnishing the Prince's new plantations there. As Noisette's reputation and his nur-

Épargne.     Cuisse Madame.

LOUIS NOISETTE
*Le Jardin fruitier* 1821
volume III plate 27
Four pears, copied from
pear plates VI, VIII, VII,
and V at page 254 of
volume II of Duhamel's
*Traité des Arbres fruitiers*
(1768)

Pl. 52

LOUIS NOISETTE
*Le Jardin fruitier* 1821
volume III plate 52
Two apples, copied
from apple plates X and
XIV at page 322 of vol‑
ume I of Duhamel's
*Traité des Arbres
fruitiers* (1768)

Reinette, franche.

Rambour, franc.

sery's stock both grew, he started a larger garden for trees and fruit at Fontenay-les-Roses, before moving to Montrouge in 1836. The Noisette nursery is credited with the introduction to France of many new North American plants, a speciality that must have been helped by Louis's brother Philippe, who was for some years a nurserymen in Charleston, South Carolina. The original Noisette rose, first raised in Charleston, was one of these introductions, in 1814, and the 'Fraisier de Caroline' in the *Jardin fruitier* is another reminder of the association.

Although Louis Noisette wrote or contributed to several other gardening books, *Le Jardin fruitier*, first published in fifteen parts from 1813 to 1821, is devoted to a subject in which the French had long been leaders, the cultivation and training of fruit trees. The history, culture, and uses of all the fruits are described, with advice on cultivation beginning with planting seeds, before going on to grafting and other methods of training and shaping trees for the best results. Of the ten plates in the first volume, six show methods of pruning and guiding the growth of trees, while the other four display the tools needed for these tasks. There is also a fruit calendar to help the gardener plan the most productive use of his ground.

The vine has a section all to itself, accompanied by seventeen of the eighty fruit plates, an accurate reflection of the grape's importance in France.

The editor of the text, Dr L. A. Gautier, does not seem to have written independently on the subject, although he is probably the author of a *Dissertation sur la bière, et principalement sur les espèces de bières fabriqués à Paris*, which was published in 1815.

The second edition of the *Jardin fruitier* appeared in twenty-six parts from 1832 to 1839. The additions include advice on pineapples, melons, and strawberries, though without illustrations of the first two of these popular fruits. The interval between the two editions allowed the author to catch up with the work of Jean Baptiste Van Mons, the Belgian nurseryman who produced many new varieties of fruit, especially pears. Several of them are added to Noisette's second edition, with comments on Van Mons's experiments in plant breeding.

Dr Patrick Neill, an Edinburgh printer and the first secretary of the Caledonian Horticultural Society, visited the Noisette nursery on 17 August 1821 and printed a long account of it in his *Journal of a Horticultural Tour* in 1823 (pages 457–68). The following extracts concentrate on the fruit trees he saw there and Noisette's treatment of them, as well as his book:

> I spent the greater part of this day in the celebrated pepiniere of L. Noisette, No. 51 Fauxbourg St Jacques, near the National Observatory. I was fortunate in finding M. Noisette at home, and on learning my name and pursuits, he immediately proposed to conduct me personally through his grounds, and he did so with the greatest attention. He has here formed an extensive arrangement of all fruit-trees adapted to the climate of this part of France. The genera and species are kept distinct, after the Jussieuan method; and the varieties of each species are arranged in the order of the maturity of their fruit, after the mode of Duhamel. Of every kind he has a specimen-tree in a bearing state; and close by this specimen-tree are placed, in general, several young trees of the same kind, budded

LOUIS NOISETTE
*Le Jardin fruitier* second
edition 1839 plate XXVI
Six plums, drawn by
Pancrace Bessa

PL. XXVI    *1 Ile verte.*         *3 Prune d'Agen.*    *5 Royale.*
            *2 Prune de S.ᵗᵉ Catherine.*  *4 Quetsche.*      *6 Prune de Briançon.*

or grafted from the bearing tree, —or else stocks ready to receive such buds or grafts . . . Doubtless, trees thus confined to very circumscribed limits, cannot be expected to afford much fruit; but they yield enough to identify the kinds, and to satisfy purchasers regarding the precise varieties which they may wish to possess . . .

The principal part of the arrangement is necessarily occupied with those kinds of fruit-trees which are generally cultivated and frequently in demand; apples, pears, plums, apricots, peaches, and cherries. It is only in the greater variety of fine pears and peaches, that this French nursery excels our English ones . . .

While examining the peaches, M. Noisette shewed me several examples of different modes of training peach-trees and grape-vines together, so as to procure to both the benefit of the same wall, and at the same time rendering them productive of fruit; and he seemed to think that this mode of training might be found useful in economising the limited space included in our vineries and peach-houses in Britain . . .

M. Noisette is about to publish "Le Jardin Fruitier," in two thin volumes 4to, with a volume of coloured plates, representing the different fruits. Some of these plates I saw in his library. In point of execution they are inferior to those of Hooker, or even of Bradshaw [that is, Brookshaw]; but as M. Noisette has a most extensive practical knowledge of the fruits of France, the work will doubtless prove highly deserving of a place in the [Caledonian] Horticultural Society's collection . . . I may add that M. Noisette, after having, with much care, studied the fruits of France for many years, expresses his high opinion of the general accuracy of the great work of Duhamel du Monceau. The execution of the engravings also is masterly. I would therefore strongly recommend to the Society to take the earliest convenient opportunity of furnishing their library with a complete copy of the splendid and expensive "Traité des Arbres Fruitiers" of that celebrated author [that is, the *Nouveau Duhamel*: see page 82].

LOUIS NOISETTE
*Le Jardin fruitier* 1821
volume II page 22
Tail-piece: a basket of
fruit with tools

## 44. LINDLEY, John (1799–1865)

Pomologia Britannica; or, Figures and Descriptions of the most important Varieties of Fruit cultivated in Great Britain. [swelled rule 1.5 cm.] By John Lindley, PH.D. F.R.S. etc. etc. etc. Professor of Botany in University College, London. [rule 2 cm.] In three volumes, Vol. I. [rule 4 cm.] London: Henry G. Bohn, York Street, Covent Garden. MDCCCXLI.

4° 24 x 14.5 cm. $A^2$ B–$N^4$ $O^2$ 104 unnumbered pages and 48 engravings, 3 of them folded, coloured by hand.

. . . Vol. II . . .

$A^2$(–A2) B–$N^4$ $O^2$ 104 unnumbered pages and 48 engravings, coloured by hand.

. . . Vol. III . . .

$a^4$ $b^4$ B–$M^4$ $N^6$ $O^6$(–O6) $P^4$(P4+1) [2] i–iii iv–xiv and 122 unnumbered pages and 56 engravings, 2 of them folded, coloured by hand.

BINDING: Half dark green morocco, marbled paper sides; spine gilt, with grapes and strawberries in compartments; all edges gilt.

PLATES: All, except five in the first volume signed by C. M. Curtis, are the work of Augusta Innes Withers (fl. 1827–1864), 'Flower Painter in Ordinary to Queen Adelaide'. S. Watts and W. Clarke engraved the drawings, and the plates are dated from November 1827 to December 1830.

JOHN LINDLEY had a model, hard-working, Victorian career, as botanist, writer, and editor. From 1822 to 1860 he was first assistant secretary, then secretary to the (Royal) Horticultural Society, whose library still bears his name. He became a Fellow of the Royal Society in 1828 and the first professor of botany at the newly founded University College London the following year. His own books ranged from popular text-books to monographs on orchids and roses, but he also helped to found the *Gardener's Chronicle* in 1841 and edited this journal until his death.

As the Horticultural Society maintained a collection of fruit trees in its Chiswick garden, Lindley was well placed to be kept informed of new varieties or variations on old ones. He also found a collaborator there, Robert Thompson (fl. 1824–1865), one of the men in charge of the fruit garden. Thompson's help was not willingly acknowledged, it seems, as he made plain in the preface to the third volume: 'This Work was originally commenced by two Officers of the Horticultural Society . . . Various causes have, however, induced that one of the Editors, upon whom at all times the greater part, and latterly the whole, of the labour of conducting the Work has fallen, to suspend it for the present, with the Third Volume, and the 152nd Plate.' He initialled the text for the last few plates, numbers 145 to 152.

The plates bear dates from November 1827 to December 1830, reflecting their first appearance in the successive parts of the *Pomological Magazine*, which Lindley started to 'make the Public accurately acquainted with those varieties of Fruit which are of sufficient importance to deserve cultivation in Great Britain; and secondly, to reconcile the discordant nomenclature of nurserymen and other cultivators'. The pattern used was the familiar one of the relevant text matching each plate, four or five of which were included in each monthly part. After the *Magazine* expired,

JOHN LINDLEY
*Pomologia Britannica*
1841 volume I plate I
The Waxed-leaved Pine-apple, drawn by Augusta Innes Withers and engraved by S. Watts

Henry Bohn bought the remaining stock, perhaps from the original publisher, J. Moyes, and reissued it in three volumes with a more appealing title.

The authors used their situation to describe new imports, among them several varieties sent to the Horticultural Society from America. Plate 54 in volume II is the President Peach, a rare exception to the author's opinion that peaches from North America were 'almost uniformly worthless in the climate of Great Britain.' In the same volume, plate 72 illustrates the Seckle Pear and the text is much more enthusiastic, quoting William Coxe (see page 151) and David Hosack, who sent this variety to the Society in 1818 and described it in the *Horticultural Society Transactions* in 1819. 'Subsequent experience in this country has amply confirmed the American account. It is found to exceed in excellence of flavour the very richest of our autumn Pears, possessing a high vinous aroma, which can scarcely be compared with anything in fruits.'

Earlier writers on fruit were consulted too, sometimes unsuccessfully, as in volume III, plate 129, 'The Purple Gage Plum . . . The origin of this variety is unknown; it must, however, be recent, as it is not mentioned by Duhamel [see page 71], or any of the older French writers, and is even omitted by Noisette in his Jardin Fruitier [see page 112].'

## 45.

Le Panier de Fruits, ou Descriptions botaniques et notices historiques des principaux fruits cultivés en France; suivies de différens morceaux de littérature et de morale; ouvrage orné de vingt-quatre planches coloriées; destiné aux jeunes gens. [rule 1.5 cm.] A Paris, Chez Perlet, rue de Tournon, n.º 6. 1807.
8º 21.5 x 13.5 cm. a⁴ 1–4⁸ 5⁶ 6–15⁸ s⁸ 17–24⁸ i–iii iv–viii 1 2–384 and 24 plates.

BINDING: Original green boards, red leather label; uncut. Bookplate of Anne W. Kavangh and her signature 'Anne' on title-page.

PLATES: All are stipple engravings, printed in colour and finished by hand. They were engraved by Maradan from drawings by J. G. Prêtre (fl. 1800–1840), except for the first, an almond, which is signed by Mademoiselle Joséphine Prêtre.

THE BOOK was first published in twelve parts, according to the signatures. The pretty plates show fruits with their leaves and flowers, from the apple to the pineapple, and the book was a sequel or rather a companion piece to *La Corbeille de Fleurs*, issued by the same publisher in the same year, though with the addition of '12 romances gravées avec accompagnement de piano. Destiné aux jeunes demoiselles'. *Le Panier de Fruits* would have been no less suitable as an amusement for young ladies, as the foreword makes clear:

En publiant la *Corbeille de Fleurs*, nous avons fait connaître le but que nous avait dirigés dans cette entreprise; celui d'offrir aux jeunes personnes des distractions innocentes et sans aucun danger, mais qui ne fuissent pas sans utilité. Cet ouvrage, destiné aux Demoiselles du premier âge, devait nécessairement être plus varié, et contenir un plus grand nombre de morceaux agréables que le *Panier de Fruits*, destiné à celles d'un âge plus avancé.

The book is sometimes attributed to Louis François Jauffret (1770–1840) who wrote several books on natural history for children. The botanical sections of *Le Panier de Fruits* are well informed and mention contemporary research, while the literary accompaniments range from a poem based on Jauffret's prose to a translation of a moral tale by Maria Edgeworth.

L'EPINEVINETTE

Dessiné par Prêtre.

Gravé par Maradan.

*Le Panier de Fruits* 1807 plate facing page 359  A barberry drawn by J. G. Prêtre and engraved by Maradan

[Engraved title-page; within a double rule] La Corbeille de Fruits, par Charles Malo. [coloured vignette of a basket of fruit 5 x 5 cm.] à Paris, Chez Janet, Libraire, Rue St Jacques, Nº 59. [1817?]
12º 12 x 8 cm. π⁴ 1–15⁶ 16⁴ 17⁴ *I* II–VIII 1 2–188 and an 8–page 'calendrier pour l'an 1818' and a frontispiece and 11 plates.

BINDING: Original pink boards; all edges gilt.

PLATES: The dozen plates of fruit are stipple engravings printed in colour. Five (numbers 1, 2, 6, 7, and 11) are signed by Pancrace Bessa (1772–1835).

THE SERIES of gift books compiled by Charles Malo between 1815 and 1821 had the unusual distinction of being illustrated by Pancrace Bessa, one of the best of Redouté's pupils, who signed five of the plates in this book and was probably responsible for all of them. Each of the fruits illustrated is described, with its history, species, and varieties, followed by notes on its uses and a selection of verses. The pattern is similar to the one used in *Le Panier de Fruits* some years earlier (see above), and the Malo books, most of which were about flowers, were presumably intended for a similar audience.

Title-page

Plate facing page 75 Greengages and plums, drawn by Pancrace Bessa

FRUIT ELSEWHERE IN EUROPE

# 47. BUSSATO, Marco (*fl.* 1578–1593)

Giardino di Agricoltura di Marco Bussato da Ravenna. Nel quale con bellissimo ordine Si tratta di tutto quello, che s'appartiene à sapere a un perfetto Giardiniero: E s'insegna per praticha la vera maniera di plantare & incalmare arbori e viti di tutti le sorti, & i varii e diversi modi ch'in ciò si tengono. Dimostrandoli oltra che con i ragionamenti, anco con appropriati Disegni e Figure, con modo tanto facile, ch'a ciascuno potrà commodamente servire; & in oltre s'insegna medicare ogni sorte di Fruttare, accioche conservino bene i lor frutti. Si mostra il modo di lavorar le terre, di mietere, e battere i Grani, & acconciar le viti, e far i vini, & altre cose necessarie all'Agricoltura. Aggiontoui nel sine una visita, che far si deve ogni mese alla campagna, con alcuni utilissimi ricordi; opera in vero molto utile e diletteuole. Con Privilegio. [vignette of Flora 5 x 5 cm.; rule] In Venetia, M D XCII. Appresso Giovanni Fiorina.

4° in gatherings of 8 21 x 15.5 cm. a⁴ A–B⁴ C–H⁸ *i–iv* 1–53 *54–56* folios, that is, 120 pages.

BINDING: Half vellum, marbled paper sides.

PLATES: 20 woodcuts, each one filling about three-quarters of a page, are scattered through the text, in identical frames of printers' flowers. A favourite illustration of a horseman talking to two men walking by him appears three times, on folios 10ᵛ, 12ʳ, and 41ʳ. The rest are more directly related to the text, with a selection of tools on folio *iv*ʳ and drawings of grafting and budding. The ten pictures of methods of grafting are free copies of those in Bussato's 1578 book (see below).

Page 13 verso  Pruning

Page 27 recto
Grafting trees

IN SPITE OF its title, Bussato's main subject is fruit trees, from seedlings in their nursery to the careful pruning of mature trees, illustrated with some of the first accurate and detailed diagrams of methods of grafting. These illustrations first appeared in the author's *Prattica historiata dell'inestare gli arbori*, a treatise on grafting alone, which was published in Ravenna in 1578. Its text was revised and included in the larger *Giardino* in 1592, which was itself enlarged for later editions in 1593 and 1612. A monthly calendar of work to be done in the garden completes the book, each month with its own head-piece showing an occupation appropriate to the season.

E. A. Bunyard, writing in 1923 in the *Journal of the Royal Horticultural Society* about early Italian gardening books, said of Bussato that 'The author was a poet, and the book is written in rather more literary style than usual in such treatises.' The elegance of its printing is equally unusual in books of this kind, though given the date and place of its publication that is perhaps less remarkable.

MARCO BUSSATO
*Giardino di Agricoltura*
1592 page 49 recto
September head-piece:
making wine

## 48. KNOOP, Johann Hermann (1700–1769)

[within a red border of printer's ornaments] Pomologia, dat is Beschryvingen en Afbeeldingen van de beste Soorten van Appels en Peeren, welke in Neder- en Hoog-Duitsland, Frankryk, Engelland en elders geagt zyn, en tot dien einde gecultiveert worden. Beschreven, Naar het Leven geteikent, en met de Natuurlyke Coleuren afgezet door Johann Hermann Knoop Hortulanus (in tempore), Mathematicus, & Scientarum Amator. Te Leeuwarden, [rule 15 cm.] By Abraham Ferwerda, Boekverkoper, 1758.
2° 38 x 26.5 cm. ★² A–Y² *i–iv 1* 2–86 *87–88* and 20 engravings of fruit, coloured by hand.

BINDING: Modern brown calf, blind stamped, with two metal clasps. The later sections of the book are bound in; all are uncut.

PLATES: 12 are of apples, 8 of pears, all showing several varieties, each labelled with its time of ripening. Knoop himself made the original drawings, which were engraved by Jan C. Philips (1700–1773) or Jacob Folkema (1692–1767). Philips signed 7 of the apple plates and 3 of the pears, while Folkema claimed 5 of each fruit. An unsigned, engraved coat of arms heads the dedication. Woodcut initials and tailpieces, often repeated, are used throughout *Pomologia* and its companions.

*With which is bound:*

[within a red border of printer's ornaments] Fructologia, of Beschryving der Vrugtbomen en Vrugten die men in de Hoven plant en onderhoud: waar by Derzelver differente Benamingen, Groey-plaatzen, Voortteeling, Cultuur, en Huishoudelyk Gebruik, als mede het Confyten en meer andere Toebereidingen der Vrugten, enz., nauwkeurig aagewezen worden. Alles Door een veeljarige Ondervinding opgestelt, ten dienste en vergenoegen der Tuin-Liefhebbers, door Johann Hermann Knoop. Met Platen, Vertonende alle Vrugten naar het leven, die in dit Werk vervat zyn. [decoration 1 x 1.5 cm.] Te Leeuwarden Gedrukt by Abraham Ferwerda en Gerrit Tresling, Boekverkopers, 1763.
2° 38 x 26.5 cm. ★² A–2K² i–iv 1–132 and 19 engravings coloured by hand.

PLATES: All are unsigned. Each shows a single fruit, with leaves: plums, peaches, cherries, nuts, and soft fruit including grapes.

[within a red border of printer's ornaments] Dendrologia, of Beschryving der Plantagie-Gewassen, Die men in de Tuinen cultiveert, zo wel om te dienen tet Cieraad, om daar van Allèes, Cingels, Heggen, Berçeaux, Cabinets, Pyramiden, Plaisier-Bosschen, enz., als tot Huishoudelyk Gebruik, te planten. Waar by Derzelver differente Benamingen, Groey-plaatzen, Aankweeking en verdere Onderhuiding, en verwolgens haar Tuin- en Huishouderlyke Gebruiken, nauwkeurig beschreeven en aangewezen worden. Alles Door een eige veeljarige Ondervinding, ten dienste en vermaak der Tuin-Beminnaars opgestelt door Johann Hermann Knoop. [decoration 1 x 1.5 cm.] Te Leeuwarden Gedrukt by Abraham Ferwerda en Gerrit Tresling, Boekverkopers, 1763.
2° 38 x 26.5 cm. ★² A–2T² i–iv 1–145 148–161 164–168 169–172 (i.e. 168, as there is no text missing).

[within a red border of printer's ornaments] Beschryving van de Moes- en Keuken-tuin, Zo van alle Vrugten, Planten en Kruiden die men in dezelve Plant. Als van de Aard-Akkers, Aard-Amandelen, Aard-Aartischokken, Aard-Besien, Aard-Noten, Agrimonie, Ajuin, Aland-wortel, Alsem, Althea, Andievie, Angelike, Anys, Artischokken, Aspergies, Averuit, Basilicum, Bernagie, Beete, Beete-Wortel, Betonie, Bies-look, Bloed-Kruid, alle zoorten van Boonen, zo Roomsche of Groote, Turksche, enz., Byvoet, Camille, Carwey, Caryophyllate, Charlotten, Chamædris, Champignons, Cicers, Cichorey-Wortel, Citrullen, Concommers, Coriander, Cumyn, Cypres-Kruid, Dille, Dragon, Duive-Kervel, Eeren-Prys, Erten,

Geers, Geele Wortels, Herts-Hoorn, Herts-Tonge, Hoppe, Huis-look, Hysop, Joden-Karzen, Kallabassen, Katte-Kruid, Kerse, Kervel, Keule of Boon-kruid, Knoflook, Kool (allerhande), Kool-Rapen, Krop- en andere Saladen, Kruize-Munt, Laurier, Lawas, Lavendel, Lepel-Kruid of Lepel-Blad, Longen-Kruid, Marjoleine en Orega, Meester-Wortel, Melde, Melisse, Meloenen, Moeder-Kruid, Mostert, Osse-Tonge, Pastinake, Patientie-Kruid, Peper, Peper-Kruid, Peper-Wortel, Peterselie, Peterselie-Wortel, Petercelie van Macedonien, Pimpinelle, Porcelein, Porrey, Radys en Rammelats, Rakette, Rapen allerhande zoort, Rapen-Kervel, Raponse, Rozemaryn, Rynvare, Salie, Salsifie, Scharley, Schordium, Schorzoneere, Seldrie, Sevengetyen-Kruid, Sinnauw, Soet-Hout, Spinagie, Steenbrek, Stek-Rape, Suiker-Wortel, Suuring, Suur-Klaver, Taraxicum, Thym, Trip-Madam, Valeriana, Veld-Cypress, Veld-Salaad, Venkel, Vrouwen-Munte, Wald-Meester, Water-Kerse, Winter-Kerse, Wyn-ruit, Zee-Venkel, enz. Waar by Derzelver differente Benamingen, Groeiplaats, Zoorten, Voorteeling, Cultuur, Broeijing. Vervroeging en Huishoudelyk gebruik, als mede hoe men dezelve Inleggen kan, als ook derzelver Kragten in de Medicynen, en voor wie gemelde Vrugten gezond of ongezond zyn. Waar agter nog gevoegt zyn verscheide Registers, als 1. Naam-lyst van de Gewassen welke tot het Keuken- en ander Huishouderlyk-gebruik dienen en in dit Werk verhandelt zyn. 2. Naam-lyst der Keuken-Gewassen, volgens het gebruik hunner Deelen, als Wortels, Kruiden, en Vrugten, met de duurring der Zaaden tot Zaaijing. 3. Naam-lyst van de Wortels, Kruiden, en Vrugten, die in Azyn met wat Zout, of in Peekel, kunnen gelegt worden. 4. Naam-lyst van de Wortels, Kruiden, en Vrugten, welke rauw met Azyn, Boom-Olie of Boter, peper en Zout, enz., als Salaad gegeten worden. 5. Naam-lyst van de Wortels, Kruiden, en Vrugten, die, week gekookt zynde, met Azyn en Boom-Olie, of Boter, Zout en Peper, enz., als Salaad kunnen gegeten worden. 6. Naam-lyst van de Kruiden die men als Toe-kruiden by Krop- en ander Salaad gebruiken kan. 7. Naam-lyst van de Kruiden welke men in het Voor-jaar tot een groen Kruid-Moes of Potagie gebruiken kan. 8. Naam-lyst van de Kruiden welke tot een geurige en gezonde Kruid- of May-Wyn kunnen gebruikt worden. Door een veeljarige Ondervinding opgestelt Door Johann Hermann Knoop Hortulanus. Te Leeuwarden By A. Ferwerda en G. Tresling, Boekverkopers. 1769.
2° 38 x 26.5 cm. π²(–π2) A–3N² i–ii 1–235 236.

TAB. XIX.

J. H. KNOOP
*Fructologia* 1763 plate XIX
Cornelian cherry

*Cornoeljes.*

KNOOP was head gardener to the Dowager Princess of Orange at Marienburg, near Leeuwarden, where his first book, a more general manual of practical horticulture, was published in 1753. This quartet of more specialized descriptions of fruit, trees and shrubs, vegetables, herbs, and salads followed ten to sixteen years later, though the last part is very rare and most sets lack this final section on the contents of the kitchen garden. A single dedication, to Epo Sjuk van Burmania, described as a forester in Friesland, apparently covers all four parts.

The fruit monographs, apples and pears in the first, plums, peaches, cherries, nuts, and soft fruit in the second, are among the earliest books on the subject to be illustrated with coloured plates, the *Pomologia* ones packed with a dozen or so varieties, each with a label giving its time of ripening. These plates, based on Knoop's own drawings, are the same size as the pages around them in the first edition, but they are larger and folded in the later Dutch edition of 1790, which also has black borders instead of red ones on the title-pages. A French edition of these catalogues was published in Amsterdam in 1771 and an enlarged German one of *Pomologia* alone in Nuremberg in the 1760s (see below). As descriptive records of varieties of fruit in cultivation, observed by a dedicated and scientific gardener late in his career, they are often cited by later authors.

## 49. KNOOP, Johann Hermann (1700–1769)

Pomologia, das ist Beschreibungen und Abbildungen der besten Sorten der Aepfel und Birnen, welche in Holland / Deutschland / Franckreich / Engeland und anderwårts in Achtung stehen, und deswegen gebauet werden. [rule 12 cm.] Beschreiben, nach dem Leben abgebildet und mit ihren naturlichen Farben erleuchtet, von Johann Hermann Knoop, Hortulanus (in tempore) Mathematicus et Scientiarum Amator. [rule 13 cm.] Aus dem Hollåndischen in das Deutsche übersetzt / von D. Georg Leonhart Huth. [rule 18 cm.] Nůrnberg, verlegt Johann Michael Seligmann. Anno 1760.
2° 38.5 x 24.5 cm. ):(² ):():(² A–R² *i–viii 1 2–56 57–68* and 20 engravings, coloured by hand.

*With which is bound:*

Pomologia, das ist Beschreibungen und Abbildungen der besten Arten der Aepfel, Birnen, Kirschen und einiger Pflaumen, welche in- und ausserhalb Deutschland in Achtung stehen und gebauet werden. [rule 15 cm.] Beschrieben, nach der Natur abgebildet und mit ihren natůr-lichen Farben abgeschildet. Oder, der von Johann Hermann Knoop herausgegeben Pomologie zweyter Theil. [double rule, lower one heavier] Nůrnberg, Im Verlag Seligmånnischen Erben. Anno 1766.
)(²)()(² A²(–A2) B–M² *i–vi 1 2–42 43–46* and 24 engravings, coloured by hand.

BINDING: Contemporary brown speckled calf.

PLATES: The first volume contains copies of the plates in the Dutch edition (see page 128), 12 of apples and 8 of pears, all except 7 signed by Johann Michael Seligmann (1720–1762) as the engraver of Knoop's drawings. Seligmann's name also appears on the first plate of the second volume, but the rest are unsigned. Seligmann appears to have died during the book's preparation, as it was published by his heirs. The extra illustrations in the second volume—13 of apples, 10 of pears, and 1 of cherries and plums, were made from drawings by Johann Christoph Sänger, a painter from Meiningen.

THE SUPPLEMENT to the German translation of Knoop's *Pomologia* was based on a manuscript by Justus Christoph Zinck, a pastor from Meiningen, adding more varieties to those described in the Dutch original (see page 128). The preface to the second volume explains the source of the extra text and illustrations.

## 50. KRAFT, Johann (*fl.* 1787–1797)

Johann Kraft Inhaber der Kaiserl. Kŏnigl. privil. Obstbaum-Pflanzschulen zu Wǎhring and Weinhaus, nǎchst Wien, Bǔrger der Kaiserl. Kŏnigl. Residenzstadt Wien, Ehrenmitglied der Kaiserl. Kŏnigl. patriotischen ŏkonomischen adelichen Gesellschaft zu Prag in Bŏhmen. Abhandlung von den Obstbǎumen worinn ihre Gestalt, Erziehung and Pflege angezeigt und beschrieben wird, mit hundert sehr feinen Abbildungen in Kupfer gestochen, und nach der Natur in Farben dargestellt. [rule 8.5 cm.] Erster Theil. [triple rule, a plain line between two decorated ones] Wien, bey Rudolph Grǎffer und Compagnie. 1792.

2° 34 x 23.5 cm. a–d² A–H² I²(I1+I★² and I★★²) K–L² M²(–M2) *i–vii* viii–xvi 1–34 35★(used on 8 pages) 35–45 *46* and a frontispiece and 100 coloured plates.

. . . Zweyter Theil. [double rule, upper one heavier] Wien, bey A. Blumauer 1796.

2° 28.5 x 23 cm. π²(–π2) A–L² M²(–M2) *i–ii* 1 2–46 and 100 coloured plates.

BINDING: Contemporary buff boards.

PLATES: Neither the frontispiece nor the fruit engravings are signed. The frontispiece, printed in sanguine, shows a walled fruit garden with putti and tools in the foreground. A panel at the bottom is lettered: 'Der Obstbaeume Erster Theil Wienn bey Rudolf Grǎffer et Compagnie.' The other engravings show fruit, each one with leaves, a flower, and a cross-section, larger fruit having a single variety on each plate and smaller ones with two or three kinds fitted in. The plates have been carefully coloured by hand, the colour occasionally heightened by light touches of varnish, especially on the fruit sections. All varieties have their German names on the plates and most have French names too.

JOHANN KRAFT'S nursery garden near Vienna must have supplied fruit trees to many of the grandest gardens in the region, for his book is dedicated to his patron, the Emperor Franz II, and the list of subscribers includes a fine selection of the local nobility and gentry. The book was first issued in twenty parts from 1787 to 1796, and reissued by Blumauer in 1797 as *Pomona Austriaca*, with the text in French. The foreword describes France as the motherland of good fruit, and says Duhamel's book on fruit trees (which was translated into German from 1775 to 1783: see page 136) had shown the author the guiding principles of his craft, so an edition in French seems an appropriate way of acknowledging the country's influence on fruit-growing in the rest of Europe.

The choice of fruit discussed by Kraft may reflect Austrian taste or the limits of local skill in gardening. The most striking omission is the lack of apples. Over half the plates are devoted to pears and the rest to plums, cherries, apricots, strawberries, nuts (mostly almonds), red, white, and black currants, gooseberries, raspberries, and mulberries. The short text contains German

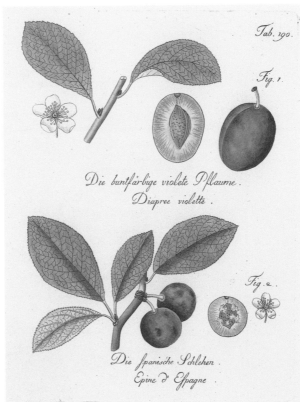

JOHANN KRAFT
*Abhandlung von den
Obstbäumen* volume II
1796 plate 129 The
Bon Chretien pear

Plate 190 Two plums

descriptions of each fruit illustrated, with Latin and French names given too. The foreword explains that the anonymous illustrations were made by the best artists available and collected over several years, though the style of them is remarkably consistent.

## 51. MAYER, Johann Prokop (1737–1804)

Pomona Franconica oder natürliche Abbildung und Beschreibung der besten und vorzüglichen Europäischen Gattungen der Obstbäume und Früchte welche in dem Hochfürstlichen Hofgarten zu Würzburg gezogen wurden. Nebst den hauptsächlichsten Anmerkungen über deren Erziehung, Pfropfung und Pflege, von Johann Mayer, Hochfürstlich Würzburgischen Hof- und Residenzgärtnern. [decorated rule 7.5 cm.] Erster Band. [decorated rule 13.5 cm.] Nürnberg, bey Adam Wolfgang Winterschmidt, Kupferstecher, Kunsthändler und Musikalienverleger, 1776.

*Followed by a second title-page:*

Pomona Franconica. [rule 10 cm.] Description des Arbres fruitiers, les plus connus et les plus éstimés en Europe, qui se cultivent maintenant au jardin de la cour de Wurzbourg; avec la représentation éxacte de leurs fruits, en figures en taille-douce, déssinées, gravées et enluminées d'après Nature. On y a joint les détails les plus interessants sur leur culture, greffe, plantation &c. Par le Sieur Jean Mayer, premier jardinier de la dite cour. [decorated rule 7 cm.] Tome premier. [decorated rule 13.4 cm.] A Nuremberg, chez Adam Wolfgang Winterschmidt, Graveur, Marchand d'Estampes et Editeur de Musique, 1776.

4° 25 x 19.5 cm. $a^4(a4^r$ signed a3) b–n⁴ A–T⁴ *I–IX* X–

JOHANN MAYER
*Pomona Franconica*
volume I 1776 plate XVII
Three plums, drawn
and engraved by
A. W. Winterschmidt

Tab. XVII.

Perdrigon violet. Die blaue Perdrigon. Ende Aug.

31.

33.

Diâprée de Roche-courbon.

Die rothe Diaprée. Mitte Sept

32.

Ste. Catherine. St. Catharinepflaume. Ende Sept.

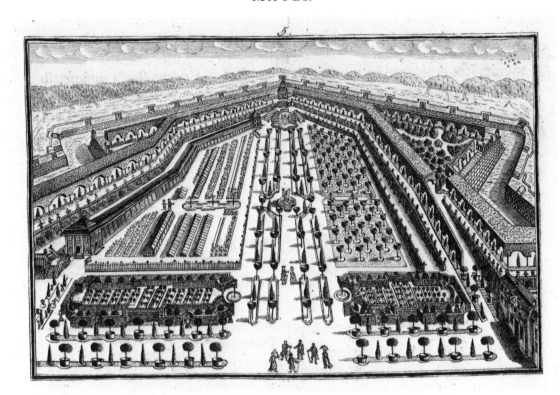

JOHANN MAYER
*Pomona Franconica*
volume I 1776 page I
Vignette of a fruit and
kitchen garden, drawn
and engraved by
A. W. Winterschmidt

CIV *1* 2–152 and a frontispiece, a folding plan, and 33 coloured plates.

. . . Tome second, avec LXXVII. Planches . . . 1779.

. . . Zweyter Band, mit LXXVII. Kupfertafeln. [rule 13.5 cm.] Herausgegeben, auf Kosten der Adam Wolfg. Winterschmidtischen Kunsthandlung, in Nürnberg 1779.
$\pi^2$ A–2Y$^4$ 2Z$^2$(2Z2+1) *i–iv* 1 2–364 [2] including a list of Winterschmidt publications on the last two pages, plus 66 coloured and 11 uncoloured plates.

BINDING: Original buff boards, red labels.

PLATES: The uncoloured frontispiece shows a glimpse of the Würzburg garden, with putti picking fruit and offering some to Athena, who is seated at the foot of an obelisk, on which is perched the Prince-Bishop's portrait. An inscription at the bottom reads: 'Dédié a Son Altesse Ré-vérendissime par Son très humble Serviteur Ad. Wolfg. Winterschmidt, Graveur et Marchand d'Estampes a Nuremberg.' A similar inscription also appears on the folding plan of the garden. Adam Wolfgang Winterschmidt (1733–1796) was also the artist and engraver responsible for the rest of the illustrations, 33 of apricots, almonds, and plums in volume I, and 66 cherries, medlars, and peaches in volume II. These were coloured by hand, but the second volume also contains 11 uncoloured engravings of pruning and shaping trees. The 10 engraved vignettes which start sections of volumes I and II are also uncoloured. A third volume of the book, published in 1801 but missing from this set, was all about apples and pears, with over 150 plates of them. Most of the original drawings, 212 watercolours, are now in the collection of the Historische Verein von Unterfranken und Aschaffenburg in Würzburg.

JOHANN MAYER was born in Prague and learned about gardening in France and England before he settled in Würzburg to look after the garden of the Prince-Bishop, Adam Frédéric, Prince of the Holy Roman Empire, Bishop of Bamberg and Würzburg, Duke of Franconia, to whom he dedicated his book, which has a bilingual text. In this copy the first volume begins with its German title-page and dedication, followed by the French version, then the preface in

French followed by its German version. In the second volume the French title-page takes precedence. Once past the preliminaries each page is divided down the middle, with one half in German and the other in French. The book was intended to raise the standard of fruit-growing in Germany, and Mayer's training in France helped him to do so. As a footnote in his preface says (page XII), 'Combien de fois, étant premier Garcon à Brunoy, n'ai je pas accompagné le feu Roy Louis XV, dans les Serres et les Potagers de ce lieu des délices? ne pouvant assez admirer sa profonde connoissance des Plantes et de tous les détails du Jardinage.'

This well-read gardener looked at fashions elsewhere too and admired certain English gardens he had seen, among them Stowe. He compared these influential new designs to changes in literary manners: 'Rien ne ressemble tant aux Parcs nouveaux que le *Tristram Shandy* de Sterne. Original comme [William] Kent, il a produit une révolution presque semblable dans la Litterature' (page XXXI). After his exploration of French and English gardens, he began work on the Würzburg one about 1770, apparently not with universal approval: 'On m'a reproché souvent d'avoir trop meublé la scêne et repandu partout la richesse et les ornements avec la prodigalité la plus indiscrette! mais je repons . . . c'est une beauté de Cour peignée, fardée, ajustée . . . qui doit paroitre dans un costume digne du Palais du Souverain qu'elle decore. Et quel Palais encore! l'un des plus beaux de l'Europe' (page XXXVI). The rather French garden Mayer planned, on a site limited by the town's fortified walls, still survives in Würzburg.

The thoroughness of Mayer's studies of gardening is reflected in a large bibliography for the fruit-growing enthusiast, printed first in French and then in German on pages LXX to XCIX of volume I. The chronological list, with annotations and the best editions specified, even refers to manuscripts too: 'Le célebre Aubriet, qui avait accompagné M. Tournefort dans quelques uns de ses voyages, a laissé 4 Vol. fol. de Plantes, Oiseaux, animaux, insectes &c. supérieurements peints en miniature, et qui se trouvent a Paris à la Biblioth. du Roi' (pages LXXVI–LXXVII). This comprehensive guide, so the author says, grew bit by bit as he rummaged in libraries, consulting books on gardening—a fine example of books forming a bridge between old gardens and new ones.

Duhamel's *Traité des Arbres fruitiers* (see page 71) was translated into German as *Pomona Gallica* and issued by Mayer's own publisher, Winterschmidt, from 1771 to 1783. The French book and its author are praised lavishly, though Mayer felt that the plates of the fruit book needed colour to give the full character of the fruit, as in his own book: 'Ce sont les fruits eux mêmes, attachés au papier, qu'on croit voir dans nos Planches.'

In the second volume of *Pomona Franconica*, the section on peaches includes a long digression on pruning, grafting, and diseases, with summaries of the methods used by gardeners like La Quintinie and Philip Miller, as well as Duhamel. Here, on pages 134–135, La Quintinie is given his place as the founding father of fruit-gardening:

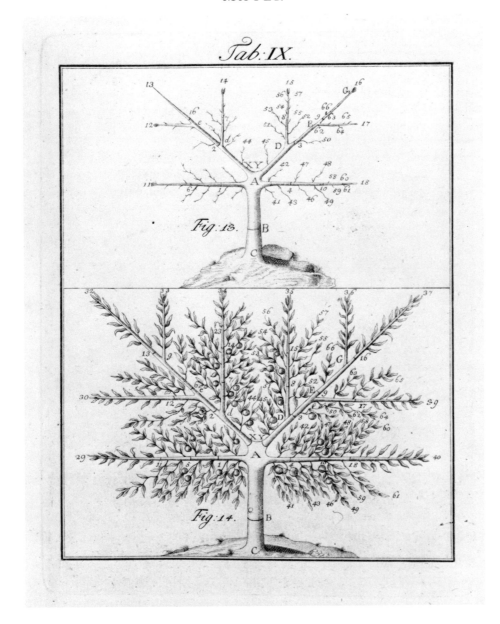

JOHANN MAYER
*Pomona Franconica*
volume II 1779
Peaches plate IX  How
to train the trees, drawn
and engraved by
A. W. Winterschmidt

M. de la Quintinye le pere du jardinage, qui est à cet Art ce que Descartes est à la Philosophie, inventa, créa, il y a cent ans environ, la taille méthodique, raisonnée, fondamentale des Arbres fruitiers; il eut pour maitre la Nature, pour guides son génie, l'observation, l'éxperience. Son livre devint le code de la taille et fut reçu dans l'Europe entiere: ceux qui se sont avisés depuis d'écrire sur cette matiere, François, Anglois, Hollandois et Allemands, tous ont pris son systeme pour base; ils cherchoient á l'étendre, le simplifier, le perfectionner: mais personne n'osoit hasarder de s'en écarter pour le fonds.

## 52. GALLESIO, Giorgio (1772–1839)

Pomona italiana ossia Trattato degli alberi fruttiferi di Giorgio Gallesio Tomo Primo Pisa Co' Caratteri de' FF. Amoretti Presso Niccolò Capurro MDCCCXVII. 2° 49 x 32 cm. Collation irregular and unsigned 192 unnumbered leaves of text and 89 coloured plates.

. . . Tomo secondo . . . MDCCCXXXIX. Collation irregular and unsigned 219 unnumbered leaves of text and 71 coloured plates.

BINDING: Half vellum, paper-covered boards.

PLATES: Aquatints, partially printed in colour and finished by hand. A copy in the library of the United States Department of Agriculture has both coloured and plain plates. Most of the plates bear dates between 1819 and 1839, but there is often a long interval between the dates of drawing and engraving. As many as twenty artists contributed, but the lion's share was done by only three: Domenico del Pino, Antonio Serantoni, and Isabella Bozzolini, with del Pino the major contributor, signing 80 plates. Nearly as many engravers were involved, fourteen of them, but most of the work was done by only four, Giuseppe Pera, Giuseppe Carocci, Tommaso Nasi, and Francesco Corsi.

BEFORE he began this enormous work, published in forty-one parts from 1817 to 1839, Gallesio had already published his *Traité du Citrus* (see page 199), which explains the reason for the lack of oranges and lemons in a catalogue of Italian fruit. The author died while his *Pomona* was still unfinished, but not before describing a collection of fruit with a different emphasis from those made further west. There are twenty-two figs, for example, the same number of pears, and twenty-six grapes and thirty-three peaches, but only eight apples, a dozen cherries, six apricots, and a handful of more exotic fruit like dates, a pomegranate, pistachios, and jujubes.

The composition of this copy matches the collation given by John Collins in the catalogue of the Arpad Plesch sale at Sotheby's in London on 17 June 1975, except for a few minor variations in the number of leaves of text. The plates are very showy, with flowers and foliage as well as fruit, and their large size has encouraged print dealers to dismember copies of the book for the sake of its pictures, so that individual plates are often found.

Gallesio's fruit garden in Savona was not his main occupation, for he was a lawyer and a civil servant as well as a botanist, whose experiments on the development of varieties of fruit were quoted later by Charles Darwin. His *Pomona* was a major contribution to the study of pomology in Italy.

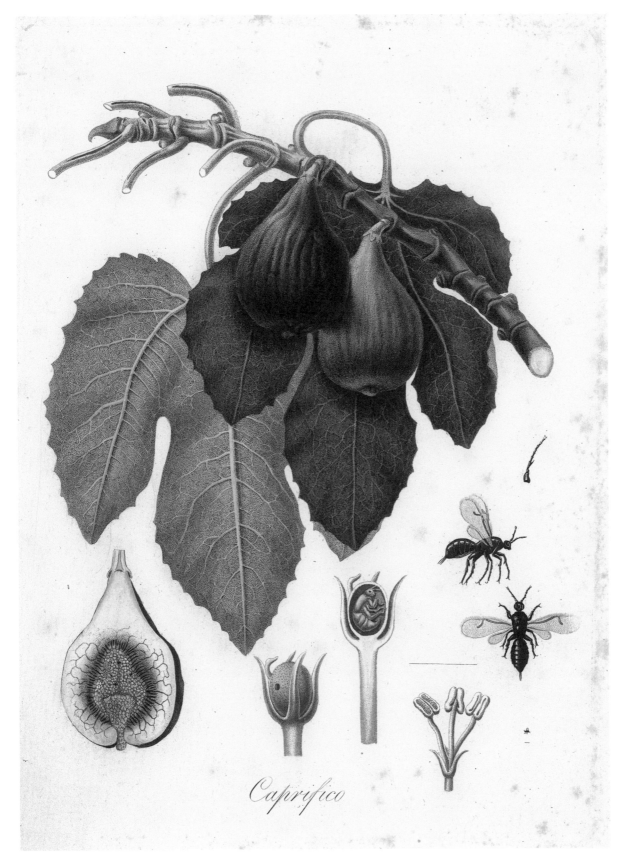

*Caprifico*

G. GALLESIO *Pomona Italiana* volume I 1817 An unsigned drawing of a caprifig, showing the wasps needed to fertilize it. The fig flower stays within the fruit, into which wasps bring pollen. Most fig trees in gardens are females with the ability to bear fruit without previous pollination, but some figs grown commercially still need the help of fig wasps. Caprifigs in each plantation act as hosts for the wasps and sources of pollen

G. GALLESIO *Pomona
Italiana* volume I 1817
A Portuguese fig drawn
by Antonio Serantoni
and engraved by Luigi
Giarre

*Fico Portoghese*

Ant. Serantoni disegnò.                    Luigi Giarre Pitt.e incise

## 53. BIVORT, Alexandre Joseph Désiré (1809–1872) and
## BAVAY, Laurent Séraph Joseph de (1795–1855)

Album de Pomologie; par A. Bivort, Membre de la Société d'Agriculture et d'Horticulture Linnéenne de Bruxelles, et de la Société d'Horticulture d'Anvers; Membre honoraire de la Société Centrale d'Horticulture du Département de la Seine-Inférieure; Membre correspondant de la Société Centrale d'Agriculture de Nancy, et de la Société des Sciences et des Arts d'Angers; [decorated rule 4.5 cm.] Bruxelles, Librairie de Deprez-Parent, rue de la Violette, 15. F. Parent, Éditeur. 1847.
2° 23 x 31 cm. π²(−π2) 2π² 1−45²46²(46:2+1) 192 unnumbered pages and 49 coloured plates.

Album de Pomologie; Par A. Bivort . . . et L.B., pomologue. [decorated rule 1.5 cm.] Tome deuxième. [decorated rule 1.5 cm.] Bruxelles, Chez F. Parent, Éditeur, Montagne de Sion, 17, près de l'église de Sainte-Gudule, Où la correspondance et les demandes d'abonnements doivent être adressées. 1849.
π² ★² 1−23² 24²(−24:2) 25² 26²(−26:2) 27−28² 29²(−29:2) 30−41² 42² (−42:2) 43−47² [4] I II−III IV 1 2−178 and 47 coloured plates, one of them double.

Album de Pomologie; Par A. Bivort, Pépiniériste, Successeur de Van Mons. Membre de la Société Centrale d'Horticulture de France; de la Société Nationale d'Horticulture de la Seine; de la Société d'Horticulture Pratique du Département du Rhone; des Sociétés d'Horticulture d'Angers, Nancy, Bruxelles, Anvers, Louvain, etc., etc.; et L.B., pomologue. [decorated rule 1.5 cm.] Tome troisième. [decorated rule 1.5 cm.] Bruxelles . . . 1850.
π² 1−43² I−IV 1 2−46 [2] 47−168 169−170 and 48 colored plates and a lithographed title-page.

Album de Pomologie; Par A. Bivort . . . Tome quatrième . . . 1851.
π² 1−21² 22²(−22:2) 23−44² I−IV 1 2−174 and 48 coloured plates and the same lithographed title-page as the previous volume. 'L.B., pomologue' is not mentioned on either title-page of this volume.

BINDING: Blue morocco, gilt and blind-stamped borders on sides. Labels of 'Js. Chs. Puls Pharmacien & Droguiste place de la Calandre N° 4 Gand' on front or back pastedowns of all four volumes. A manuscript note on the front pastedown of the first volume reads: 'L'ouvrage est l'un des rares exemplaires tires sur papier superfin a 9 francs la livraison. L'Edition ordinaire a ete publiee au prix de fr.6.00 la livraison. JB.'

PLATES: The fruits described are illustrated in 184 lithographs, coloured by hand, though a few of the plates in volumes 3 and 4 have some leaves or fruits left uncoloured. Neither artist nor lithographer has signed them, but the lithographed title-pages added to volumes 3 and 4 are signed by V. de Doncker. They show an array of fruit in the foreground against a background of a garden scene, surrounded with trellis bearing vines and bunches of grapes. A gardener stands on the left, Pomona on the right. Most of the plates show two varieties of fruit side by side, often with leaves or twigs. The pear is the overwhelming favourite, with 139 plates, about three-quarters of the total. Of the remainder, 13 are devoted to apples, 5 to grapes, and the rest to a few plums, peaches, cherries, gooseberries, strawberries, raspberries, a medlar, and a nectarine.

ACCORDING to E. A. Bunyard in his 'Guide to the Literature of Pomology' (*Journal of the Royal Horticultural Society*, 1915, volume 40, page 441), Alexandre Bivort's *Album de Pomologie*, published in monthly parts over four years, 'is of great value as it contains coloured plates and accurate descriptions of many of Van Mons' seedlings, and it forms a wonderful record of the great number of new fruits which were at this time being raised in Belgium.' As Van Mons' successor, Bivort was certainly well informed about new Belgian varieties of fruit. Several of the plates in the earlier volumes of the *Album* have numbered references to a 'Catalogue Général', which seems to be the *Catalogue descriptif abrégé, contenant une partie des arbres fruitiers qui depuis 1798 jusqu'en 1823 ont formé la collection de J. B. van Mons*, which was published in Louvain in 1823. Patrick Neill's *Journal of a Horticultural Tour . . . in the Autumn of 1817*, also published in 1823, contains a brief description of Jean Baptiste Van Mons (1765–1842) in the entry dated 11 September (pages 301–302):

> M. Van Mons [in Brussels] is well known as a chemist, and he has likewise distinguished himself by his labours in horticulture, particularly in raising new varieties of fruit from the seed . . . He mentioned, that horticulture had been the favourite employment of his hours of relaxation for fourteen years past, and that he had, during that period, raised several hundreds of new pears, besides a good many apples, plums, cherries, and peaches. Of new seedling varieties of good pears, raised chiefly by himself and by M. Duquesne of Mons, he considers his present collection as extending to about 800!

This preference for pears was also justified in Bivort's 'Postface', inserted after the title-page of volume 1, in which he also gave reasons for establishing his new journal:

> En réunissant dans une publication spéciale tout ce qui peut intéresser le pomologiste, nous avons cru remplir une lacune que nous n'avons pas été les seuls à signaler . . . On ne s'étonnera pas de nous voir donner la préférence au genre *Poire*; la prééminence de ce fruit parmi ceux qu'on peut cultiver en plein vent en Belgique n'est pas contestable . . . Nous avons pris pour règle de n'admettre dans notre *Album* que les productions dont le mérite nous est connu; à côté des produits étrangers, récents ou anciens, nous avons cru pouvoir faire une large part aux fruits provenant des sujets semés par Van Mons d'après une théorie raisonnée et dont les premiers résultats ont été appreciés dans toute l'Europe.

The Van Mons pears were greeted enthusiastically in America too, where they were imported by André Parmentier and P.J.A. Berckmans. In the spring of 1834, for example, more than 300 varieties of pears were sent to Boston where they were welcomed by local enthusiasts, among them Robert Manning (see page 154). The traffic in new fruit was not entirely in one direction, for Bivort's *Album* includes the Seckle pear in its first volume, an American plum in its third, and an American peach, the President, in its fourth. Several of the descriptions in this last volume are signed by J. de Jonghe, who seems to have replaced Laurent de Bavay as Bivort's collaborator.

The lithographic printing so beautifully demonstrated in the plates of the *Album de Pomologie* was well established in Ghent and Brussels by about 1830, with the help of craftsmen from the Netherlands. It was such a stimulus to botanical and horticultural illustration that one leading nurseryman, Louis Van Houtte, added a lithographic printing plant to his garden and published twenty-three volumes of *Flore des Serres et des Jardins de l'Europe* from 1845 to 1880.

Not many complete sets of the *Album* seem to have survived. The de Belder copy, sold at Sotheby's in London on 27 April 1987 and described in the sale catalogue (lot 27) as 'a pomolog-

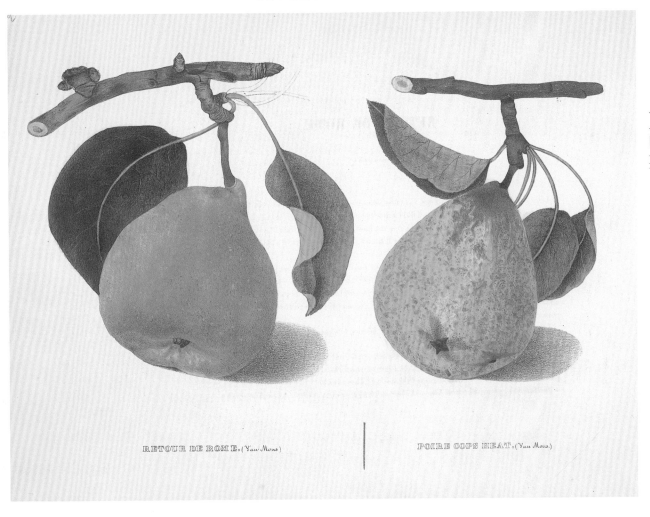

RETOUR DE ROME. (Van Mons)

POIRE COPS HEAT. (Van Mons)

A. BIVORT *Album de Pomologie* volume 1 1847 [plate 12] Two of the pears developed by J. B. Van Mons

ical rarity', had only three volumes and 137 plates, like the copy in the Lindley Library of the Royal Horticultural Society. There is no copy at all in the British Library, the library of the British Museum (Natural History), or the library of the Royal Botanic Gardens, Kew, but there is at least one other full set in America, in the library of the Massachusetts Horticultural Society in Boston.

FRUIT IN AMERICA

An anonymous
French watercolour of
a black walnut from
Virginia, made early in
the nineteenth century
when the tree was
being naturalized
in France

*Juglans nigra. Virginiana.*

54.

A Black Walnut. Juglans nigra Virginiana. Early nineteenth century.  53 x 41.5 cm. Watercolour and pen and ink.

THIS FRENCH DRAWING of a black walnut from Virginia has a pencilled note in the bottom right-hand corner of the sheet: 'Ce noyer a jusqua 21 folioles. L'impaire souvent avortie' ('This walnut has as many as 21 leaflets [in its compound leaves]. The odd one often fails to develop'). In this drawing the stems, fruits, and cross-sections have been coloured, the leaflets left in black and white. By 1807 the black walnut was naturalized in France, where it was praised for its beauty as well as its fast growth and fine wood.

F. A. Michaux's *North American Sylva* (1819, volume I, page 155) describes the fruit of the black walnut as 'of a sweet and agreeable taste, though inferior to that of the European walnut. The size of the fruit varies considerably, and depends upon the vigour of the tree, and upon the nature of the soil and of the climate.' The strong, durable timber, which is dark enough to give the tree its name, has been used for furniture, gun stocks, and boat-building. Michaux's description of the tree ends with a comparison of the European walnut and its American cousin:

Nuts of the European Walnut and of the Black Walnut have been planted at the same time in the same soil; those of the Black Walnut are observed to shoot more vigorously, and to grow in a given time to a greater height. By grafting the European upon the American species . . . their advantages, with respect to the quality both of wood and fruit, might be united.

## 55. FORSYTH, William (1737–1804) and COBBETT, William (1762–1835)

A Treatise on the Culture and Management of Fruit Trees; in which a new Method of Pruning and Training is fully described. Together with Observations on the Diseases, Defects and Injuries, in all kinds of Fruit and Forest Trees; as also, an Account of a particular Method of Cure, made public by order of the British Government. [swelled rule 3 cm.] By William Forsyth, F.A.S. & F.S.A. Gardener to his Majesty at Kensington and St. James'. [swelled rule 3 cm.] To which are added, an introduction and notes, adapting the rules of the treatise to the Climates and Seasons of the United States of America. [row of dots 2.5 cm.] By William Cobbett. [row of dots 2.5 cm.] Albany: Printed for and sold by D. & S. Whiting, at the Albany Book Store, no 45, State-street. Sold also by Thomas & Andrews, Boston; A. & A. Stansbury, N. York; O. Penniman & Co. Troy; S. P. Goodrich, Utica; J. Glover & Co. Oxford, and H. Chapin, Canandaigua. 1803. 8° in half-sheets 21 x 12.5 cm. A⁴ B–2C⁴ 2E–2M⁴ *i–v*

vi–xii *13* 14–280 and 13 unsigned engravings (as in the
English editions).

BINDING: Tree calf. Signature of 'J. P. Wendell 24.th Oct.r
1803' on front pastedown.

FORSYTH and
COBBETT
*Fruit Trees* 1803
Title-page

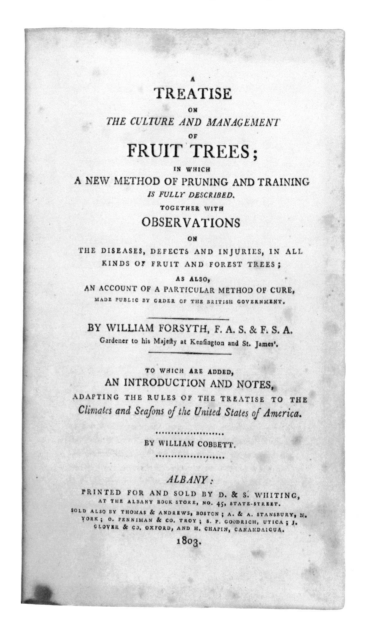

A
**TREATISE**
ON
*THE CULTURE AND MANAGEMENT*
OF
**FRUIT TREES;**
IN WHICH
**A NEW METHOD OF PRUNING AND TRAINING**
*IS FULLY DESCRIBED.*
TOGETHER WITH
**OBSERVATIONS**
ON
THE DISEASES, DEFECTS AND INJURIES, IN ALL
KINDS OF FRUIT AND FOREST TREES;
AS ALSO,
AN ACCOUNT OF A PARTICULAR METHOD OF CURE,
MADE PUBLIC BY ORDER OF THE BRITISH GOVERNMENT.

BY WILLIAM FORSYTH, F. A. S. & F. S. A.
Gardener to his Majesty at Kensington and St. James'.

TO WHICH ARE ADDED,
AN INTRODUCTION AND NOTES,
ADAPTING THE RULES OF THE TREATISE TO THE
*Climates and Seasons of the United States of America.*

. . . . . . . . . . . . . . . . . . . .
BY WILLIAM COBBETT.
. . . . . . . . . . . . . . . . . . . .

ALBANY:
PRINTED FOR AND SOLD BY D. & S. WHITING,
AT THE ALBANY BOOK STORE, NO. 45, STATE-STREET.
SOLD ALSO BY THOMAS & ANDREWS, BOSTON; A. & A. STANSBURY, N.
YORK; O. PENNIMAN & CO. TROY; S. P. GOODRICH, UTICA; J.
GLOVER & CO. OXFORD, AND H. CHAPIN, CANANDAIGUA.
1803.

WHATEVER the merits of William Forsyth's advice (see page 99), he had the good
fortune to find a large number of readers for his book on fruit trees, a market extended
even further by the version that William Cobbett annotated for American gardeners and published in New York and Philadelphia in 1802, the same year as the first edition of the original
book, and again in Albany in 1803. This adaptation, according to Hedrick, was the first book

devoted to fruit alone to be published in America. The dedication, addressed to Mr James Paul, Senior, of Bustleton, Pennsylvania, explained Cobbett's eagerness to pass on Forsyth's directions:

> The smallness and inferior quality of the fruit of the Peach-Tree, in particular, and the swift decay of the tree itself, have, for many years past, been a subject of general regret in the middle states of America; and, it appears to me, that whoever shall communicate to you a method of removing this evil, will render you no unacceptable service . . . During the last summer, (1801) I went with a party of friends, to be an eye witness of the effects (of which I had heard such wonders related) of this gentleman's mode of cultivating and curing trees; and, though my mind had received strong prepossession in its favor, what I saw very far surpassed my expectation.

Forsyth's method of pruning, which he called heading-down, recommended cutting back to three or four buds in the spring, shortening the new shoots the following year, and gradually removing old branches after that. Both the quantity and the quality of fruit were improved by this treatment. An appendix to this edition prints a letter from Peter W. Yates of Albany to the publishers, saying how well Forsyth's method had worked for him. The American editions of the book also retained the appendix about the allegedly miracle-working mixture Forsyth had prepared to treat diseased trees, though this compound was eventually proved to be useless.

After an earlier stay in Nova Scotia as a soldier, Cobbett emigrated in 1792 to Philadelphia, where he taught English, opened a bookshop, and began to produce political pamphlets and periodicals. Later on he moved to New York, before returning to England in 1800. His knowledge of American conditions, and the way in which they differed from English ones, must have encouraged him to make an appropriate adaptation of Forsyth's book. The process was reversed with his own book, *The American Gardener* (1821), written after his second visit to the country from 1817 to 1819, and later adapted to become *The English Gardener*, first published in 1829, with several later editions. Cobbett's early years included a short spell of work at Kew, and his interest in farming and gardening lasted throughout his life. Among the multitude of his activities after his second return from America, he established a nursery in Kensington, where he grew and sold large numbers of North American trees as cheaply as possible. As well as forest trees, he imported American apples too, according to John Claudius Loudon, who visited the nursery and described it in his *Gardener's Magazine* (1828, volume 3, page 364): 'Mr. Cobbett propagates 38 sorts of American apples, which he severally describes and recommends. The Newtown Pippin, Rhode Island Greening, and Fall Pippin, he says, are decidedly the best in point of flavour and keeping.'

Cobbett's epitome
of Forsyth 1803
Title-page

AN

EPITOME

OF

*MR. FORSYTH'S TREATISE*

ON THE

CULTURE AND MANAGEMENT

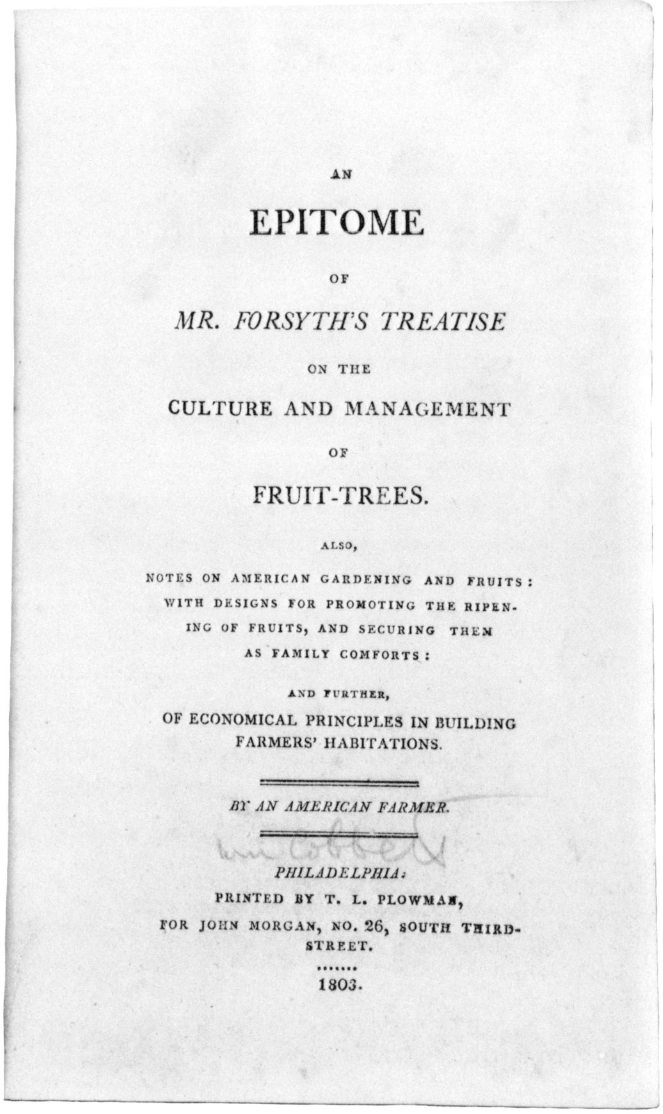

OF

FRUIT-TREES.

ALSO,

NOTES ON AMERICAN GARDENING AND FRUITS: WITH DESIGNS FOR PROMOTING THE RIPENING OF FRUITS, AND SECURING THEM AS FAMILY COMFORTS:

AND FURTHER,

OF ECONOMICAL PRINCIPLES IN BUILDING FARMERS' HABITATIONS.

*BY AN AMERICAN FARMER.*

*PHILADELPHIA:*

PRINTED BY T. L. PLOWMAN,

FOR JOHN MORGAN, NO. 26, SOUTH THIRD-STREET.

.......

1803.

## 56. [COBBETT, William (1762–1835)]

An Epitome of Mr. Forsyth's Treatise on the Culture and Management of Fruit-Trees. Also, Notes on American Gardening and Fruits: with Designs for Promoting the Ripening of Fruits, and Securing them as Family Comforts: and further, of Economical Principles in Building Farmers' Habitations. [double rule, upper one heavier] By an American Farmer. [double rule, lower one heavier] Philadelphia: Printed by T. L. Plowman, for John Morgan, No. 26, South Third-Street [row of stars] 1803.

8° in half-sheets 20.5 x 12.5 cm. *$A^2$* B–$2A^4$ (including both U and V; gatherings Q and P misbound) *i–iv 1* 2–186 *187–192* (pages 105–112, 97–104 misbound) and 13 unsigned engravings (as in English editions of Forsyth's book) plus 2 more showing plans for houses; most are folded.

BINDING: Contemporary calf.

WILLIAM COBBETT annotated Forsyth's *Treatise* (see page 147) for American gardeners and published the result in New York and Philadelphia in 1802, the same year as the first edition of the original book. In 1803 another edition was published in Albany too. The *Epitome of Mr. Forsyth's Treatise* by 'An American Farmer' has also been attributed to Cobbett, though it seems strange that he should publish an anonymous abbreviation after using his own name on another version of the same book. Ian MacPhail (in *Huntia* 1965, volume 2, page 88) suggested that John Beale Bordley (1727–1804) who was indeed an American farmer and a lawyer, might have been the man behind the pseudonym, but the case is not conclusively proved. Meanwhile, it seems reasonable to allow Cobbett the credit for cutting back Forsyth's verbiage to reveal the essence of his message.

## 57. COXE, William (1762–1831)

A View of the Cultivation of Fruit Trees, and the Management of Orchards and Cider; with accurate descriptions of the most estimable varieties of native and foreign Apples, Pears, Peaches, Plums, and Cherries, cultivated in the middle states of America: illustrated by Cuts of two hundred kinds of Fruits of the natural size; intended to explain Some of the errors which exist relative to the origin, popular names, and character of many of our fruits; to identify them by accurate descriptions of their properties, and correct delineations of the full size and natural formation of each variety; and to exhibit a system of practice adapted to our climate, in the successive stages of a nursery, orchard, and cider establishment. [swelled rule 1 cm.] By William Coxe, Esq., Of Burlington, New Jersey. [swelled rule 1 cm.] Philadelphia: Published by M. Carey and Son. Nov. 1, 1817. [swelled rule 1 cm.] D. Allinson, Printer.

4° 21.5 x 13.5 cm. $\pi^2$ 1–33⁴ *i–iii* iv 5 6–253 *254–268* and 77 plates.

BINDING: Contemporary calf. Signature of Matthew Comstock on front pastedown and pencil notes in his hand on fly-leaf and throughout, especially in the section on pears.

PLATES: Each one contains two or more woodcuts. There are 44 of apples (100 varieties), 22 of pears (63 varieties), 6 of peaches (15 varieties), 3 of plums (17 varieties), and 1 each of apricots (3 varieties) and nectarines (2 varieties).

WILLIAM COXE, who was born in Philadelphia, wrote the first home-grown American book on fruit-growing. He was a merchant, though his fruit farm at Burlington, New Jersey, was one of his main interests. There he grew most European and American varieties available, importing several from France or Holland besides developing new ones. He was also a member of the New Jersey state legislature and later of Congress, where he became a friend of Daniel Webster, 'a horticulturist of note' as well as a politician.

In New Jersey there were large orchards, as the nearby cities, including Philadelphia and Baltimore, offered markets for their crops. Nurseries to supply the orchards also flourished. In Burlington in 1806 David Smith's catalogue offered 151 apple varieties, 98 pears, 67 peaches, 43 cherries, 20 plums, 16 nectarines, and 10 apricots.

WILLIAM COXE
*A View of the Cultivation
of Fruit Trees* 1817 plates
between pages 104 and
105 Five apples

No. 4. Summer Queen.

No. 8. Rambour D'Ete.

No. 6. Summer Rose.

No. 7. Summer Pearmain.

No. 9. Codling.

Coxe used his own experience to provide relevant advice for others, as he explained in his preface (page 6): 'Having been for many years actively engaged in the rearing, planting, and cultivating fruit trees, on a scale more extensive than has been attempted by any other individual of this country, I have too often had occasion to regret the difficulty, and not unfrequently the impossibility of obtaining from my own countrymen, information on which I could rely respecting the objects of my pursuit.' His elaborate descriptions are linked to the relevant drawings, though not all the varieties described are illustrated.

Cider was an important by-product of apple orchards from the early settlements in America to well into the nineteenth century, as many farmers had cider presses and used their own fruit. New England even exported cider to the southern colonies and the West Indies. In October 1823 the plant-collector David Douglas visited Coxe's orchard, where he was given 'several varieties of fruit trees as well as two bottles of seventeen-year-old cider—presents to the President and the Secretary of the [Horticultural] Society' of which Coxe was an honorary member. The gifts are recorded in H. R. Fletcher's history of the Royal Horticultural Society (1969, page 100).

## 58. MANNING, Robert (1784–1842)

Book of Fruits: being a descriptive catalogue of the most valuable varieties of the Pear, Apple, Peach, Plum & Cherry, for New-England culture. [rule 1 cm.] By Robert Manning. [rule 1 cm.] To which is added the Gooseberry, Currant, Raspberry, Strawberry, and the Grape; with modes of culture. Also, hardy ornamental Trees and Shrubs. [rule 1 cm.] With Plates. [rule 1 cm.] First Series for 1838. [double rule, upper one heavier, 1 cm.] Salem: Published by Ives & Jewett. And for sale at the different book-stores and seed establishments in New-England. [rule 1.5 cm.] 1838.

12° in sixes. 18 x 11.5 cm. $A^6$ B–$J^6$ $K^6$ *1–5* 6–120 and an 'Advertising Sheet' of 12 pages, the last one blank, plus a frontispiece and 3 other plates.

BINDING: Worn light brown stamped cloth. The name 'H. R. Lott' is written in pencil on the front pastedown, and there are many notes in the same hand throughout the catalogues of fruit.

PLATES: Uncoloured lithographs, all signed 'Moore's Lith. Boston', that is, printed by Thomas Moore, who worked independently in Boston from 1835 to 1841 as the successor to William S. Pendleton. A printed note on page 4 says that the plates 'were furnished by Mr. John M. Ives', who went on to edit two later editions of the book. There is also a woodcut of a dwarf pear tree grafted on a quince on page 29.

Easter Beurrée Pear.

Easter Beurrée Pear, drawn by John M. Ives and lithographed by Thomas Moore, and page 95, with copious annotations

ROBERT MANNING, one of the founders of the Massachusetts Horticultural Society, began to plant his 'Pomological Garden' in Dearborn Street, Salem, in 1823. Here he tried to cultivate all the varieties of fruit 'hardy enough to endure the inclemency of a northern winter', eventually collecting more than two thousand kinds, of which a thousand were pears, the largest collection in America. Many of them came from Jean Baptiste Van Mons in Belgium, but others, pears, apples, and some of the rest of the fruit, came from the Horticultural Society in London or 'the first European establishments'. Home-grown American varieties had their place too.

Manning emphasized his accurate descriptions, made from trees and fruit carefully identified and successfully grown in his garden. In the so-called 'Desultory Remarks' which form a preface to his book he says:

> There is one circumstance to which we venture to call the attention of our readers—that while some recent works on Pomology are compiled from earlier authors, or from information derived at second-hand, . . . we have in these pages described no specimen which we have not actually identified, beyond a reasonable doubt of its genuineness . . . The innumerable errors in the names of fruits, and the perplexity and disappointment arising from this cause, are inconceivable to any but a collector . . . A better state of things is, however, beginning to prevail, especially in the United States, where a knowledge of the subject is widely diffused, and a laudable solicitude is felt that catalogues should contain no varieties but what are actually cultivated, and ascertained to be identically the kinds which their titles proclaim them to be.

Amid the confusion caused by several names being used for some kinds of fruit, this attempt to standardize those used in America at once became an accepted authority, superseding Coxe's book (see page 151) and holding its own until the first edition of Downing's larger book was published in 1845 (see page 158). Although Manning intended his little book to be the first of a series, to be 'published at the close of every fruit season', it had no successors. Two enlarged editions were issued after his death, the second as the *New England Fruit Book* in 1844 and the third as the *New England Book of Fruit* in 1847, both edited by John M. Ives.

The annotations in this copy are concentrated on the apples and pears, which the former owner of the book seems to have studied with care. His comments on the flavour and keeping qualities of the fruit, variant names, and comparisons with Downing are thickly scattered on margins and blank pages. The advertisements at the end of the book offer 'fruit trees, vines, shrubs, and ornamental trees' from Manning's Pomological Garden and 'John M. Ives' adjoining Nursery', with seeds and plants from other local nurserymen too, among them Hovey & Co. of Boston (see page 160) and William Kenrick of Newton, who specialized in 'Mulberries for Silk, at a liberal discount, by the hundred or thousand'.

The Orchardist's Companion [vignette 13 x 18 cm. of Pomona being crowned by a nymph and given baskets of fruit by attendant gardeners] A quarterly journal, devoted to the history, character, properties, modes of cultivation, and all other matters appertaining to the Fruits of the United States, embellished with richly colored designs of the natural size, painted from the actual fruits when in their finest condition, and represented appended to a portion of the branch, with leaves and other characteristics as seen when on the tree. Also, the flowers, cut fruits and stones. [rule 1 cm.] Vol. 1.——April. [rule 1 cm.] A. Hoffy, Editor and Proprietor, 41 Chestnut Street, Philadelphia. 1841.

*With which is bound:*

Hoffy's Orchardist's Companion or, Fruits of the United States, a quarterly journal . . . Volume 2. A. Hoffy, Editor and Publisher, Philadelphia, 1842–3.

4° 28 x 23 cm. Collation irregular and unsigned The contents of this copy are bound as follows: [6] *i–v* vi–xv *xvi 17* 18–20 [2 including a second title-page for a volume of plates, just like the first except for 'Vol. 2'] 12 unnumbered coloured lithographs, each with a leaf of text facing it *31* 32–49 *50* 12 more plates and their text [4] *51* 52–68 [2 including the contents of the first year's four issues in two sections] 12 more plates and their text *i–viii* including a title-page for volume 2, 1842–3, *1* 2–16 12 more plates.

BINDING: Half leather, cloth sides. 'Russell' in ink, repeated in pencil, on the first title-page.

PLATES: All 48 were printed by P. S. Duval's Lithographic Press in Philadelphia and coloured by hand, probably by Hoffy's pupils. Hoffy himself drew and engraved all the first 12; thereafter two of his students, D. S. Quinton and Edward Quayle, helped him. Quinton drew and engraved 5 of the second dozen and engraved 2 more. In the third batch he drew and engraved 9 of the 12 and engraved the other 3 from Hoffy's drawings. In the fourth group Hoffy drew and engraved 1 and drew 3 more; Quinton drew and engraved 2 and engraved 1 more; and Edward Quayle drew and engraved 6 and engraved 2 more. The title-page vignettes were drawn by Hoffy and engraved by J. H. Brightly.

ALFRED HOFFY worked for several printers of lithographs in Philadelphia. Among other subjects, he drew several portraits, including one of the original Siamese twins, Eng and Chang, in 1837, but his enthusiasm for recording fruit seems to have taken up a good deal of his time. His *Orchardist's Companion* was the first American journal completely devoted to fruit and its cultivation, and it was dedicated to the President and Members of the Pennsylvania Horticultural Society. Hoffy's preface helps to explain the order of the contents of this copy:

*The First Title Page, marked Vol.* 1, is intended to precede and embody the preliminaries, together with all the letter press matter, treating of the practical operations in the cultivation of fruit trees &c., and finally to constitute the *First Volume* of this work. *The Second Title Page, marked Vol.* 2, is intended to be placed in advance of the *Plates* and their *descriptive pages*, and in due time to constitute the *Second Volume of this work.* Each portion may be readily separated . . . and placed appropriately and distinctly together under their *specific Title Pages*, when about to be formed and bound into Volumes.

That might have been clear enough until the journal moved on into its second year and another volume 2, but that was almost the end of its life, in spite of the patronage of the Society and its members.

ALFRED HOFFY *The Orchardist's Companion* 1841  Robinson's Washington Pear, drawn and lithographed by Hoffy

*Painted from Nature & Lithographed by A. Hoffy.*

Robinson's Washington Pear.

*P. S. Duvals Lith. Press, Philª*

One of these members was a local nurseryman, Robert Buist (1805–1880), who had been trained in the Royal Botanic Garden, Edinburgh, before coming to Philadelphia in the 1820s. There his garden became a centre for the introduction of new plants and seeds, and he wrote several books as well. In a 'Notice' dated March 1842 'A. Hoffy is doing himself the honor of announcing to his friends, subscribers, patrons and the public, that Mr. Robert Buist has kindly accepted at his hands the future Editorial department of the "Orchardist's Companion," at the same time cannot omit expressing his feelings of satisfaction and pride in the opportunity of presenting to them so valuable an acquisition to the views of this work.' The verso of the same leaf bears a letter dated 22 February from Buist himself:

> The proprietor . . . having applied to me to undertake the Editorial Department of this permanently useful and popular publication, I have accepted it, hoping that my endeavours and practical knowledge of the subject will not detract from its established merits . . . We are beginning an age when actions will speak louder than words, and we fondly anticipate that our amateurs and practitioners will *water* us copiously with their richest ideas and practical observations . . . to promote the grand object in view of generally diffusing a taste for the choicest products of Pomona throughout the length and breadth of the Union.

There were indeed several contributions from readers, but Buist's collaboration seems to have been short-lived, for on the volume 2 title-page, dated 1842–3, Hoffy is described as 'editor and publisher'.

William Draper Brincklé (1799–1863), a local physician and a keen amateur pomologist, may have been another helper; he certainly edited Hoffy's two later attempts at producing similar journals—*The American Pomologist* (1851, with ten fruit plates) and *The North American Pomologist* (1860, with thirty-six plates, including the ten issued in 1851). All three journals seem to have foundered because of the limited market for these beautiful but expensive portraits of fruit, though they were issued either plain or coloured. The cost of the *Orchardist's Companion* was 'Seven dollars per annum in advance, when paid punctually on the delivery or receipt of the first number of the volume, after which the full price of Two dollars per number will be charged, making Eight dollars per annum' for the 'Best or Colored Edition'. The plain one was four dollars in advance or one dollar twenty-five cents for each issue.

The fruit illustrated in the *Orchardist's* plates was usually supplied from gardens near Philadelphia. The total number is made up of fourteen pears, eleven apples, eight peaches, seven plums, three grapes, two cherries, two strawberries, and a single apricot.

## 60. DOWNING, Andrew Jackson (1815–1852)

The Fruits and Fruit Trees of America: or, The Culture, Propagation, and Management, in the Garden and Orchard, of Fruit Trees Generally; with descriptions of all the finest varieties of fruit, native and foreign, cultivated in this country. [wavy line 2.5 cm.] By A. J. Downing. Corresponding member of the Royal Botanic Society of London; and of the Horticultural Societies of Berlin; the Low Countries; Massachusetts; Pennsylvania; Indiana; Cincinnati, etc. [wavy line 2.5 cm.] What wondrous life is this I lead Ripe apples drop about my head; the lusci[o]us [c]lusters of the vine Upon my mouth do crush their wine; The nectarine and curious peach Into my hands themselves do reach. Marvell. [that is, Andrew Marvell's poem, *The Garden*, written before 1678; wavy line 2.5 cm.] Illustrated with many engravings. [wavy line 2.5 cm.] New-York & London. Wiley and Putnam. [rule 1 cm.] 1845.

12° in 6s 19.5 x 11.5 cm. $\pi^8$ $1^6$(1:3 signed 1★, 1:4 signed 2) 2–38⁶ 39¹² 40–43¹² 44⁴ 45¹² [2] *i–v* vi–xiv *1* 2–594 595–*598 i* ii–x (the last 14 pages contain advertisements).

BINDING: Brown publisher's cloth, blind rules on sides, gilt lettering and grape cluster on spine. The signature of 'M. Hampton Columbia Sept 10. 1845' is on the fly-leaf, and 'M. Hampton Sep 10 1845' on the following leaf.

The Fruits and Fruit Trees of America . . . [rule 3 cm.] . . . [rule 3 cm.; Marvell quotation corrected; rule 2 cm.] Illustrated with coloured engravings. [rule 2 cm.] New York: John Wiley, 161 Broadway, and 13 Paternoster Row, London. [rule 2 cm.] 1850.

12° in 6s 23.5 x 15 cm. $\pi^2(-\pi 2)$ $2\pi^6$ $1^6$(1:3 signed 1★, 1:4 signed 2) 2–49⁶ 50⁴(−50:4) *i–v* vi–xiv *1* 2–594 and 69 plates.

BINDING: Original half green morocco, gilt spine with bowls of fruit in compartments. Label of J. W. Moore, bookseller of 195 Chestnut Street, Philadelphia. Bookplate of Arpad Plesch (1890–1974), whose library of botanical books was sold in London in 1975 and 1976. Label of W. H. Stewart on the fly-leaf and his stamp, with 'La Carolina' added to his name, on the title-page.

PLATES: This edition and most subsequent ones contain 69 unsigned lithographs, printed in colour and finished by hand, in addition to many woodcuts in the text, as in the 1845 first edition. Several of the pear plates, 17 of them, are also found in *The Illustrated Pear Culturist*, by An Amateur, published in 1858 (see page 225). In that case two bear the name of the New York lithographer William Boell, who may have been concerned in printing the Downing plates too. The 1850 edition was printed from stereotyped plates of the first edition, except for the title-page, therefore the text contains no references to the coloured plates.

ALTHOUGH Downing is remembered now mainly as a leading American landscape gardener—his *Treatise on the Theory and Practice of Landscape Gardening* was published in 1841—he was also well known as an expert on fruit. His father, Samuel, started a nursery at Newburgh, in the Hudson Valley, in 1801, and was succeeded there by his son Charles in 1822. The youngest son of the family, Andrew, joined his elder brother as a partner in 1834 and became the nursery's sole owner in 1839, when Charles (1802–1885) began to concentrate on fruit alone, eventually setting up his own experimental orchard to test new varieties. At its best, about 1840, the Downing nursery could offer 140 apple varieties, 106 pears, 47 peaches, 31 cherries, and many soft fruits, as well as shrubs, roses, climbers, bulbs, and perennials, and Andrew used its resources to furnish his garden designs with ornamental plants. As the preface to his fruit book says (page v): 'A man born in one of the largest gardens, and upon the banks of one of the noblest rivers in America, ought to have a natural right to talk about fruit trees.' The satisfaction of

*Beurré d'Aremberg*

growing fruit was one he tried to share, for 'I heartily desire that every man should cultivate an orchard, or at least a tree, of good fruit.' That aim was probably endorsed by the man to whom the book was dedicated, Marshall P. Wilder, President of the Massachusetts Horticultural Society.

An advertisement for Downing's fruit book at the end of the first edition has a footnote saying 'This will be the most complete work on the subject ever published, and will, it is hoped, supply a desideratum long felt by amateurs and cultivators.' The hope of the book's becoming the standard American one on its subject must have been fulfilled by the long series of editions, up to the twentieth in 1900, edited and revised by Charles Downing after his brother's early death in a steamboat accident in 1852. Right from the beginning the text had frequent references to other important writers on fruit, among them Duhamel (both old and new versions), Loudon (especially the *Arboretum*), the *Transactions of the Horticultural Society* in London, and, for American comments, the books of Cobbett, Coxe, and William Prince. (Most of these are described elsewhere in the *Oak Spring Pomona*.)

Downing's silhouette illustrations of fruit, much copied in later books, are explained in the preface (page ix): 'Many of the more important varieties of fruit are shown in outline. I have chosen this method as likely to give the most correct idea of the form of a fruit, and because I believe that the mere outline of a fruit, like a profile of the human face, will often be found more characteristic than a highly finished portrait in colour.' There must have been some second thoughts, or perhaps a demand from publisher or readers, for coloured plates were soon added. A memoir of Downing by G. W. Curtis, published as an introduction to a collection called *Rural Essays* in 1853, talks about the fruit book on page xxvii: 'The duodecimo edition has only lineal [*sic*] drawings. The large octavo was illustrated with finely coloured plates, executed in Paris from drawings made in this country from the original fruits. It is a masterly resumé of the results of American experience in the history, character, and growth of fruit.' The so-called 'lineal' drawings are line drawings, of course, and the difference between duodecimo and octavo editions is one of size rather than format, but the information on the source of the illustrations may be more accurate. Curtis brought together the monthly leader columns contributed by Downing to the *Horticulturist*, which he edited from its foundation in 1846 to his sudden death.

## 61. HOVEY, Charles Mason (1810–1887)

The Fruits of America, containing richly colored figures, and Full Descriptions of all the choicest Varieties cultivated in the United States. [vignette 8.5 x 10.5 cm. of four putti holding a basket of fruit] By C. M. Hovey, Editor of the Magazine of Horticulture; Corresponding Member of the Cincinnati Horticultural Society, Ohio; of the Cleaveland Horticultural Society, etc.; and Honorary Member of the Horticultural Societies of New Haven, Conn.; Pittsburg, Pa.; Rochester, N.Y.; Steubenville, Ohio; Burlington, Iowa; Columbus, Ohio; New Bedford, Mass., etc. [rule 4.5 cm.] Volume I. [rule 4.5 cm.] Boston: Hovey and Co., Merchants' Row. New York: D. Appleton and Co. 1852.

4° 26.5 x 18 cm. Collation irregular and unsigned *i–v* vi–viii 1–100 and an uncoloured portrait frontispiece and 48 coloured plates.

. . . Volume II. [rule 4.5 cm.] Boston: Published by Hovey and Co., Merchants Row. 1856.

*i–iii* iv 1–96 and an uncoloured portrait frontispiece and 48 coloured plates.

An incomplete third volume, of which three parts were issued, is missing from this copy, but a supplementary volume (38 x 27.5 cm.) contains 28 leaves of proofs of 29 of the plates, 27 of them printed on India paper, then mounted on heavier paper, the other two printed on the same page of the thicker paper.

BINDING: Dark brown diced leather, gilt borders and spine, all edges gilt. Bookplate of Paul Mellon. The proofs are bound in half dark brown leather with brown cloth sides.

PLATES: The woodcut vignettes on the title-pages are signed by A. Roberts. Two uncoloured lithographed portraits of C. M. Hovey in volume I and William Sharp in volume II are signed 'W. Sharp' and 'WS'. The coloured plates are all labelled 'Drawn from Nature & Chromolith<sup>d</sup> by W. Sharp & Son' with variants naming 'W. Sharp' or 'Sharp & Son'. William Sharp worked in Boston from 1840 to 1885. He made many experiments in colour lithography and some of his fruit prints also appeared in the first issue of *Transactions of the Massachusetts Horticultural Society* in July 1847. As well as the coloured plates, Hovey's book is thickly scattered with woodcuts of trees, flowers, and fruit.

HOVEY was a nurseryman in Cambridge, Massachusetts, where his collection of fruit trees about 1845 included a thousand pears and four hundred apples, as well as other fruit. The variety of strawberry bearing his name, which he developed and introduced in 1838, grew large, firm fruit on more productive plants, and its popularity lasted for about fifty years. His experiments in plant breeding produced new varieties of camellia too, and he also founded the *American Gardeners' Magazine* in 1834. This was soon transformed into the *Magazine of Horticulture*, a popular gardening journal, which Hovey edited until 1868, when it ceased publication.

*The Fruits of America* was issued in twenty-eight parts from 1847 to 1856. Two volumes were completed, but only three parts and twelve plates of the third appeared before the work was abandoned. The first volume was dedicated 'To all lovers of pomological science, but more especially to the subscribers to The Fruits of America, whose aid and encouragement have insured its success'. In retrospect, the author's thanks to his subscribers look a little premature, as it seems likely that the cost of preparing the book's plates helped to make it too expensive for its possible buyers. The proof plates kept with this copy demonstrate the care taken to make accurate illustrations of the fruit, and the book has a place in the history of American printing as well as American pomology.

The two complete volumes describe and illustrate ninety-six varieties of fruit—fifty-three pears, twenty apples, seven cherries, seven peaches, six plums, and three strawberries. The history of each one is given, with a full description of the plant, its habit, flower, and fruit, and advice on its cultivation. References at the start of each entry lead on to the standard European and American books and periodicals: Duhamel, the fruit catalogue of the Horticultural Society of London, Lindley, Downing, and others. Hovey was also concerned about the multitude of names attached to some varieties, as his preface explains:

> By the labors of Van Mons and his Belgian associates, — of Noisette and his countrymen, — of Knight and other English cultivators, — as well as by the aid of our own amateur and practical Horticulturists, the well-known fruits of the last century, with a few exceptions, have given way to those of the present . . . But with this great accumulation of kinds, — and along with the multitude of names, — has followed a confusion of nomenclature which has greatly retarded the general cultivation of the newer and more valuable varieties; and the labors of the most ardent Pomologists have long been devoted

C. M. HOVEY *Fruits of America* 1847–56 Proof plates: The Rhode-Island Greening Apple (printed facing page 79 in volume II) drawn and lithographed by William Sharp

THE RHODE ISLAND GREENING APPLE.

Fruits of America, Plate Nº                    Drawn from Nature & Chromo Lithᵈ by W. Sharp.

to the attempt to reduce the chaos of names to something like order . . . I do not think it necessary to enter into any argument to show the great importance and value of colored drawings in identifying fruits, and detecting synonymes. They are now generally acknowledged, when accurately and truthfully executed, —and accompanied with faithful descriptions, —to be the only safe and reliable means of arriving at certain and satisfactory conclusions. The high estimation in which the elegant folios of Duhamel and Poiteau, and the splendidly-colored drawings in the Transactions of the London Horticultural Society, and the Pomological Magazine, are held by all Pomologists, attest this . . . There is a national pride, too, which I feel in the publication of a work like this; and that is, that the delicious fruits which have been produced in our own country, many of them surpassed by none of foreign growth, —and which are rendered doubly the more valuable, because inured to our climate and adapted to our soil, —will be here beautifully depicted; and thus show to the cultivators of the world that, though yet in the infancy of the art, the skill of our Pomologists, unaided, too, by the experience which cultivators abroad may so well claim, has already given them a fair start on the road to success; and, favored by Providence with a genial atmosphere and a cloudless sky, with the enterprise, intelligence, and perseverance, so characteristic of our people, why may we not hope that they will make the most rapid advance in a science whose results are so conducive to the health, the comfort, and the luxury of mankind.

## 62. COLE, Samuel W. (1796–1851)

A Book for Every Body. [rule] The American Fruit Book; containing directions for raising, propagating, and managing Fruit Trees, Shrubs, and Plants; with a description of the best varieties of fruit, including new and valuable kinds; embellished and illustrated with numerous engravings of fruits, trees, insects, grafting, budding, training, &c., &c. [rule 1.5 cm.] By S. W. Cole, editor of the New England Farmer, late editor of the Boston Cultivator, author of The American Veterinarian, and formerly editor of the Yankee Farmer, and Farmer's Journal. [rule 1.5 cm.] Boston: Published by John P. Jewett, No. 23, Cornhill. New York: C. M. Saxton. 1849.
12° 15.5 x 9.5 cm. $I^6$ 2–24$^6$ $i$–$v$ vi–xxiv (8, 14, 15 with Arabic numerals) 25 26–288 and a frontispiece.

BINDING: Contemporary calf, rebacked. The signature 'Robert D. Hill' is in pencil on the front pastedown.

PLATES: The frontispiece is printed on both sides, with a wood engraving of the Hubbardston Nonsuch apple on the recto and one of the Flemish Beauty pear on the verso, facing the title-page. A note on the verso of the title-page reads: 'The engravings in this work have been done by Mr. S. E. Brown, a skilful artist.' Throughout the text there are many more examples of his work, including fruit silhouettes apparently modelled on those in A. J. Downing's book, *The Fruits and Fruit Trees of America* (see page 158).

BEFORE farming claimed most of his attention about 1835, Samuel Cole had already published a spelling book and a volume of poems. From 1840 to 1850 he had a nursery at Chelsea, Massachusetts, and during this decade he was a leading member of the Massachusetts Horticultural Society. He came from Maine, where he used to test fruit trees, according to a note

S. W. COLE
*The American Fruit Book*
1849 pages 106–07
Apple silhouettes
drawn by S. E.
Brown

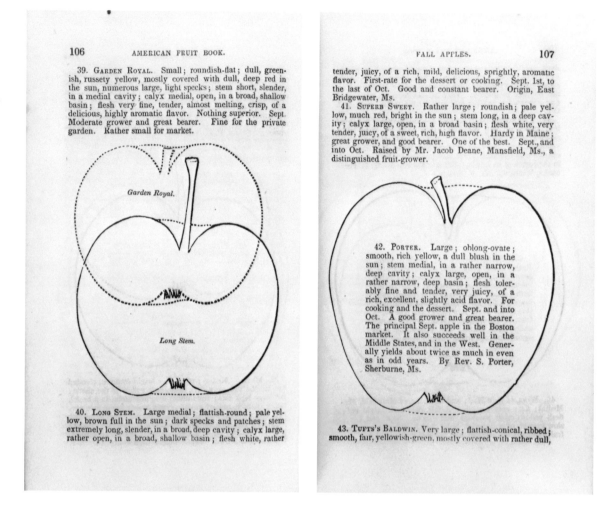

on the back of the title-page of *The American Fruit Book*: 'We have occasionally made remarks on the hardiness of fruits in Maine, as we have a specimen orchard there, where we try many varieties.' The preface to the book spelled out the author's aims:

> Our object has been, to furnish a book adapted to the wants, and within the means, of every family in the country—emphatically a work for the MILLION—containing all the practical information necessary for the production and successful management of trees, and the selection of the best varieties of fruit, in order to excite greater attention, both in cultivator and consumer, in raising more and superior fruits, and in their extensive use as wholesome food, an improving ingredient in various culinary preparations, and not only a harmless, but a healthful luxury.

This proclamation may have been directed at the Downing book on American fruit, first published in 1845, and certainly a more elegant and more expensive production than Cole's chunky little handbook, though he did indeed try to make his book useful across the continent.

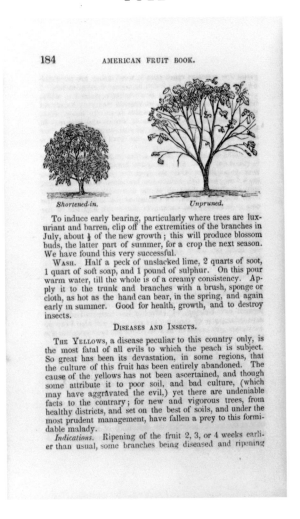

S. W. COLE *The American Fruit Book* 1849 page 184 Pruned and unpruned peach trees, drawn by S. E. Brown

Among those whose help is acknowledged on the back of the title-page are 'Mr. Ernst, of Cincinnati . . . [who] has politely furnished . . . a list of fruits adapted to that section' and 'Mr. Elliott, of Cleveland . . . [who] has furnished a list adapted to that region, selected for this work, by Prof. Kirtland and himself'.

## 63. NURSERYMEN'S PLATES

[Album of Fruit and Flowers. Probably Rochester, New York, *c.*1860.]
29.5 x 23 cm. 63 unnumbered leaves, 5 blank, 58 coloured plates.
BINDING: Modern brown cloth.

PLATES: 52 watercolours, some possibly theorem paintings using stencils, 6 lithographs coloured or finished by hand, three of which, Diana, Concord, and Rebecca grapes, have 'Published by E. Darrow & Brother, Rochester, New York' printed below the name of the variety.

Album of Fruit
and Flowers *c.* 1860
Cherries

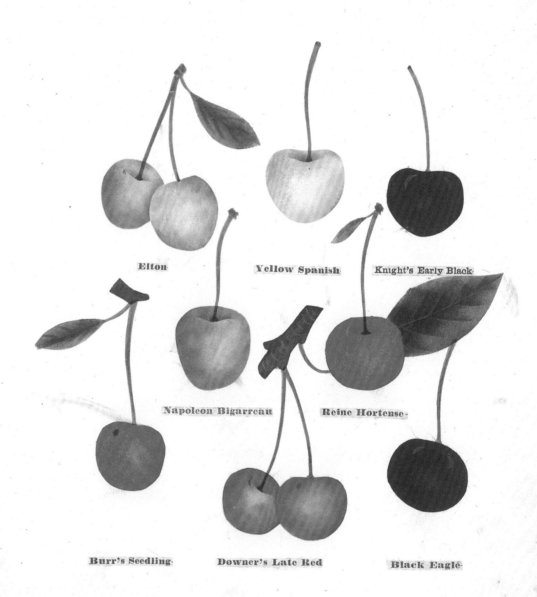

Elton          Yellow Spanish          Knight's Early Black

Napoleon Bigarreau          Reine Hortense

Burr's Seedling          Downer's Late Red          Black Eagle

CHERRIES.

Erastus Darrow (1823–1909) was in partnership with his brother Wallace from 1856 to 1866, publishing fruit and flower plates, among other prints (see Charles van Ravenswaay, *Drawn from Nature* (1984) page 121 note 97). The other prints are the Isabella grape, the New Rochelle (or Lawton) blackberry, and the rose Géant des Batailles, and all three have printed labels. One of the three raspberries (Brinckle's Orange) on the plate devoted to that fruit also has a lithographed picture beneath its colour, but this plate and all the remainder have labels snipped from a printed list of fruit and ornamental plants and stuck to the relevant leaves of the album.

Of the watercolours, three seem to be copies of plates by Joseph Prestele (1796–1867) or his son Gottlieb (1827–1892) reproduced in van Ravenswaay's book *Drawn from Nature*, which is about the work of this family of artists. The Swaar apple corresponds to plate 43 (Gottlieb), the White Smith gooseberry to plate 62 (Gottlieb), and the Persian Yellow rose to plate 75 (Joseph), while the rose Caroline de Sansel is a variant of plate 73 (Joseph). The Early Strawberry apple also shows signs of a Prestele model, as the whole fruit and half a second one, sliced from top to bottom, is an echo of several Prestele apples, as well as those in earlier fruit books. The bleeding heart, *Dielytra spectabilis*, is also similar to plate 94 in the Prestele book, though the version in this album is earlier. The unknown artist and W. H. Prestele may have been copying the same model. The *Weigelea rosea* plate is identical to one published by D. M. Dewey in 1859 and used by him for at least another twenty years.

FROM THE 1850s, as Rochester became an important centre of nursery gardening, another local industry grew up to provide illustrations of fruit, flowers, shrubs, and trees, selections of which were used as catalogues by travelling 'tree peddlers' who sold plants from the nurseries they represented to farmers and gardeners in the territories they visited. The earliest illustrations of this kind were watercolours copied by local artists, but soon their production was made more efficient by the use of stencils to produce theorem paintings of flowers or fruit. Printed outlines or lithographs were also coloured by hand until chromolithographs added colour to the basic process, though even then they were often finished by hand.

This album may have been made by one of the artists involved in making coloured plates for nurserymen quite early in the large-scale development of their production, to judge from the varieties illustrated and links between some of these drawings and other dated ones. Some of these links are with plates known to have been issued by D. M. Dewey, a major figure in the trade (see page 168), and the anonymous artist might have been one employed by him. Charles van Ravenswaay, in 'Drawn and Colored from Nature' (*Antiques*, March 1983, pages 594–99) describes 'painted nurserymen's plates' as 'more akin to folk painting than to the commercial art of their time'. The same author's book *A Nineteenth-Century Garden* (1977, page 20) extends the comparison: 'To the average American of the time, scarcely aware of fashionable art, these plates, with their simplified designs and sparkling colors, were akin to the stylized art with which he was familiar: the stenciled chairs, the portraits by itinerant, unschooled artists, and the flower and fruit paintings by schoolgirls.' The decorative quality of the watercolours in this album underlines the attractions of these plates. Gardeners are still willing to hope that the plants and seeds they order from illustrated catalogues will always turn out as well as the pictures. The customers of the nineteenth-century tree peddlers must have been no less eager to believe in the horticultural treasures they were offered.

There are more useful plants than purely ornamental ones in the album: seventeen apples, twelve pears, four grapes, four cherries, three plums, two peaches, and single plates of an apricot, a quince, currants, a blackberry, gooseberries, raspberries, and strawberries. Six roses, two other flowering shrubs, and 'the finest herbaceous plant in cultivation', bleeding heart (*Dielytra spectabilis*) follow the fruit, perhaps intended to furnish a small flower garden near the orchard.

## 64. DEWEY, Dellon Marcus (1819–1889)

[lithographed title-page] The Specimen Book of Fruits, Flowers and Ornamental Trees. Carefully Drawn and Colored from Nature, for the use of Nurserymen. Rochester, N.Y. Published by D. M. Dewey, Ag.ᵗ [*c.* 1866.]

28.5 x 22.5 cm. 38 coloured plates, including the title-page.

BINDING: Quarter brown leather, brown cloth sides, stamped in gold on front cover with a cluster of pears (the twin of the one on the cover of Field's *Pear Culture*, 1859: see page 223) and 'Dewey's Colored Fruit & Flowers', with a decorated rectangular label for a name beneath the pears. Bookplate of Paul Mellon. Title-page inscribed in pencil 'Store Oct 66'.

PLATES: The title-page, which has panels of lettering within a border of flowers and fruit, the larger panel with a garden scene in its lower part, and 12 of the plates are signed 'Lith. of E. B. & E. C. Kellogg. Hartford Conn.' Edmund Burke Kellogg (b. 1809) and Elijah Chapman Kellogg (1811–1881) were two of a family of four brothers, all lithographers, who produced a large quantity of prints of many kinds — portraits, historical scenes, and even a temperance series, as well as fruit and flowers. Most of the rest of the plates have been coloured by hand, using stencils. All the plates are lettered 'D. M. Dewey's Series of Fruits, Flowers & Ornamental Trees. Rochester, N.Y.'

[A selection of coloured plates, mostly fruit, from Dewey's series of 'American Fruits and Flowers', *c.* 1880.] 22 x 14 cm. 65 coloured plates.

BINDING: Half red leather, marbled paper sides.

PLATES: A mixture of chromolithographs, some finished by hand, and about 10 theorem pictures coloured with stencils, most of these being flowering shrubs. The plate of Sharpless' Seedling Strawberry mentions a specimen exhibited in Rochester on 20 June 1878. Nearly all the plates are labelled 'D. M. Dewey's Series, Colored from Nature. American Fruits and Flowers' but a few are tagged 'Dewey's Medium Series' or 'Dewey's Pocket Series' instead. Several have prices pencilled in below the captions.

AS ROCHESTER's gardening flourished a local bookseller with an interest in the subject, D. M. Dewey, began to collect and publish coloured plates of fruit, flowers, shrubs, and fruit-bearing or purely ornamental trees. Selections of these plates were used as illustrated catalogues by travelling salesmen who peddled the stock of the nurseries they represented. These groups of the plates sold by Dewey and others from the 1850s to the last decade of the century were usually bound into pocket-sized books about ten by six inches (25.5 x 15 cm.) with stout leather covers, often stamped with the name of the nursery or the salesman offering the plants portrayed within. Dewey also recognized the wider appeal of the coloured plates described by Charles van Ravenswaay as 'an innovation in American popular art' (*A Nineteenth-Century Garden*, 1977, page 20. See page 167 for further references to his other work on nurserymen's plates.) Their polychrome attractions were extended to a larger audience in small selections from

Brincle's Orange.  Ohio Everbearing.  Catawissa.

D. M. DEWEY'S Series of Fruits, Flowers and Ornamental Trees, Rochester, N. Y.

D. M. DEWEY
*The Specimen Book of Fruits, Flowers, and Ornamental Trees*
*c.* 1866  Raspberries

a larger-sized series presented in decorative bindings, like the first of the pair described here. They were intended for prizes at horticultural shows or fairs, or even for display on parlour tables, beside the family Bible and photograph album, as Dewey suggested in an 1871 catalogue of his coloured plates. His collection of them included several thousands by the time of his last catalogue in 1888. Whatever their source, and some of Dewey's plates were bought from other printers, all were labelled with his name, as well as that of the plant or the variety of fruit, with a short caption giving a brief description of its qualities and its season of ripeness.

The earliest plates were simple watercolours, but later, as the demand grew, the technique of theorem paintings coloured with the help of stencils was used to multiply the number of copies as quickly and as cheaply as possible. Later still, engraved or lithographed outlines were coloured by hand, and finally chromolithographs printed in colour began to replace more laborious procedures, though some of these were finished by hand too. Most of these processes involved the labour of teams of artists and colourists, one or two of whom went on to establish themselves as rivals to Dewey, though none achieved the same success.

Each of the selections described here has more useful plants than purely ornamental ones. The first has twenty-five fruit plates to eight of roses, other flowering shrubs, or trees, while the second, larger, selection has forty-five fruit plates and twenty roses, other shrubs, or trees. In both groups the apple is the favourite fruit with most varieties available, followed by pears, plums, peaches (or apricots or nectarines), cherries, grapes, strawberries, raspberries, gooseberries, and currants, more or less in that order of frequency, reflecting the demands of the gardeners to whom they were sold.

Dewey supplied labels, tools, and other equipment for nurserymen as well, and in 1875 he even published a manual for their salesmen, *The Tree Agents' Private Guide*, a little book full of advice on everything from the pronunciation of plant names to how to dress to make a favourable impression and how to make sure of a prospective sale.

## 65. ANDREWS, O.

[A collection of fruit plates. Rochester, New York, *c.*1881.]
22 x 14.5 cm. 143 (of 152) coloured plates.

BINDING: The plates are divided into two groups of 57 and 86, each group made up of rows of four joined by tapes and backed by a second row of four, so that eight are visible on each opening. The whole set folds down to the length and breadth of a single plate, and the linked collection is attached to a black leather box-shaped case with movable sides. 'O. Andrews, Great Barrington, Mass. Fruits' is stamped in gilt on the front flap of this leather wallet. The metal clasp of the case is marked 'Pat$^{d.}$ Feb. 26, March 12.78'.

PLATES: A mixture of chromolithographs, some finished by hand, and the hand-coloured plates, with or without printed outlines, which were a speciality of the Thompson

O. ANDREWS
A Collection of Fruit
Plates *c.* 1881  The set
unfolded, showing
some of the plates

O. ANDREWS
A Collection of Fruit Plates *c.* 1881  The folded set in its case

company in the 1870s. Most bear the name of J. W. Thompson & Co., a company active in Rochester, New York, from 1876 to 1891, or the Nicholson company, for Charles F. Nicholson was a local competitor and the eventual successor of John W. Thompson. One of the gaps in the set has been filled by a later, inferior, chromolithograph of the Winchell Grape, its name added in shaky capitals beneath the inserted picture.

THIS large collection of fruit plates, showing the stock of O. Andrews of Great Barrington, a town in the south-western corner of Massachusetts, reflects similar preferences to the smaller groups described above. The favourite fruit is the apple, with fifty-seven plates in the upper section of this folding display. The lower part holds pictures of plums, pears, cherries, peaches, strawberries, raspberries, blackberries, grapes, currants, gooseberries, quinces, a dewberry, a mulberry, 'Eaton's New Peach Flavored Pie Plant' (or rhubarb), and a solitary vegetable, 'Conover's Colossal Asparagus', just the thing for anyone misguided enough to want asparagus stalks that might grow to as much as an inch and a half in diameter.

Some of the brief captions beneath the glowing pictures of the fruit help to date this collection. The Russian mulberry is said to have been introduced from seed sown in 1875, bearing fruit from the time the little trees were two years old, while the Hansell raspberry, a variety grown for its early fruit, had ripe berries by the middle of June in 1881. The two plates showing the Cuthbert or Queen of the Market red raspberry and the Golden Queen yellow one are also embellished with lace-cuffed hands, one to each plate, holding little heaps of red or yellow berries.

## 66. STUART, Charles W. & Co.

[A collection of coloured plates, mostly fruit, c.1888.] 22.5 x 14.5 cm. 76 coloured plates.

BINDING: Brown calf, front cover lettered 'Chas. W. Stuart & Co. Newark, N.Y. No. 967'. A large label on the front pastedown reads: 'Special. Do not mark prices on plates, under any circumstances. Chas. W. Stuart & Co.'

PLATES: 76 chromolithographs, one signed 'The Henderson-Achert Co. Lith. Cin'ti' and nearly all the rest either 'Stecher Lith. Co. Roch. N.Y.' or 'F. A. Stecher Lith. Roch. N.Y.' The Stecher Lithographic Company of Rochester published the *Horticultural Art Journal* from 1886 to 1891, and a few of these plates also bear the journal's name. Four also bear copyright dates of 1887 or 1888.

THE firm direction inside the front cover, instructing the salesman using the plates never to add prices to them, would have allowed the illustrations to be used year after year without prospective customers making embarrassing comparisons between current prices and those of earlier seasons.

During the 1870s chromolithographed plates of fruit and flowers frequently replaced hand-coloured ones, as they were less expensive to produce in the quantities needed. Twenty-one of the plates in this selection are devoted to ornamental plants—eight roses, six other shrubs, and seven trees, the last group shown with the addition of seats and little landscapes round their trunks. Among the fruit are a dozen varieties of apple, eight peaches, six pears, six grapes, six raspberries (black, red, or white), five cherries, five plums, two quinces, two currants (black and white), two gooseberries, and an apricot.

A nineteenth-century American box, made of wood covered with paper and painted with vignettes of fruit. 'Miss Nancy Barnum' is written in pencil inside the lid

CITRUS FRUIT

G. B. FERRARI *Hesperides* 1646 page 147
An arcade of oranges
with a protective roof
in the garden of Cardinal Carlo Pio, drawn by
Philippe Gagliard and
engraved by C. Cungi

# 67. FERRARI, Giovanni Battista (1584–1655)

Hesperides sive De malorvm avreorvm cvltvra et vsv Libri Quatuor Io: Baptistae Ferrarii Senensis e Societate Iesv. [I.H.S. (i.e., Jesus) and a crucifix within a sun, 5.5 x 5.5 cm.] Romae, Sumptibus Hermanni Scheus. M D C X L V I. [rule 15 cm.] Svperiorvm permissv. 2º in 4s 35.5 x 23 cm. ✱⁶ A–3Q⁴ *i–xii 1–480 481–496* including an engraved frontispiece and 101 engraved plates.

BINDING: Contemporary vellum. Armorial bookplate of the Honourable Charles Hamilton (1704–1786), who designed his own garden at Painshill in Surrey, and advised the owners of other great gardens of the period, like Bowood and Stourhead.

PLATES: The title-page cum frontispiece was drawn by Pietro da Cortona (1596–1669) and engraved by J. F. Greuter. On a stepped terrace in front of a temple Hercules leans on a block of stone bearing the inscription 'Hesperides sive Malorvm avreorvm cvltvra et vsvs'. The block is topped with Hercules' discarded lion-skin. One of the Hesperides is timidly offering him a laurel wreath, while between them a neatly coiled dragon, the guardian of the golden apples, writhes on the ground.

The 80 fruit plates are the work of Cornelis Bloemaert (*c.*1603–1683). Gavin Bridson has pointed out (in *Printing in the Service of Botany*, 1986, page 45) that all the fruit plates except one are etched, the exception (the lemon on page 269) being a fine example of Bloemaert's line engraving. He also engraved most of the remainder, signed by Andrea Sacchi, Nicolas Poussin, Pietro Paolo Ubaldini (2), F. Perier, Francesco Albani, Philippe Gagliard (4), F. Romanelli, Guido Reni, Dominic Zampieri (Domenichino), and H. Rinaldi. R. Goyrand and J. F. Greuter each engraved at least one of the plates not showing fruit. Of these 7 are devoted to statues and other images of Hercules, while the rest show mythological scenes, garden buildings, orangeries, tools, and tubs. The original drawing for the Poussin engraving on page 97, showing the Hesperides bringing their fruit to the Italian lakes, is in the Royal Library, Windsor, with Domenichino's drawing for the plate of Myrrha's metamorphosis on page 419. The drawing for Guido Reni's orange garden on page 343, with the Hesperides and several gardeners at work, is in the Ashmolean Museum, Oxford.

GIOVANNI BATTISTA FERRARI was born and died in Siena, where he became a Jesuit at the age of eighteen. For nearly thirty years he taught Hebrew in a seminary in Rome, where he also seems to have cultivated an interest in gardening. In 1633 his lavishly illustrated book *De Florum*, describing flowers and their culture, was published in Rome, followed five years later by an edition in Italian, and later still by a pirated version produced in Amsterdam. From flowers Ferrari turned to citrus fruit, publishing in 1646 his *Hesperides*, the first book completely devoted to oranges, lemons, citrons, and limes in a multitude of varieties. Incidentally, by his choice of artists—one of whom, Poussin, is praised on page 99—Ferrari produced a splendid example of baroque book illustration too.

The book begins with Hercules hunting the golden apples in the garden of the Hesperides, the daughters of Hesperus (or Night) who, with the help of a dragon, defended the garden in the far west of the known world. As the theft of the apples was the last of Hercules' twelve labours before joining the gods, he is described as both hero and deity, with engravings of both

G. B. FERRARI
*Hesperides* 1646 page
391 A double-flowered
orange, drawn and
engraved by Cor-
nelis Bloemaert

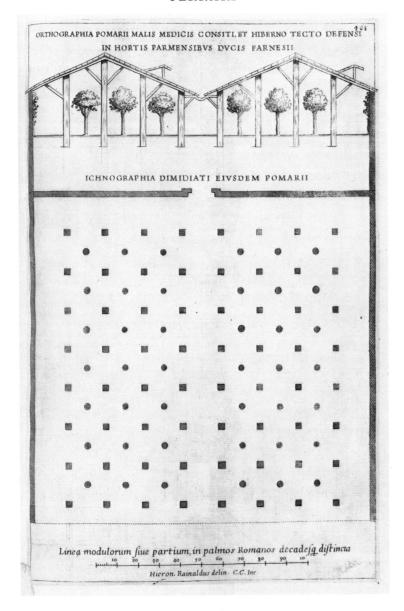

ORTHOGRAPHIA POMARII MALIS MEDICIS CONSITI, ET HIBERNO TECTO DEFENSI
IN HORTIS PARMENSIBVS DVCIS FARNESII

ICHNOGRAPHIA DIMIDIATI EIVSDEM POMARII

Linea modulorum siue partium, in palmos Romanos decadesq distincta

Hieron. Rainaldus delin · C.C. Inc

G. B. FERRARI *Hesperides* 1646 page 461 The ground plan and a section of the Farnese nursery on the Palatine Hill in Rome, drawn by H. Rinaldi and engraved by C. Cungi

statues and coins to confirm his status. Two of these plates (pages 11 and 27) were reproduced by J. C. Volkamer in the second volume of his *Nürnbergische Hesperides* (1714, folios 3–4; see page 191), a book that reflects in many ways the author's exploration of his predecessor's work. This first part of Ferrari's book is also packed with quotations from Pliny, Varro, and many others, tracking golden apples through classical literature.

Following this 'approach to the Hesperides' the book is divided into three sections, each named for one of the daughters of Hesperus. Aegle presides over citrons, Arethusa over lemons, and Erythia over oranges, with a strong hint that their paradise garden might be recreated in Italy if their 'golden apples' were interpreted as oranges and other citrus fruits. Ferrari's detailed descriptions of individual varieties of these fruits, many of them monstrous-looking objects with strangely distorted shapes or very thick bumpy skin, are illustrated by plates showing them in their full size, often with flowers and leaves. The names are inscribed on ribbons winding round the twigs and across the plates, which usually show a cross or transverse section below the whole fruit. The artist and engraver Cornelis Bloemaert had been apprenticed to the Dutchman Crispijn van de Passe (the artist of the *Hortus Floridus*, a beautiful and popular flower book) but he spent the last part of his life in Italy, where his patrons included the Barberini family and Pietro da Cortona. For Ferrari he illustrated eight citrons, thirty-nine lemons, nine strange fruits grouped with the lemons but four of which look more like grapefruit (at a date when the West Indian parents of modern grapefruit were unknown in Europe), four limes, and twenty oranges, among them a couple of precursors of the navel kind (pages 315 and 405).

The Italian climate offered a comfortable setting for the cultivation of citrus fruits, and many kinds were naturalized there long before Ferrari's day, especially once the sweet orange from China arrived in the fifteenth century. The decorative trees, with their evergreen leaves and scented blossoms, needed protection from cold during the winter and sometimes shelter from too much sun in the summer. Their delicacy and their beauty were good reasons for displaying them in orangeries, glazed and often heated conservatories that were the ancestors of more sophisticated greenhouses. The plate on page 457 of the *Hesperides* shows the Aldobrandini family's magnificent vaulted orangery. In the warmest weather airy sheds with slatted wooden walls stopped the trees and their fruit from being roasted, and these are illustrated on pages 461 and 463, in a form closely related to modern versions of similar buildings.

As well as cataloguing so many varieties of citrus fruit, Ferrari also talks about the gardens in which they were grown, mostly those of the nobility or others rich enough to collect and cosset demanding plants. The last few pages of the book deal with the uses of the trees, flowers, and fruit: oils distilled from leaves, orange flower water, and even an ardent spirit for medicinal purposes.

## 68. COMMELIN, Jan (1629–1692)

Nederlantze Hesperides, Dat is, Oeffening en Gebruik Van de Limoen- en Oranje-boomen; Gestelt na den Aardt, en Climaat der Nederlanden. Met kopere Platen verçiert, Door J. Commelyn. [triangular vignette 5 x 6 cm.] Tot Amsterdam, [rule 13 cm.] By Marcus Doornik, Boek-verkooper op den Vygen-dam. 1676. Met Privilegie.
2° 31.5 x 20 cm. *A*² B–O² *i–iv* 1–47 *48–52* and an engraved title-page and 26 other plates.

BINDING: As usual, bound with Hendrick Cause's *De Koninglycke Hovenier* 1676, in contemporary vellum with the bookplates of A.P.M. de Kluijs and Arpad Plesch (1890–1974). This copy was bought at the Plesch sale at Sotheby's in London on 16 June 1975.

PLATES: The unsigned, engraved title-page shows gardeners planting and potting citrus trees, watched by a goddess and a cluster of putti, all holding fruit. The lettering repeats that of the title-page with slight variations, of which the most important is the addition of three words at the end, so that 'Met Privilegie' is modified by 'voor Vyftien Iaaren'. The 20 fine engravings of fruit or citrus flowers are signed by Cornelis Kick (1635–1681), a local painter of fruit and flowers. Of the 6 engravings showing pots and orangeries, the fourth and fifth are signed 'De Vree', probably Nicolaes de Vree (1645–1702), an Amsterdam painter of landscapes and flowers, who may also have been responsible for the rest of the plates and the title-page.

JAN COMMELIN
*Nederlandtze Hesperides*
1676 Head-piece
starting the preface

JAN COMMELIN, an Amsterdam merchant dealing in spices and other exotic imports, was easily able to keep track of the plants from Dutch colonies that were imported with more commercial cargoes. Most of them came from the East or West Indies or the Cape of Good Hope, and the Amsterdam botanic garden became one of the foremost in Europe, receiving these newcomers and in some cases passing on seeds or cuttings of them to other gardens, especially the university one at Leiden. About 1682, when the Amsterdam garden was re-established on a new site, Commelin took charge of it on behalf of the city authorities. The first volume of a catalogue of its plants which he compiled, concentrating on those from the East and West Indies, was published in 1697, thanks to his nephew Caspar, another botanist, who put together a second volume, mainly on African plants, which appeared four years after the first.

The fashion for growing citrus fruit and other tender evergreens in pots which could be moved indoors to conservatories or orangeries during the winter may have paved the way for the successful cultivation of new plants from tropical countries. Improvements in both the ability to control the temperature of glass-fronted greenhouses (that is, houses for evergreens) and the skill needed to care for unfamiliar and demanding plants must have helped the introduction of new exotic flowers and fruits. In France, according to Madame de Sévigné in a letter of 1657, roses, jasmine, carnations, or tuberoses were sometimes planted round the pots or boxes to hide the containers holding the orange or lemon trees, but some of the pots or the even larger stone urns were so decorative that they can hardly have been intended to be concealed.

Commelin had his own orangery, which is illustrated in one of the plates of his *Hesperides*. Several of his friends shared his interest in citrus fruit, and their heated conservatories are also illustrated or mentioned in the text, as well as predecessors like the Italian Ferrari, whose own *Hesperides* (see page 177) is constantly quoted, as a rich source of advice on the history, classification, and cultivation of oranges and lemons. Another writer quoted, a contemporary called Frans van Sterbeeck, lent the manuscript of his book *Citricultura* to Commelin, who may have used it

JAN COMMELIN *Neder-landtze Hesperides* 1676 plate facing page 18 An orange branch with small fruit and half another orange, drawn and engraved by Cornelis Kick

Oranje-boom met de Kleine vrught
Anders Naantje.

Fol: 18.

C. Kick Pinx.

to enrich the *Nederlantze Hesperides*, which he was writing at the time. In April 1677 Commelin returned the manuscript to van Sterbeeck with a copy of his own newly published book on the same subject. Van Sterbeeck's *Citricultura* (see page 185) was not published until 1682, when it was printed in Antwerp, with a preface describing the loan of the manuscript to Commelin, who might have spoiled the market for his friend's book.

Recipes for orange brandy, candied orange-blossom, orange-flower water, preserves, pastilles, and ointment, and similar lemon preparations, plus lemonade, end the *Hesperides*, following descriptions of various kinds of orange and lemon, their transport, cultivation, pruning, and protection during the northern winter.

## 69. COMMELIN, Jan (1629–1692)

[within a border of double rules] The Belgick, or Netherlandish Hesperides. That is. The Management, Ordering, and Use of the Limon and Orange Trees, Fitted to the Nature and Climate of the Netherlands. [rule] By S. Commelyn. [rule] Made English by G.V.N. [rule] London, Printed for J. Holford Bookseller, at the Crown in the Pall-mall, and are to be Sold by Langly Curtis, 1683. 8° 17.5 x 11 cm. A–N⁸ *i–x 1–194 195–198*.

BINDING: Calf, rebacked, stamped 'Clarke & Bedford'; all edges red. The cut-out signature of John Aubrey (1626–1697), antiquary and gossip, is stuck on the front pastedown, above the bookplate of Donald E. Roy. On the verso of the title-page is the bookplate of 'William Penn Esqʳ Proprietor of Pennsylvania: 1703'.

THIS plain little book, with no illustrations at all, is a great contrast to the original Dutch edition, with its fine plates of fruit and conservatories. The unidentified translator, G.V.N., dedicated 'This *Belgick Hesperides* (in an English Dress)' to Thomas Belasyse, the 2nd Viscount Fauconberg (1628–1700), whose house at Sutton Court, Chiswick, by the river Thames near London, was described by John Gibson in 1691 as being 'very well furnished with good greens' in both garden and greenhouse.

The earliest orange trees in England were said to have been grown at Beddington in Surrey about 1560 by Sir Francis Carew. These rarities were described by John Aubrey as imports from Italy, but their owner bought trees in France too, and his oranges may have been sent home from Paris. On 27 September 1658 John Evelyn visited 'that antient Seate of the Carews, a faire old hall, but a scambling house: famous for the first *Orange* garden of *England*, being now overgrowne trees, & planted in the ground, & secur'd in winter with a wooden tabernacle & stoves'. The Beddington oranges lived on until 1740, and the enthusiasm for growing oranges and lemons survived them.

G.V.N.'s translation of Commelin's advice to Dutch gardeners passed on directions as to the best source of trees (pages 82–83):

JAN COMMELIN *The Belgick, or Netherlandish Hesperides* translated by G.V.N. 1683 William Penn's bookplate and the dedication

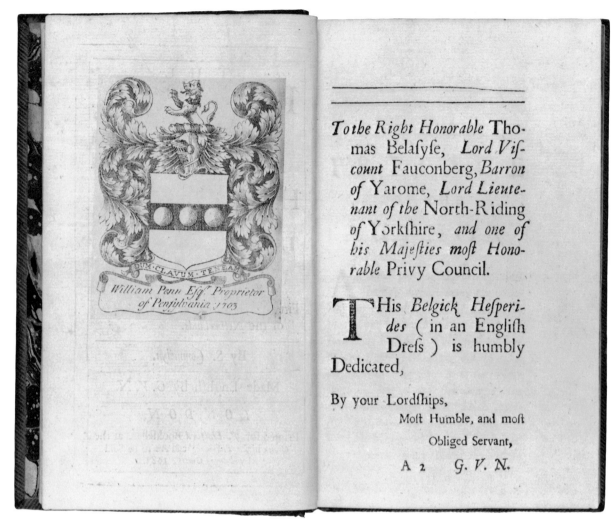

To the Right Honorable Thomas Belasyse, *Lord Viscount* Fauconberg, *Barron of Yarome, Lord Lieutenant of the* North-Riding *of* Yorkshire, *and one of his Majesties most Honorable* Privy Council.

THis *Belgick Hesperides* ( in an English Drefs ) is humbly Dedicated,

By your Lordfhips,

Most Humble, and most

Obliged Servant,

A 2      *G. V. N.*

The place whence they must be fetched, is St. *Remo*, Situated by or upon the River *Nervi*, whence they are brought to *Genoa*. We must bring no Trees out of any other climates to Plant or Order here in our Netherlands, because the Condition of that place, doth, above all other places in *Italy*, agree best with our Climate . . . If Trees be brought out of any other Countries, as Spain, or Portugal, it will certainly be in Vain and to no Purpose; because they cannot well endure our cold changeable and uncertain Air.

The Mediterranean coast on either side of the border between France and Italy is still thickly scattered with lemon and orange trees, and San Remo would still be a good place to look for healthy young ones.

The first chapter of the book sums up its purpose:

Being the Ordering or Management of the Limon and Orange Trees is much increased within these few Years, by many inhabitants of our Country, and would yet Increase more, if Ignorance and unskilfulness were not in the Cause. To open the Door to this Science, this *Hesperides* is come to Light, offering her Golden Apples to every one, tho not without prudent Labour: Which we shall here Propound in order. *First*, A short Introduction shall be given to the Knowledg of the Trees and Fruits, which are Described every one in their particular Kinds and Parts. *Secondly*, the Ordering and Use of the Fruits, with their most excellent Profit and Usefulness, which are all shortly and plainly Communicated to all Managers.

## 70. STERBEECK, Frans van (1631–1693)

Citricultura oft Regeringhe der uythemsche Boomen te weten Oranien, Citroenen, Limoenen, Granatum, Laurieren en andere. Waer in beschreven is de gedaente ende kennisse der Boomen, met hunne bloemen, bladeren en vruchten: van ieder geflacht in het besonder. Als oock van den Ranck-appel, oprechten Laurier van America, Den Caneel-boom: Ende besonderlijck van den Verboden Adams oft Paradys-appel. Daer beneffens de natuere, kracht, en ghebruyck, haer deught en ondeught van ieder vrucht en plant. Waer by oock grondigh gheleert wordt het Zaeyen, Mesten, Planten, Oculeren, Inten, Afsuyghen, Inlegghen, Besnoeyen, en Begieten. Oock de kennisse van het treuren ofte sieckten der Boomē, ende haere behulp-middelen. Met alle het ghene dese Boomen (soo wel in den winter, als in den somer) tot welstandt zijn versoeckende. Ende dat alles naer den eysch van ons Nederlandts Climaet. By lanckdurighe ondervindinghe in het licht ghegheven ende met kopere platen verciert door Franciscus van Sterbeeck Priester. [Maltese cross 0.5 x 0.5 cm.] T'Antwerpen, By Joseph Jacops, in de Borse-straet naest den hoeck van de Langhe Nieu-straet. Anno 1682. Met Gratie en Privilegie.

4° 20.5 x 15.5 cm. $\pi^2(-\pi2)$ §–4§⁴(4§3 wrongly signed ★★★★) ★★★★★⁴(★★★★★1 wrongly signed §§§§) A–I⁴ K⁴(K1+1) L–2R⁴ 2S² *i–xlii* 1–74 [2] 75–296 *297–324* (56 printed upside-down, corrected by hand; 174 printed as 147, corrected by hand) and an engraved half-title and 16 other engravings.

BINDING: Modern vellum. Bookplates of V. de la Montagne, Frans and Joop Verdoorn. Professor Frans Verdoorn (1906–1984) was a Dutch botanist and historian of natural history. An earlier label reads 'Desen Boeck hoort toe aen de Sodalityt der Getraude, onder den Titel van Onse L. V. Boedtschap der Societyt Jesus tot Antwerpen Anno 1721' ('This book belongs to a guild of the faithful

A tail-piece of a basket of flowers from the prefatory poems

in the name of the Annunciation of Our Lady, representing the Society of Jesus in Antwerp, 1721').

PLATES: The engraved half-title, showing a tree being tucked into a tub, with smaller potted trees on balustrades and walls in the background, is signed by the artist Charles Emmanuel Biset (1633–c.1686) and the engraver Frans Ertinger (1640–1710), who also signed the coat of arms facing the start of the dedication. Ertinger also worked in Rome and Paris, where he was a 'graveur du roi' in 1667. Both signatures appear on the portrait of Sterbeeck following the list of contents. Ertinger's name alone is on plates 1 to 3 and 5 to 7, and for several of these he made the drawings as well as engraving them. The rest are unsigned. Plates 1, 2, 3, and 5 appear to be based on parts of several illustrations of citrus fruit in Ferrari's *Hesperides* (see page 177), Sterbeeck's plate 1 echoing Ferrari's pages 369 and 377, plate 2 pages 59, 61, and 63, plate 3 pages 307, 311, 313, and 315, and plate 5 pages 189 and 229. Plate 4 is a banana, both plant and fruit, plate 6 shows methods of grafting, with a garden background, plate 7 equipment for taking unwanted curves out of the trunks of trees in pots, plate 8 a pomegranate (branch, flowers, and fruit), plate 9 a passionflower and its fruit, plates 10 to 13 various laurels, from the classical bay to the more exotic kinds, as twigs or potted trees, and plate 14 cinnamon twigs, leaves, flowers, and fruit.

VAN STERBEECK was a Jesuit priest, though the English botanist John Ray, who visited his garden on 5 May 1663 ('We saw many rare plants') described him as a Franciscan. His book about citrus fruit and other exotic plants starts with five congratulatory poems, some in Flemish, some in Latin, all by various local worthies of Antwerp praising their friend for his achievement. The extra leaf between pages 74 and 75 contains another poem, in couplets, called 'Weeninge van Adam', a lament for Eden, following a chapter of speculation on the identity of Adam's apple, the forbidden fruit—an apple, a fig, or even a banana? A lengthy bibliography and a list of contents follow before the main text, a first part on oranges, a second on citrons and grapefruit, a third on lemons, and a fourth on exotic trees, grafting, and pests. The last section deals with pomegranates, passionflowers, laurels, cinnamon, and the oleander.

Just as Ferrari began by describing citrus fruit in Italy, his own country, van Sterbeeck starts with the Netherlands, acknowledging local predecessors like Clusius, Dodoens, and l'Obel. He also mentions the work of his friend in Amsterdam, Jan Commelin, whose *Nederlantze Hesperides* (see page 180) was published in Amsterdam in 1676, after its author had borrowed van Sterbeeck's manuscript for an early view of his work. According to *Citricultura*'s preface, their correspondence left Sterbeeck unable to refuse the loan of his notes, which he had been collecting for a long time. They were returned on 16 April 1677 with gratitude and a copy of Commelin's *Hesperides*. The preface continues (in translation):

I thought it necessary to add the details above solely in order to prevent the slander that my *Description of Exotic Trees* has been borrowed or copied from these *Dutch Hesperides*, for my notes and experiments in this matter go back thirty years, as will be clear to the reader. Hence everything I have borrowed from other esteemed authors and experienced practitioners is mentioned and noted in its proper place, not concealed or suppressed.

The text is very well stuffed with historical references too.

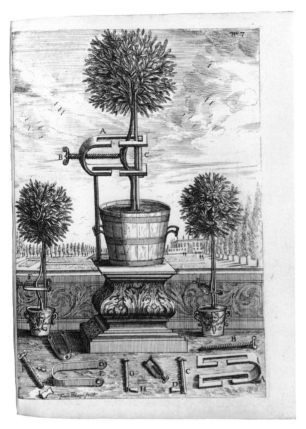

The part of the book on the management of exotic trees, indoors in winter or out of doors in summer, describes how to keep them happy in tubs or pots, and even how to cope with insects, mice, or rats in greenhouses. The whole book is dedicated to Justus de Nobelaer, Knight, whose palatial greenhouse is described on page 167, where Commelin's is also mentioned.

This copy of *Citricultura* is frequently interleaved with extra notes, and there is a great deal of marginal annotation throughout, with extra cross-references inserted and misprints corrected. The whole effect is that of an author thinking of a possible new edition of his book, and keeping the printed text up to date as well as he could. The Jesuit connection mentioned in the label on the front pastedown makes it seem very likely indeed that this was the author's copy. A second edition, so-called, of his book was published in Antwerp in 1712, but not revised at all, for it is only the printed sheets of the original edition bound up with a new title-page. The same publisher brought out in the same year another edition of van Sterbeeck's *Theatrum Fungorum*, his pioneering book on mushrooms first published in 1675.

## 71. [MORIN, Pierre (*fl.* 1619–1658) alleged author]

Nouveau Traité des Orangers et Citronniers, contenant La manière de les connoître, les façons qu'il leur faut faire pour les bien cultiver, & la vraie methode qu'on doit garder pour les conserver. [vignette 3 x 3 cm. of crowned clasped hands holding a medallion bearing the initials CDS] A Paris, Chez Charles de Sercy, au sixiéme Pilier de la Grand' Salle du Palais, vis-à-vis la Montée de la Cour des Aydes, à la Bonne Foy couronnée. [rule] M. DC. XCII. Avec Privilege du Roi.

12° 15 x 8 cm.  ã⁴ ẽ² A–Q in alternate gatherings of 8 and 4 leaves  *i–xii 1* 2–187 *188–192*

BINDING: Mottled brown calf, rebacked. Bookplate of Rachel McMasters Miller Hunt (1882–1963), whose botanical library is now the core of the Hunt Institute in Pittsburgh.

Title-page

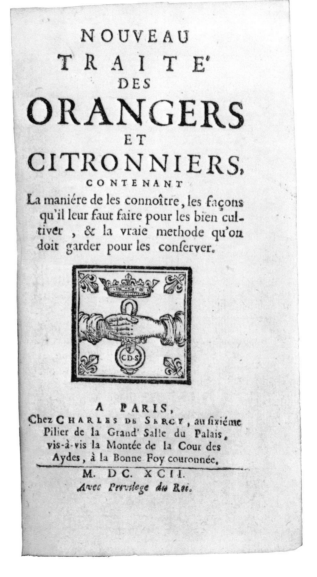

WHEN this book was first published, in 1674 as *Instruction facile, pour connoistre toutes sortes d'orangers et citronniers*, the name of Pierre Morin appeared on its title-page as the author, an attribution repeated in a second issue of 1680. The posthumous value of Morin's name may have been great, but he did not write the book, and its 1692 edition no longer pretends that he did.

Pierre Morin 'le jeune, dit troisieme'—the third because both his father and his oldest brother bore the same name—was a member of a family of nurserymen. Late in his life he wrote about the culture of flowers, in a book published by Charles de Sercy in 1658, and he also issued a catalogue of tulips, ranunculus, iris, and anemones in his own garden in 1651. John Evelyn visited him there on 1 April 1644, when he was sightseeing in Paris.

> The next morning I was had by a friend to Monsieur Morines Garden; a person who from an ordinary Gardner, is ariv'd to be one of the most skillful & Curious Persons of France for his rare collection of Shells, Flowers & Insects: His Garden is of an exact Oval figure planted with Cypresse, cutt flat & set as even as a Wall could have form'd it: The Tulips, Anemonies, Ranunculus's, Crocus's &c being of the most exquisite; were held for the rarest in the World, which constantly drew all the Virtuosi of that kind to his house, during the season; even Persons of the most illustrious quality: He lived in a kind of Hermitage at one side of his Garden.

Both the *Nouveau traité des orangers* and the *Nouveau traité pour la culture des fleurs* were published by Charles de Sercy in 1674, and both were based on an Italian book, Agostino Mandirola's *Manuale de' giardinieri*, of which two editions appeared in Macerata in 1649 and 1658. It gave directions for the culture of rare flowers and bulbs, as well as the nurture of oranges. Both the French books derived from it were listed among others in a document giving permission to Sercy to reprint Morin's *Remarques necessaires pour la culture des fleurs*, which he did in 1694, and, as no other author was mentioned, Morin was credited with almost all the books on the list. Presumably Sercy commissioned an anonymous writer to translate the Italian book and adapt its contents to the new setting.

The publisher's preface to the 1692 edition of the *Traité des orangers* makes it clear how fashionable the subject was: 'La matiere dont il traite y concourt de sa part, étant également noble & curieuse; puisque les Arbres de la culture desquels il s'agit, sont les principaux ornemens des Jardins un peu distinguez. L'estime qu'on a pour eux leur fait même tenir un rang separé chez les plus grands Seigneurs, par les Orangeries qu'on y voit, comme si le reste n'étoit pas digne de paroître en leur compagnie.' This edition was revised by 'Monsieur Gilles Ballon Directeur des Jardins du Roi' and 'M. Garnier Jardinier du Roi a la Pepiniere'. The little book gives full directions for the cultivation of orange and lemon trees from seeds or grafts onwards, indoors or out, in tubs or in open ground. The last chapter even recommends jasmine, myrtle, bay, and other shrubs to decorate greenhouses or gardens when the citrus fruits were past their best. The *Traité* has its own decorations too, with small woodcut tailpieces and bands of printers' flowers.

## 72. MUNARI, Cristoforo (1667–1720)

A quince, an apple, two lemons, and three blue and white cups, *c.*1700.   28 x 39 cm.   Oil on canvas.

BY 1703 Cristoforo Munari was working in Rome, where he seems to have absorbed the influence of Dutch painters of still lives in his choice of subject-matter, though the density of some of his backgrounds looks less close to these examples. The elegantly peeled lemon and the Delft cups in this little picture raise Dutch echoes, and Munari's other surviving work adds musical instruments, books, silver, or glasses to the fruit and cups shown here. The bowl-shaped cups, right side up, upside-down, or tipped on their sides, are favourite components of many of his pictures. Some of them also include a variety of citrus fruit, with some of the monstrous oddities so carefully cultivated in Italy.

In 1706 Munari arrived in Florence, where he painted still lives and *trompe l'oeil* compositions for local patrons. In 1715 he was called to Pisa to work on the restoration of pictures in the cathedral there.

# 73. VOLKAMER (or VOLCKAMER), Johann Christoph (1644–1720)

Nůrnbergische Hesperides, Oder Gründliche Beschreibung Der Edlen Citronat- Citroen- und Pomeranzen-Früchte / Wie solche in selbiger und benachbarten Gegend / recht mögen eingesetzt / gewartet / erhalten und fortgebracht werden / Samt Einer ausführlichen Erzehlung der meisten Sorten / welche theils zu Nůrnberg würklich gewachsen / theils von verschiedenen fremden Orten dahin gebracht worden, auf das accurateste in Kupffer gestochen / in Vier Theile eingetheilet und mit nůsslichen Anmerckungen erklåret. Beneben der Flora, Oder Curiosen Vorstellung verschiedener raren Blumen, Samt Einer Zugabe etlicher anderer Gewåchse / und ausführlichen Bericht / wie eine richtigzutreffende Sonnen-Uhr im Garten-Feld von Bur anzulegen / und die Gårten nach der Perspectiv leichtlich aufzureissen, Wie auch einem Bericht von denen in des Authoris Garten stehenden Columnis Milliaribus, herausgegeben von Johann Christoph Volkamer. ★ ★ ★ Mit Rôm. Kåyserl. Maj. allergnådigst-verliehenem Privilegio. [rule 15.5 cm.] Nůrnberg / zu finden bei dem Authore, und Zu Franckfurth und Leipzig / bei Johann Andreå Endters seel. Sohn und Erben. M DCC VIII.

4° 37 x 23.5 cm. )(⁴A–2K⁴ A–C² D²(D2+1) *i–viii 1 2–255 256–264 1 2–17 18* and a frontispiece and 116 engravings (including 6 double and 3 folding ones).

Continuation der Nůrnbergischen Hesperidum, Oder: Fernere gründliche Beschreibung Der Edlen Citronat- Citronen- und Pomeranzen-Früchte, mit einem ausführlichen Bericht / wie solche am besten zu warten und zuerhalten senn; Worbei diejenigen Sorten / so theils zu Nůrnberg gewachsen / theils von verschiedenen fremden Orten dahin gelanget / auf das accurateste in Kupffer gestochen und nachgezeichnet worden; abermals in vier Theile eingetheilet / und mit gehörigen Anmerkungen erlåutert; Benebenst einem Anhang von etlichen raren und fremden Gewåchsen / Der Ananas / des Palm-Baums / der Coccus-Nůssa / der Baum-Wolle / u.a.m. welche ebenfalls in Kupffer-Rissen vorgestellt sind; Herausgegeben von Johann Christoph Volkamer. ★ ★ ★ Mit Rôm. Kaiserl. Maj. allergnådigstem Privilegio. [rule] Nůrnberg / zu finden bei dem Authore, und Zu Franckfurth und Leipzig / bei Johann Andreå Endters seel, Sohn und Erben. M DCC XIIII.

π²(–π2) a–e⁴ A–2G⁴ *i–xxi 1–161 162a–b 163–175 176a–b 177–226 227a–b 228–232 232–239 240–241* folios (*not* pages) including a frontispiece and 134 engravings, several of them double and/or folding.

BINDING: Contemporary sprinkled calf, gilt spine. Armorial bookplate of 'Rudolf Graf von Abensperg und

Page 76 Vignette of tools, trees, and a gardener

191

Traun, K.K. würklicher Camerer', that is, the Emperor's treasurer, with his crowned monogram stamped on title-pages.

PLATES: In volume I only 30 of the plates bear an artist's signature, 14 of them that of Paul Decker the elder (1677–1713) and 7 that of J. C. Steinberger (1680–1727). Joseph à Montalegre (*fl.* 1708–1715) signed a single plate in volume I and over half—67—in volume II, in which Paul Decker the younger (1685–1742) signed the frontispiece and one other plate. Others identified as artists or engravers of occasional plates include J. C. Steinberger, C. F. Krieger, L. C. Glotsch, B. Kenkel, S. Leonhard, W. Pfau, T. G. Beckh, J. A. Delsenbach, J. C. Dehne, and F. P. Lindner, but many of the plates are based on Volkamer's own drawings or those of his younger brother (see below). The vignettes and tailpieces, about 30 of them, are so attractive that they have often been borrowed to decorate later books.

JOHANN CHRISTOPH VOLKAMER was the son of Johann Georg Volkamer I (1616–1693), physician, botanist, and gardener, who visited Italy and studied at Padua from 1638 to 1641, soon after the establishment of the botanic garden there. When he returned to Nuremberg he built a large greenhouse in his garden at Gostenhof, the house and garden later inherited by his oldest son, Johann Christoph, who shared his father's love of both Italy and gardening. During his youth he spent several years in Italy, perhaps as many as ten after arriving in Verona in 1660. He visited many gardens in the neighbourhood and further afield as far as Venice and Bologna, beginning to study the endless varieties of citrus fruit he saw. Even after his return to Germany his friends among Italian gardeners and nurserymen supplied him with citrus trees and kept him informed of new developments.

The *Nürnbergische Hesperides* was a slow-growing book. Its genesis is reflected in two albums of Volkamer's drawings for it in the Germanisches Nationalmuseum, Nuremberg. About two hundred of these drawings have survived, and others were probably destroyed during World War II with parts of the family archive. As well as collecting and commissioning the work of other artists, both Johann Christoph Volkamer and his brother, Johann Georg II, another naturalist, drew some of the fruit and gardens illustrated in the *Hesperides*. It is clear that the book was modelled on an earlier *Hesperides*, Ferrari's of 1646 (see page 177), the first book entirely devoted to citrus fruit. Not only the title but the divisions, the allegorical plates referring to appropriate myths, and the style of the fruit drawings echo the earlier book, but the perspective drawings of gardens added to the fruit plates—mostly German gardens from the Nuremberg region in the first volume and Italian ones in the second—demonstrate Volkamer's broader

J. C. VOLKAMER
*Nürnbergische Hesperides*
1708 page 188a A de-
tail showing the village
of Hummelstein

interests. A third volume, on gardens and greenhouses elsewhere in Europe, was planned but never finished.

The first part was a great success, its appearance followed by a quick reprint and a translation into Latin, which was published in 1713, in time to draw attention to the second volume, which came out the following year. The views of Italian houses and gardens in this volume are mostly taken from the country round Venice, the Brenta, the Euganean hills and those near Bologna. So valuable are they as records of early eighteenth-century Italy that a selection of them was reprinted there in 1979. Among the non-Italian gardens in this volume are Schönbrunn in Vienna and Volkamer's own garden in Nuremberg, a town that welcomed both French and Italian influences in the design of its gardens and the plants used to furnish them.

Directions for the cultivation of citrus fruit show little advance on Ferrari or Commelin (see page 180), but many more varieties are illustrated, among them quantities of the ornamental oddities produced in Italy during the seventeenth century and introduced into Germany to test the skill of gardeners there. Other botanical treasures are drawn and described too—olive and bay trees, the strawberry tree, a vast aubergine or egg-plant, and a double plate of the night-blooming cereus in volume I, with favourites from Volkamer's garden like choice auriculas and pag.194.b.

Aranzo da Portugal

In Hr. Wurzelbaurs Garten.

I. C. Steinberger fecit.

J. C. VOLKAMER
*Nürnbergische Hesperides*
1708 page 194b A Portugal orange and Herr Wurzelbaur's garden, signed by J. C. Steinberger

Aranzo Limonato.

Des Herren von Lempen Hauß-Garten.

I. C. Steinberger fecit.

J. C. VOLKAMER
*Nürnbergische Hesperides*
1708 page 202a  An
orange lemon and the
courtyard of Herr von
Lempen's garden, filled
with tubbed or potted
trees, signed by J. C.
Steinberger

J. C. VOLKAMER
*Nürnbergische Hesperides*
1708 page 216b Auriculas from the garden of J. G. Volkamer II and the Bretzen garden, signed by J. C. Steinberger

Melanzana

pag. 244 a.

Prospect im Lochnerischen Garten.

J. C. VOLKAMER
*Nürnbergische Hesperides*
1708 page 244a  An au-
bergine or egg-plant
from Italy and the
Lochnerische garden

J. C. VOLKAMER
*Continuation der Nürn-
bergische Hesperidum* 1714
page 73  A lemon from
Salerno and a village
near Verona, drawn and
engraved by Joseph a
Montalegre

primroses. In the *Continuation* the plants are even more exotic, with five showy double plates of pineapples to confirm Lady Mary Wortley Montagu's contemporary observations on German skill in the management of this demanding fruit and the heated glasshouses it needed (see page xxxi). There is also a date palm, a coconut (with a Chinese vignette beneath the fruit), a dragon tree, and even a cotton plant. Plans and drawings of orangeries and a sun-dial are also found in the first volume, with a special supplementary description (with drawings) of an obelisk from Constantinople, an overgrown milestone transported to Volkamer's own garden.

The fruit and gardens in most of the plates—spherical oranges, lemons, and citrons drifting like eccentric balloons above miniature landscapes—make pleasingly surreal compositions, so that individual plates have frequently been taken from dismembered copies of the book. Occasionally these have been coloured too, but engraving as fine as this is not really improved by colour, sometimes quite the reverse.

J. C. VOLKAMER
*Nürnbergische Hesperides*
1708 page 87 A tail-
piece with a dish of fruit

## 74. GALLESIO, Georges (i.e. Giorgio) (1772–1839)

Traité du Citrus par Georges Gallesio, Auditeur au Conseil d'État et Sous-Préfet à Savone. Omnia . . . Paullatim crescunt, ut par est, semine certo; Crescendoque genus servant, ut noscere possis Quæque sua de materia grandescere, alique. Tit. Luc. Car. liv.I.v.189. ['Each mean observer sees Things grow from certain Seeds by just degrees, And growing keep their Kind, and hence we know That things from proper Matter rise, and grow; By proper Matter fed, and nourish't too.' Lucretius *De Rerum Natura* translated by Thomas Creech, 1682; decoration 1.5 x 1.5

cm.] A Paris, Chez Louis Fantin, Libraire, Quai des Augustins, nº 55. De l'Imprimerie de P. Didot l'aîné. M DCCC XI.

8º 22 x 14 cm.  $\pi^2(-\pi 2)$ $2\pi^8$ $1-22^8 23^6$ *i–vii* viii–xviii *1 2–363 364* and a folding 'tableau synoptique'.
BINDING: Buff paper wrappers; uncut.

BEFORE beginning to publish his huge *Pomona Italiana* in 1817 (see page 138), Gallesio wrote this monograph on citrus fruit, which he dedicated to the comte Chabrol de Volvic, 'préfet du département de Montenotte', who recommended his work to the appropriate Minister in Paris. Another quotation from Lucretius accompanies the dedication, translated thus by Thomas Creech, in a favourite version a copy of which was in Thomas Jefferson's library:

> Yet for respect of You with great delight
> I meet these dangers, and I wake all night
> Labouring [fit Numbers and fit Words to find
> To make Things plain.]

Gallesio was born in Liguria and later lived in Savona, on the coast west of Genoa, still a good region for citrus fruit. In his garden he grew and studied many fruit trees, trying to classify their species, varieties, and hybrids, but he was specially devoted to oranges, as he explains in his preface:

> Favorisé par un climat heureux, par la commodité d'une propriété vaste, bien exposée et fertile, j'ai examiné les caprices de ces végétaux depuis leur naissance jusqu'à leur fructification . . . Ces arbres charmants réunissent à-la-fois les avantages des plantes d'agrément, et ceux des plantes utiles: rien n'égale la beauté de leur feuillage, l'odeur suave de leurs fleurs, l'éclat et le goût de leurs fruits . . . tout enfin, dans ces arbres, charme les yeux, satisfait l'odorat, pique le goût, nourrit le luxe et les arts, et présente à l'homme étonné la réunion de tous les plaisirs. Des qualités aussi brillantes les ont rendus les arbres de tous les climats: . . . dans les pays froids, ils ont donné naissance à ces bâtiments destinés par le luxe à entretenir un climat artificiel au milieu d'hiver.

After studying the work of earlier writers on citrus fruit, among them Ferrari (see page 177), Commelin (page 180), and Volkamer (page 191), and admiring the fine illustrations in these books, Gallesio decided there was still room for further exploration, concentrating on the classification of the species and varieties and based on experiments and dissections as well as knowledge of their history. His book begins with the classification he developed, one that takes account of all countries in which citrus fruit was cultivated. He visited oranges and lemons in gardens in France too, including Versailles, where the most venerable tree was called François I or *grand Bourbon*, and the Jardin des Plantes, and others in Italy and Spain. There are constant references to Ferrari and Volkamer, supplemented by Hans Sloane and Philip Miller for later descriptions of West Indian citrus fruits, and many other travellers and botanists from classical times on, all helping to shed light on citrus history, from the bitter and then the sweet oranges

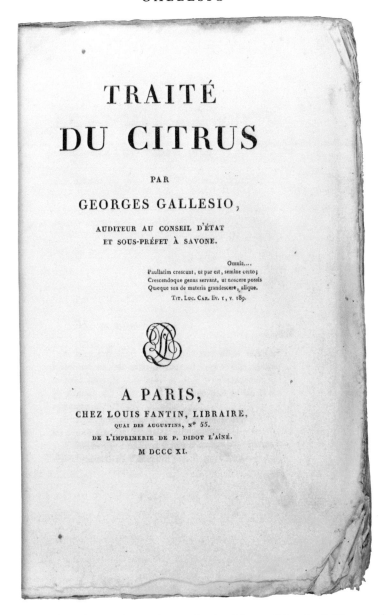

G. GALLESIO
*Traité du Citrus* 1811
Title-page

emerging from China and India and on through Arabia to North Africa and Europe to the teratological monsters so popular in Italian gardens in the seventeenth century. His theories about the development of citrus fruit, based on such exhaustive study and observation of them, were later used by Charles Darwin. A translation of the first chapters of the *Traité du Citrus* into Italian was published in 1816 as *Teoria della Riproduzione vegetale*.

## 75. MICHEL, Etienne (*fl.*1800–1820)

Traité du Citronier, redige Par M. Étienne Michel, Éditeur du Nouveau Duhamel, Associé libre et Correspondant de la Société des Amis des Sciences, Belles-Lettres, Agriculture et Arts d'Aix, département des Bouches-du-Rhône; de la Société d'Émulation de Rouen, et autres. Les dessins en sont faits sur la nature par M$^r$. P. Bessa, Peintre de Fleurs et d'Histoire Naturelle, et Professeur. [on right of page, between a pair of wavy lines 4 cm. long] Utile dulci. ['useful and pleasant'; monogram of M and B 5.5 x 5 cm.] A Paris, Chez [bracket] L'Auteur-Éditeur, rue Saint-Louis, n°. 42, au Marais; Arthus Bertrand, Libraire-Éditeur, rue Hautefeuille, n°. 23; Deterville, rue Hautefeuille, n°. 8 [double rule 6 cm.] C. Ballard, Imprimeur du Roi, rue J. J. Rousseau, n°. 8. [wavy line 3 cm.] 1816.

2° 52 x 35 cm.  $\pi^2$ A–D$^2$(D2+D*bis*1) E–V$^2$ *i–iv 1* 2–82 and 21 coloured plates.

BINDING: Quarter dark brown leather, black and white paper-covered boards.

PLATES: The plates, which were printed in colour, are copies of numbers 22 to 42 in volume 7 of the *Nouveau Duhamel* (see page 83). Pancrace Bessa's drawings, which were made into stipple engravings by Gabriel (12 of them), Dubreuil (2), Jarry (6), or Mademoiselle Augustine Dufour (a single one), show single fruits with sections, flowers, and leaves (11), collections of fruit (9), or, in plate 18, rooted orange leaves.

E TIENNE MICHEL was a major contributor and the main editor of the *Nouveau Duhamel*, the revised and greatly expanded edition of Duhamel's *Traité des Arbres et Arbustes* which was published from 1800 to 1819 and illustrated by Redouté and Bessa (see pages 82–87). The text of Michel's *Traité du Citronier* is taken from pages 67–148 of the last volume of this bigger book, accompanied by twenty-one of Bessa's drawings (plates 22–42) of citrus fruits, citrons, oranges, and grapefruit as well as lemons. There are frequent references to the work of Ferrari, Commelin, Volkamer, and Gallesio, those earlier students of citrus fruit, and Michel uses a classification proposed by Antoine Risso, whose own *Histoire naturelle des Orangers* was published in 1818. Risso's paper on the uses of citrus fruit, given to the Académie des Sciences and ordered to be printed in its *Mémoires des Savans étrangers*, is quoted on pages 64–68 of Michel's book. The paper cited appears to be part of a long one by Risso on the natural history of citrus fruit, published in 1813 in volume XX of the *Annales du Muséum d'histoire naturelle* (pages 169–212, 401–31).

ETIENNE MICHEL
*Traité du Citronier* 1816
BM monogram from
title-page

202

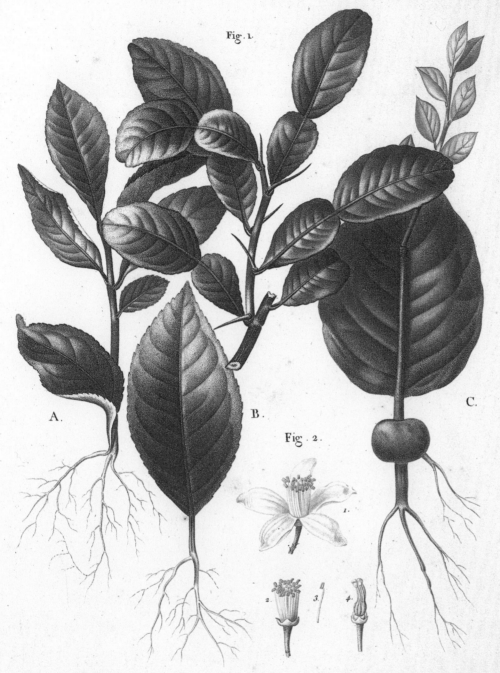

Fig. 1.

A.

B.

Fig. 2.

C.

*1.*

*2.* *3.* *4.*

Fig. 1. **CITRUS** Histrix.　　**CITRONIER** Hérisson.

Fig. 2. Fleurs de l'Oranger.　　A . B . C . Feuilles enracinées.

P. Bessa pinx.　　Gabriel sculp.

**ETIENNE MICHEL**
*Traité du Citronier* 1816
plate 18  Orange flowers
and rooted leaves, drawn
by Pancrace Bessa and
engraved by
Gabriel

ETIENNE MICHEL
*Traité du Citronier* 1816
plate 21 Citrus Decu-
mana, drawn by
Pancrace Bessa and
engraved by Jarry

**CITRUS** Decumana.      **CITRONIER** Pompelmous.

P. Bessa pinx.      Jarry sculp.

## 76. RISSO, Antoine (1777–1845) and POITEAU, Antoine (1766–1854)

Histoire naturelle des Orangers, par A. Risso, Ancien Professeur des Sciences physiques et naturelles au Lycée de Nice, membre associé des Académies de Turin, d'Italie, de Genève, de Marseille, de Florence, des Sociétés philomatique de Paris, des naturalistes de Genève, d'histoire naturelle d'Arau, etc., etc., et A. Poiteau, Botaniste, peintre d'histoire naturelle, jardinier en chef des Pépinières royales de Versailles, member de la Société d'agriculture et des arts de Seine et Oise. Ouvrage orné de figures peintes d'après nature. [ornament 3.5 x 3.5 cm. of twin coats of arms, crowned, encircled by a wreath of orange blossom] Paris, Imprimerie de M^me Hérissant Le Doux, Imprimaire ordinaire du Roi et des Musées royaux, rue Sainte-Anne, n° 20. [double rule 2 cm.] 1818.

2° 45.5 x 30.5 cm. $\pi^2$ $1^2$ $2$–$70^2$ i–iv 1–3 4–280 and 109 coloured engravings (plate 15 wrongly numbered 21 and corrected in pencil).

BINDING: Deep pink paper-covered boards.

PLATES: The stipple engravings made from Poiteau's drawings are printed in colour and finished by hand. Nine engravers worked on the book, but nearly two-thirds of the plates are signed by Louis or Georges François Marie Gabriel and fifteen more by Theodor Susémihl.

ANTOINE RISSO was a naturalist who spent all his life in Nice. He became an apothecary, but he studied several other branches of natural history too, exploring the Alpes Maritimes and the Mediterranean coast, where he is commemorated by the animal still known as Risso's dolphin. He wrote a guide for visitors to Nice and a study of the fishes of the region, as well as a local flora. He directed the Jardin de Naturalisation founded at Nice in 1828 and also demonstrated his interest in economic plants by investigating insects harmful to olive trees. Later on he taught 'medical chemistry' at a local college. After the publication of the *Histoire naturelle des Orangers*, which appeared in parts from 1818 to 1822, he planned a similar monograph on figs, although this was left unfinished at his death.

The text of the *Orangers* deals with the origins, characteristics, classification, and nomenclature of the whole group, with two plates of anatomical details, before turning to individual descriptions of over seventy varieties of sweet or bitter oranges, nearly fifty lemons, and smaller numbers of limes, citrons, and grapefruit. Separate chapters cover methods of cultivation, in both the region round Paris and the south of the country, diseases that may attack citrus fruit, and the uses of wood, leaves, and flowers, as well as the fruit itself. Even products like candied lemon peel (*zeste d'Italie*), orange flower water, orangeade, and the liqueur named as *curasow* are described. Local nurserymen in Nice can hardly have objected to their wares being advertised in the price lists of wild or grafted trees of different sizes that were offered for sale by them.

The book is dedicated to the Duchesse de Berri, Charles X's Italian daughter-in-law, whose patronage is indicated by the crowned coats of arms on the title-page, as well as the flowery words:

En daignant accorder votre protection à l'*Histoire naturelle des Orangers*, et nous permettre de la faire paraître sous vos auspices, Votre Altesse Royale a fixé d'avance le suffrage du Public, qui sait apprécier son goût éclairé pour les beaux arts. Puisse cet ouvrage offrir quelques délassemens a Votre Altesse

ANTOINE RISSO and
ANTOINE POITEAU
*Histoire naturelle des
Orangers* 1818 plate 2
Citrus anatomy, drawn
by Poiteau and en-
graved by Gabriel

Plate 4  A China
orange, drawn by
Poiteau and engraved
by Gabriel

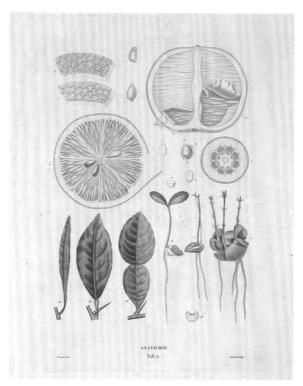

Royale, en retraçant à ses yeux l'image des fruits qu'elle cueillit souvent de sa propre main sous le beau ciel de l'Italie: puisse-t-il engager à les cultiver dans la Patrie que vous avez adoptée.

The book itself may be seen as a collaboration between France and Italy too, for at the time Risso's town of Nice was still Italian territory. A second edition, revised by A. du Breuil and called *Histoire et Culture des Orangers*, was published in 1872.

Antoine Poiteau began his career as an apprentice gardener at the Jardin des Plantes, where he was also taught botany. After a period of plant-collecting in the Caribbean, especially Haiti, he returned to Paris in 1800 and, during the next thirty years, illustrated many books, using the skill developed during his travels, which was modelled, at least in its early days, on prints of van Spaendonck's drawings. 'Cet habile iconographe', as he is described in Michaud's biographical dictionary, realized the need for accurate drawings to complement written descriptions of new plants, to such an extent that his descriptions were sometimes altered in the light of observations made while he was drawing. As well as illustrating the citrus fruits in the *Orangers*, Poiteau contributed to the descriptions of the tropical varieties, using knowledge of them gained from his earlier career.

No French botanical artist of the period can have escaped the influence of Redouté, and Poiteau was among the group associated with him. These oranges and lemons and their relations, with leaves, flowers, and often cross-sections as well as whole fruits, form one of the most beautiful and complete records of the varieties known in the nineteenth century.

206

APPLES AND PEARS

## 77. LAWRENCE, Anthony (*fl.* 1670s) and BEALE, John (1603–1682?)

[within a border of double rules] Nurseries, Orchards, Profitable Gardens, and Vineyards Encouraged, The present Obstructions removed, and probable Expedients for the better Progress proposed; For the general benefit of his Majesties Dominions, and more particularly of Cambridge, and the Champain-Countries, and Northern parts of England. In Several Letters out of the Country, Directed to Henry Oldenburg, Esq; Secretary to the Royal Society. [rule] The first Letter from Anthony Lawrence; All the rest from John Beale, D.D. and Fellow of the Royal Society. [rule] London, Printed for Henry Brome at the Gun in St. Pauls Church-Yard, the West End. 1677.

4° 19.5 x 14 cm. A–D⁴ *i–ii* 1–28 *29–30*.

BINDING: Quarter tan morocco, cloth sides.

Title-page

ANTHONY LAWRENCE seems virtually unknown, except for his contribution to this volume, which includes praise for the Oxford nurseryman, Ralph Austen, whose *Treatise of Fruit-Trees* was first published in 1653 (see page 19). A letter of 29 November 1676 from John Beale to Robert Boyle commends Lawrence for 'transporting many thousands of grafts of apples and pears of the best cyder fruit out of Herefordshire and Worcestershire, into Somersetshire, Dorsetshire, Devonshire, and Cornwall; and . . . riding up and down to give instructions and encouragements'.

John Beale's life is more fully recorded. He came from Hereford and was the rector of Yeovil in Somerset for over twenty years and a chaplain to Charles II for nearly as long. In 1657 he published *Herefordshire Orchards: a Pattern for all England*, printing letters on the subject he had sent to Samuel Hartlib. So useful was this little book that it was reprinted much later, in 1724, and Hereford's orchards and its reputation as a cider-producing county still flourish.

Beale was also a Fellow of the Royal Society and contributed 'Aphorisms concerning cider' to John Evelyn's *Pomona*, a supplement to his *Sylva*. The dedication of *Nurseries* to Henry Oldenburg mentions the interest of the young Royal Society in gardening and horticulture: 'Hortulan Affairs are not the least of our Inland Commodities; and they have been the serious engagement of the said Royal Society from the first year of their Institution.' With Evelyn and Beale among its earliest Fellows, the Society could hardly have neglected these subjects.

## 78. WORLIDGE, John (*fl.* 1677–1700)

[within a border of double rules] Vinetum Britannicum: or A Treatise of Cider, And other Wines and Drinks extracted from Fruits Growing in this Kingdom. With the Method of Propagating all sorts of Vinous Fruit-Trees. And a Description of the New-Invented Ingenio or Mill, For the more expeditious making of Cider. And also the right way of making Metheglin and Birch-Wine. [rule] The Third Impression, much Enlarged. To which is added, A Discourse teaching the best way of Improving Bees. [rule] With Copper Plates. [rule] By J. Worlidge. Gent. [rule] London, Printed for Thomas Dring, over against the Inner-Temple-gate in Fleet-street. 1691.

*The part on bees has a separate title-page:*

Apiarium; or A Discourse of the Government and Ordering of Bees, with their Nature and Properties, Tending to the best Way of Improving them, and to the Discovery of the Fallacies that are imposed by some, for private Lucre, on the credulous Lovers and Admirers of these Insects. [rule] The Third Edition. [rule] Written by J. W. Gent. [rule] London, Printed for and Sold by Thomas Dring, Bookseller, at the Sign of the Harrow at Chancery-lane end in Fleet-street. MDCXCI.

8° 17 x 10 cm. *A⁴ B–V⁸ X⁴ i–xxiv 1–236 i–x 1–42 43–50* and two engraved frontispieces.

BINDING: Contemporary brown calf, rebacked. Bookplate of Washington Sewallis, Earl Ferrers.

PLATES: The unsigned frontispiece of the *Vinetum* shows two cider presses; that of the *Apiarium* a beehive. There are also three full-page engraved figures in the text, on pages 97, 105, and 115, showing various machines connected with the production of cider.

JOHN WORLIDGE
*Vinetum Britannicum*
third edition 1691 page
105 A cider mill

JOHN WORLIDGE, of Petersfield in Hampshire, also wrote on agriculture and gardening. The first edition of his *Vinetum* was published in 1676, the second in 1678, with *Apiarium* attached. In spite of the separate title-page and pagination of *Apiarium*, the index on the last eight pages of the book covers both sections, on cider and bees. The book is dedicated to 'Elias Ashmole Esquire, Fellow of the Royal-Society', who presented his own and the Tradescants' collections to the University of Oxford as the nucleus of the Ashmolean Museum.

Worlidge summed up his book at the end of its preface:

You have not only here presented to you the Art of Propagating the Apple-tree, and preparing the Juice of its Fruit; but some select Observations and Experiments in the Planting and Propagating several other Vinous Fruit-bearing Trees . . . And also a Corollary of the Names and Natures of most Fruits flourishing in this Isle.

## 79. [PHILIPS, John (1676–1709)]

[within a border of double rules] Cyder. A Poem. In Two Books. [rule]—Honos erit huic quoq; Pomo? Virg. ['Honour will be given to the apple too' *Eclogues* II; rule] London: Printed for Jacob Tonson, within Grays-Inn Gate next Grays-Inn Lane. 1708.

8° 19 x 11.5 cm. *A² B–F⁸ G⁴ H² i–vi 1 2–89 90* (44, 46, 62 signed ★, 61 signed †) including an engraved frontispiece.

BINDING: Brown calf, rebacked, new endpapers. Crowned armorial bookplate of Bradby Hall (a shield within the buckled garter representing the Order of the Garter and bearing its motto 'Honi soit qui mal y pense').

PLATES: The frontispiece (part of the plate-mark of which is visible on the inner edge of the title-page) shows a grove of trees divided by a path, with a fountain at its crossing and a building ending the vista. Three men are in the foreground, one planting a seedling, the second digging a hole, and the third pruning an apple tree. It is signed by the engraver Michael van der Gucht and labelled

'Geo. 2. L. 1.' referring to the first line of the second of Virgil's *Georgics*, which John Dryden translated in 1697:

> Thus far of Tillage, and of Heav'nly Signs;
> Now sing my Muse the growth of gen'rous Vines:
> The shady Groves, the Woodland Progeny,
> And the slow Product of Minerva's Tree.

There are bands of printer's ornaments on pages 1 and 49 at the start of each book of the poem.

ABOUT 1750 John Philips was christened 'Pomona's Bard' by another poet, James Thomson. Philips's family came from Herefordshire, still a county linked with apples and cider, which provided the subject for his longest poem. He began writing it during his university days at Oxford, but it was not finished and published until 1708, not long before his early death. A signed agreement with its publisher is dated 27 November 1707. The poet was paid forty guineas for it on 24 January 1708 and received a hundred copies on large paper and two special dedication copies bound in Turkey leather. Once in print it was reissued in Tonson's *Annual Miscellany* in 1708 and again in Philips's collected works in 1720. A separate 1720 issue only 71 pages long, lacking the frontispiece but with pictorial head-pieces at the start of each book, has been described by Peter Stageman in the *Garden* (1988, volume 113, pages 483–87).

Philips considered his poem to be Miltonic blank verse in imitation of Virgil, describing the culture of the apple tree and the manufacture of cider. Philip Miller, the curator of the Chelsea Physic Garden for most of the eighteenth century, gave it his blessing, saying that 'There were many books written on the same subject in prose which do not contain so much truth as that poem.' It begins with the right soil for apples:

> What Soil the Apple loves, what Care is due
> To Orchats, timeliest when to press the Fruits,
> Thy Gift, *Pomona*, in *Miltonian* verse
> Adventrous I presume to sing; of Verse
> Nor skill'd, nor studious: But my Native Soil
> Invites me, and the Theme as yet unsung.

After a dedication to one Mostyn, 'such a matchless Friend', the poet goes on to tell 'How Nature's Gifts may be improv'd by Art', that is, pruning, thinning out the buds, and protecting the trees from insects and other pests, not omitting to observe other plants often found growing among apple trees:

> The *Herefordian* Plant
> Caresses freely the contiguous *Peach*,
> *Hazel*, and weight-resisting *Palm*, and likes

JOHN PHILIPS
*Cyder* 1708 Frontispiece,
drawn and engraved by
Michael van der Gucht,
and title-page

T' approach the *Quince*, and th'*Elder*'s pithy Stem;
Uneasie, seated by funereal *Yeugh*,
Or *Walnut*, (whose malignant Touch impairs
All generous Fruits), or near the bitter Dews
Of *Cherries*. Therefore, weigh the Habits well
Of Plants, how they associate best, nor let
Ill Neighbourhood corrupt thy hopeful Graffs.

The poem continues with a roll-call of apple varieties, especially the favourite Redstreak, 'improved by Scudamore's skilful Hand', and a few pears too. Other apple growers are praised: James Brydges, Duke of Chandos, Lords Beaufort and Weymouth. The second book begins with worries about the travels in Italy of the first Lord Harcourt, the poet's friend, whose journey provided subjects for the head-pieces in the 1720 issue of *Cyder*. His absence is lamented, and the author hopes he will not learn to reject his native cider for continental wine.

A rather lumbering account of picking apples and pressing their juice follows, with even the left-over pulp being used:

Nor shalt thou now
reject the *Apple-Cheese*, tho' quite exhaust,
Ev'n now 'twill cherish, and improve the Roots
Of sickly Plants.

Apples are compared with crops of other countries, then various kinds of cider are described, with instructions about filtering and storing them before the farmer can share his product with his friends. This occasion for celebration leads to a brisk account of British monarchs and recent battles, with a final flourish:

Where-e'er the *British* spread
Triumphant Banners, or their Fame has reach'd
Diffusive, to the utmost Bounds of this
Wide Universe, *Silurian* Cyder borne
Shall please all Tasts, and triumph o'er the Vine.

## 80. KNIGHT, Thomas Andrew (1759–1838)

Pomona Herefordiensis; containing coloured engravings of the old Cider and Perry Fruits of Herefordshire. With such new fruits as have been found to possess superior excellence. Accompanied with a descriptive account of each variety, [rule 2.5 cm.] By Thomas Andrew Knight, Esq. F.R.S. & L.S. and President of the Horticultural Society of London. [rule 2.5 cm.] Published by the Agricultural Society of Herefordshire. London: [double rule, lower one heavier, 2.5 cm.] Printed for the Agricultural Society of Herefordshire, by W. Bulmer and Co. Cleveland-row, St. James's; and sold by W. Hooker, 75, John-street, Fitzroy-square; White and Cochrane, Fleet-street; and J. Harding, St. James's-street. 1811.

4° 30.5 x 24 cm. *a*¹ b⁴ and 30 unsigned leaves [2] *i* ii–viii and 60 unnumbered pages accompanying 30 engravings coloured by hand.

BINDING: Russia leather, rebacked; all edges gilt.

PLATES: William Hooker engraved and coloured the aquatints of apples and pears after drawings by Elizabeth Matthews of Belmont, who did twenty-seven, and Frances Knight, the author's daughter, who did the remaining three. The first plate, showing the Redstreak apple, is signed by Matthews and Hooker. The latter's own fruit book, *Pomona Londinensis*, was published in 1818 (see page 110).

THOMAS ANDREW KNIGHT was the younger brother of Richard Payne Knight, the promoter of the picturesque style of landscape gardening, but his interests were rather more practical. From his days at Oxford his work in the natural sciences led to experiments in breeding both animals and plants, while his friendship with Sir Joseph Banks introduced him to others

The Foxley Apple.

T.A. KNIGHT *Pomona Herefordiensis* 1811 plate XIV The Foxley Apple, drawn by Elizabeth Matthews and engraved by William Hooker

concerned with similar subjects. He became a Fellow of the Linnean Society in 1807 and of the Royal Society in 1805, and he was President of the Horticultural Society from 1811 until his death, as he had been among the original members. The *Transactions* of the latter two societies published many of Knight's papers on plant physiology and horticulture; so useful were they that a selection of them, chosen by George Bentham and John Lindley, leading members of the next generation of botanists, was reprinted in 1841.

As Knight was born in Herefordshire and spent most of his life near Ludlow, at Elton Hall and then Downton Castle, his work on fruit trees was set in a county still associated with growing apples and making cider. Even the *Pomona*'s printer, William Bulmer, was a London member of a family whose name is still attached to a large quantity of the cider that comes from Hereford. The preface to the *Pomona* contains an outline of cider-making, with a reference to the third edition of the author's *Treatise on the Culture of the Apple and Pear* (1808). This *Treatise*, first published in 1797, reached a fifth edition in 1818, and recommended raising new varieties from seed to improve orchards, instead of grafting on older varieties, which often failed to produce healthy trees.

*Pomona Herefordiensis* was published in ten parts with three plates each, starting in 1808. Knight was a founder member of the Agricultural Society of Herefordshire, which sponsored the book, though his own name must have been a sufficient guarantee of its quality. The plates were important, as the preface explains (page ii):

> The Agricultural Society of Herefordshire proposed the publication of coloured Plates of those old varieties to which their county has been indebted for its fame, and also of a few new varieties, which have been introduced under their patronage, and are believed to be not inferior to the old. Written descriptions have proved generally sufficient to enable the botanist to distinguish one original species of plants [*sic*] from another; but coloured Plates alone are capable of pointing out those slight discriminations of character, which often distinguish one variety of fruit from another, of any given species.

> The decay of every variety of the apple and pear, which has been long cultivated, is now very generally accepted; and therefore a more particular account, than has hitherto been given, of the means by which the most valuable new varieties have been obtained, may probably not be unacceptable.

## 81. RONALDS, Hugh (1759–1833)

Pyrus Malus Brentfordiensis: or, A Concise Description of Selected Apples. By Hugh Ronalds, F.H.S. Nurseryman, Brentford. With a figure of each sort drawn from nature on stone by his daughter. [rule 5.5 cm.] "Sunt nobis mitia poma." Virg. ['The Fruit is theirs, the Labour only mine.' *Eclogues* I, translated by John Dryden, 1697.] "Let every tree in every garden own The Red-streak as supreme, whose pulpous fruit With gold irradiate and vermilion shines." Phillips. [see page 211] ". . . . . . . . . . the fragrant stores Of apples, which the lusty-handed year, Innumerous, o'er the blushing orchard shakes: A various spirit, fresh, delicious, keen, Dwells in their gelid pores."

Thomson. [*The Seasons*; rule 5.5 cm.] London: Printed by Richard Taylor, Red Lion Court, Fleet Street; for Longman, Rees, Orme, Brown, and Green, Paternoster-row. [rule 1 cm.] 1831.

4° 32 x 24.5 cm. $A^4$ $B^2$ and 46 unsigned leaves *i–vii* viii–xii *1* 2–91 *92* and 42 lithographs coloured by hand.

BINDING: Modern half dark green morocco, marbled paper sides.

PLATES: The lithographs were drawn by Elizabeth Ronalds and printed by Charles Hullmandel. Only the first plate is signed.

HUGH RONALDS 'summed up his life's experience of apples in *Pyrus Malus Brentfordiensis*' (Miles Hadfield, *Gardening in Britain*, 1950, page 294). He chose a good moment to do so, for the number of varieties available had increased sharply during his career. His daughter illustrated the fruit of 179 of them for the book, adding leaves only on plate 34, which shows a cluster of Nonpareils. Many of the new kinds were recent imports, and the book describes several

No. 1 Api Petit.
2 American Plate.
3 Robinson's.
4 Isle of Wight Golden Pippin.
No. 5 Ashmeads Kernel.
6 Grange.
7 Moor Hen.
8 Reinette Grise.
9 Golden Knob.

HUGH RONALDS
*Pyrus Malus Brentfordiensis*
1831 plate XXXII Nine
apples, including Lady
Apple and Ashmead's
Kernel, drawn by Eliza-
beth Ronalds and litho-
graphed by Charles
Hullmandel

American varieties, like the Newtown Spitzenburg on plate 10: 'A large beautiful American sauce apple . . . . This is a very estimable variety.' In 1828 William Cobbett was offering nearly forty American apples for sale in his Kensington nursery (see page 149).

The last eight pages of Ronalds's book contain lists of varieties recommended for particular purposes or positions, as well as an index and an advertisement for his nursery:

> Should this prove a favourable season (1831), we shall have a fine display of fruit, both on the trees and in the fruit-room; among them some new and excellent sorts, not yet sufficiently ascertained for description. I shall have much pleasure in showing them, from September till the spring, to any persons interested on [*sic*] the subject who may please to call and inspect them.

## 82. HOGG, Robert (1818–1897) and BULL, Henry Graves (*c.* 1818–1885)

The Herefordshire Pomona, containing original figures and descriptions of the most esteemed kinds of Apples and Pears. [rule 5 cm.] The illustrations drawn and coloured from nature by Miss Ellis and Miss Bull [rule 5 cm.] Technical Editor: Robert Hogg, LL.D., F.L.S., Honorary Member of the Woolhope Naturalists' Field Club; Vice-President of the Royal Horticultural Society; Author of 'The Fruit Manual'; 'British Pomology'; 'The Vegetable Kingdom and its Products', &c., &c. [circular badge of the Woolhope Club 4 cm. in diameter] "Hope on. Hope ever.' "Ζεφυρίη πνείουσα τὰ μὲν φύει ἄλλα δέ πέσσει ὄγχνη ἐπ' ὄγχνη γηράσκει, μῆλον δ' ἐπὶ μήλῳ, αὐτὰρ ἐπὶ σταφυλῇ σταφυλῆ, σῦκον δ'ἐπὶ συκῷ." Homer Odyssey vii. 119–22. ['The balmy spirit of the western gale, Eternal breathes on fruits untaught to fail; Each dropping pear, a following pear supplies, On apples apples, figs on figs arise,' translated by Alexander Pope, 1725–26; rule 3 cm.] General Editor: Henry Graves Bull, M.D., &c., J.P. for the City and County of Hereford, Membre Honoraire de la Société Centrale d'Horticulture de la Seine-Inférieure, France. [rule 2 cm.] Volume I. [rule 2 cm.] Hereford: Jakeman and Carver, High Town. London: Journal of Horticulture Office, 171, Fleet Street, E.C. [rule 1 cm.] 1876 [i.e. 1878]–1885.

4° 36.5 x 28.5 cm. Collation irregular and unsigned [8+ 'Important Corrections' slip] *I* II–XIX *XX* [2] *1* 2–62 [2] *63* 64–92 [2] *93* 94–112 [2] *113* 114–160 then 158 pages matching plates I–XXX and numbered as the plates, followed by 6 pages of 'Index to the Introductory Papers'; 31 coloured and 4

uncoloured plates. (Plate LXXVII of Norman apples is bound between pages XII and XIII of the general introduction, with the description of these newly imported apples; plates I–XXX follow the historical papers.)

. . . Volume II . . .

Collation irregular and unsigned 322 pages including 6 preliminaries, 290 numbered to match plates XXXI–LXXVI, and 26 containing lists of cider apples and perry pears, followed by indexes of the names of all the varieties described; 45 coloured plates.

BINDING: Half red morocco, red cloth sides, spine with gilt apples in compartments, marbled end-papers. 'Bound by Bayntun-Riviere Bath England' stamped on top left corner of the free front end-paper of volume I.

PLATES: Nearly all are from drawings by Edith E. Bull (*fl.* 1840s–1880s), the daughter of H. G. Bull, and Alice B. Ellis (*fl.* 1870s–1880s). One exception is the Eggleton Styre apple on plate XXIX, which was drawn by Frances Stackhouse Acton (d. 1882), the eldest daughter of Thomas Andrew Knight. She made the drawing in 1878, seventy years after making many others for her father's *Pomona Herefordiensis* (see page 214). Of the four uncolored plates in volume I, the two portraits (T. A. Knight facing page 29 and Lord Scudamore facing page 63) are signed 'W.G.S.' and 'W. G. Smith', possibly indicating that Worthington George Smith (1835–1917), a member of the Woolhope Club who was better known as a botanical illustrator, engraved them both. The chromolithographs of the fruit, most with several apples or pears on each plate and sometimes leaves and flowers as well, were printed in Brussels by G. Severeyns. The original drawings for them, assembled into patchwork plates, are now in the Museum of Cider in Hereford. The line drawings of cross-sections of fruit in the text are not signed.

THE Woolhope Naturalists' Field Club, based in Hereford, the main town of a county famous for apples and cider, turned its attention to neglected orchards in the 1870s, once the 'Fungus Forays' started in 1867 had found that decaying apple trees were often the hosts of the fungi being hunted. After the 1872 foray the Reverend M. J. Berkeley, an eminent mycologist as well as a prominent councillor of the Royal Horticultural Society, arranged a gift of ninety-two grafts of apple trees from the Society's garden in Chiswick to the Woolhope Club. Prompted by this donation, the club formed a Pomology Committee, with the Reverend Charles Henry Bulmer as one of its leading members. A little later, in 1887, Bulmer's two sons, Henry Percival and Edward Frederick, founded the company which is now the largest cider-maker in the world, and nearly a hundred years later the company, in its turn, supported the establishment of the Museum of Cider in Hereford.

The possibility of publishing a *Herefordshire Pomona* was considered at a special meeting of the Woolhope Club in 1876, two years after regular exhibitions of apples and pears had been established. In October 1877, according to the club's *Transactions* (page 42) 'about 1200 plates of fruit were exhibited' and Dr Hogg 'reserved those varieties which will be required for description and figuring in the present and future numbers of the new *Herefordshire Pomona*, which is shortly to appear.' The background to this development is described in the introduction to the *Pomona* (page 11):

> The study of Pomology is rather beyond the domain of a strictly Scientific Society; but the members of the Woolhope Club had become strongly impressed with the necessity of some great effort to restore Herefordshire to its fruit-growing supremacy; to call the attention of the growers to the best varieties of fruit for the table and the press; to improve the methods followed in the manufacture of Cider and Perry, and the quality of those products; and thus to increase in every way the marketable value of its orchard products.

The book was dedicated to Lord Bateman, the lord lieutenant of the county, 'as a tribute to the cordial interest he has shown in this effort to improve the productions of Herefordshire'. The first of seven parts was published in the autumn of 1878 and the rest followed annually until the last, which was delayed until the results of an Anglo-French pomological meeting in October 1884 could be incorporated. Dr Bull's preface is dated January 1885, while a note after it, thanking him for all his work, is dated March 1885. The Woolhope Club's annual general meeting in April of that year was given a financial statement about the whole book (printed on pages 273–75 of the club's *Transactions 1883–1885*), so it seems that the last part was issued in the

ROBERT HOGG and
H. G. BULL *The
Herefordshire Pomona*
part VI 1883
plate LIV American
Mother, Ashmead's
Kernel, and other apples,
drawn by Edith E. Bull
and Alice B. Ellis, and
lithographed by G.
Severeyns

Plate LIV

3 Gogar Pippin.

2 American Mother

1 Wyken Pippin

4 Cockle's Pippin.

5 Ashmead's Kernel

9 Wanstall

6 Brownlee's Russet

7 Aromatic Russet    8 Boston Russet.

G. Severeyns, Chromolith Brussels

Alice B. Ellis & Edith E. Bull del.
for The Woolhope Club.

spring of 1885. The statement accounts for a sum of almost 2000 pounds, the cost of printing 600 copies of seven parts containing six, eight, ten, twelve, twelve, thirteen, and sixteen plates. In the Lindley Library of the Royal Horticultural Society is a set of the *Pomona* in its original parts, with grey paper wrappers, dated and divided as follows:

I 1878 pages *i–iv* 1–46 *47–48* plates I–VI and their text

II 1879 pages *i–iv* 49–98 plates VII–XIV and their text

III 1880 pages *i–iv* 101–130 plates XV–XXIV and their text

IV 1881 pages *i–ii* 131–160 plates XXV–XXXVI and their text

V 1882 pages *i–ii* plates XXXVII–XLVIII and their text

VI 1883 pages *i–ii* plates XLIV–LXI and their text

VII 1884 [i.e. spring 1885] title-pages to volumes I and II, dedication, tables of contents, general introduction (pages I–XX), lists and indexes; plates LXII–LXXVII and their text

The artists needed 'all the sunshiny hours of eight autumnal sessions in succession' to record 432 varieties of apples and pears contributed by members of the Pomona Committee, exhibitors at fruit shows, nurserymen, gardeners, and other enthusiasts. The descriptions that accompany the plates were the work of Dr Robert Hogg, the man who had supervised the replanting of the Horticultural Society's fruit garden at Chiswick and the author of *The Fruit Manual*, the later editions of which provided a basis for the *Pomona* descriptions. The acidity of the juice of several of the fruits was measured and reported by G. H. With of Trinity College Dublin, who also provided a 'valuable recipe for Orchard Manure'.

Most of the historical essays at the beginning of the book were written by the general editor, Dr Henry Bull, who dealt with the early history of the apple and the pear, modern apple lore, Thomas Andrew Knight and his work, and the life of John, 1st Viscount Scudamore, of Holme Lacey, who discovered the Redstreak apple about 1630 and used all his influence to encourage its propagation and its long reign as the pre-eminent cider apple. A strong tradition also gives him credit for the introduction of several other cider apples from Normandy. Another member of the same family, Sir Henry Scudamore Stanhope (later the Earl of Chesterfield), added an essay on the cordon method of growing pears at Holme Lacey, a garden that also supplied some of the fruit illustrated in the *Herefordshire Pomona*. Edwin Lees contributed an account of crab-apples, and the last essay, on 'The Orchard and its Products, Cider and Perry', was the work of the Reverend Charles Bulmer and the Pomona Committee. A thick garnish of literary quotations is scattered throughout these historical papers, starting with Homer and Virgil, ending with Tennyson, and paying proper attention to John Philips's long poem, *Cyder*, first published in 1708 (see page 211), not long before the author's early death and the burial of 'Pomona's Bard', as James Thomson called him, in Hereford Cathedral.

Philips was writing at the time when cider was still considered the patriotic alternative to imported wine or even to beer made from grain that might have been used for bread. Evelyn's *Pomona* (1664), a supplement to his *Sylva*, and Worlidge's *Vinetum Britannicum* (1676: see page 210) both speak of the value of this national drink and its production in the West Country. A tax imposed on it in 1763 made cider rather less popular, but by the time the Woolhope Club began its crusade for the revival of the local orchards a renewed interest in apples and cider was growing fast, in France as well as England.

The last part of the *Herefordshire Pomona* was held back for a few months to allow a report of a visit to a meeting of French pomological societies, held in Rouen in October 1884, to be added to the introduction. The Woolhope Club collected a gold medal for an exhibit of fifty-seven varieties of eating apples, a similar number of cookers, and thirty-six kinds of pears, as well as a bronze medal for a second group of fifty-six cider apples and forty-two perry pears. The first six parts of the *Pomona* were also exhibited and given a 'Diplôme d'Honneur', while Dr Hogg was awarded a special gold medal 'for his life-long work in Pomology'. The Woolhope visitors compared some Herefordshire apples known as 'Norman' with French fruit, a test that led to the English ones being rechristened as 'Hereford' varieties. Eight true Norman cider apples were brought back to Hereford from this visit, with last-minute drawings and descriptions of them included in an appendix to the introduction published with the last instalment of the *Pomona*.

The indexes of apple and pear names that finish off the book are still valuable as a way of tracking down the variety of labels used in different times and places for the same fruit, though the reader is easily distracted by the historical associations of many of the names, which have a rich flavour of their own. In the end, the co-operative effort of the writers, artists, and other members of the Woolhope Club produced a book that is virtually an encyclopaedia of apples and pears.

The most recent in the long series of apple books from Herefordshire is *Bulmer's Pomona*, published in 1987 to mark the centenary of H. P. Bulmer Limited, the cider-making company. This collection of thirty-five reproductions of watercolours of cider apples, with the leaves and flowers of their trees, by Caroline Todhunter, is accompanied by line drawings of cross-sections by Rodney Shackell, while Ray Williams has described each apple and not only the acidity of its juice but the flavour of the cider made from it. Cider and the apples from which it is made are once again enjoying a revived popularity.

## 83. DIETZSCH, Barbara Regina (1706–1783)

Two Quinces on a Branch, *c.*1750.  28 x 20 cm.  Gouache on a black ground. (See frontispiece.)

BARBARA DIETZSCH belonged to a family of painters and musicians in Nuremberg, where several members of it were employed by the Court. Her brother and sister were also botanical artists, and the pictures of all three were often painted on dark grounds, adding a sharp contrast to the flowers or fruit depicted. Barbara Dietzsch painted birds and insects as well as plants, and her work was valued by contemporary collectors.

The Nuremberg physician Christoph Jacob Trew (1695–1769), a great patron of botany, commissioned several artists to record flowering plants, some from his own garden. These drawings were often used later to illustrate his books. Barbara Dietzsch and her sister Margaretha were among the artists who contributed in this way to Trew's *Hortus Nitidissimis* (1750–86), edited by J. M. Seligmann and A. L. Wirsing and including nearly two hundred spectacular plates of garden flowers.

The quince has never been as popular as its close relation, the pear, perhaps because its hard fruit has to be cooked before being eaten, but it is often used as a stock for grafting pear trees. Once picked and brought indoors, the fruit releases a distinctive warm scent a little like that of ripe citrus fruit.

## 84. FIELD, Thomas Warren (1821–1881)

Pear Culture. [rule 2 cm.] A Manual for the Propagation, Planting, Cultivation, and Management of the Pear Tree. With descriptions and illustrations of the most productive of the finer varieties, and selections of kinds most profitably grown for market. By Thos. W. Field. [two verses side by side, with a vertical rule 1 cm. long between them] The golden-dropping Pear, the reddening glow Upon the cheek of Beauty, and the Peach, Have common source and end. The Dust We till, we are. The nodding flower, the Elm, Arching in cloisters and in vaulted aisles, Are man, or beast, or worm, in other forms. No marble dumb, or crumbling tomb shall rear Their pale chill walls o'er me. The tree I plan Shall monument my dust—itself the tree, Refined in leaf, and fruit, and flower: that when The immaterial part puts matter on Again, it is more fit for Heaven. New York: A. O. Moore, Agricultural Book Publisher, 140 Fulton Street. 1859.

12° 19 x 12 cm. $1^{10}$ $2$–$12^{12}$ *i–iv* 5 vi–viii *13* (no text missing) 14–286 *287–288* 1–12 ('Catalogue of Books on Agriculture and Horticulture published by A. O. Moore & Co.') and a frontispiece and 3 plates.

BINDING: Brown publisher's cloth, blind-stamped design; gilt bunches of pears on front and spine.

PLATES: The coloured frontispiece is a lithograph of five pears by A. Hochstein, printed by Sarony, Major, and Knapp, who worked in New York, singly or together, from 1843 to 1871. The other three plates are uncoloured woodcuts, the first, opposite page 188, a collection of superimposed pear silhouettes 'Selected and Drawn by Mr. L. Berckmans'. The other two are unsigned and show individual pears, Duchesse d'Angoulême opposite page 212 and Beurré Clairgeau opposite page 234.

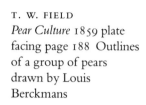

T. W. FIELD
*Pear Culture* 1859 plate
facing page 188  Outlines
of a group of pears
drawn by Louis
Berckmans

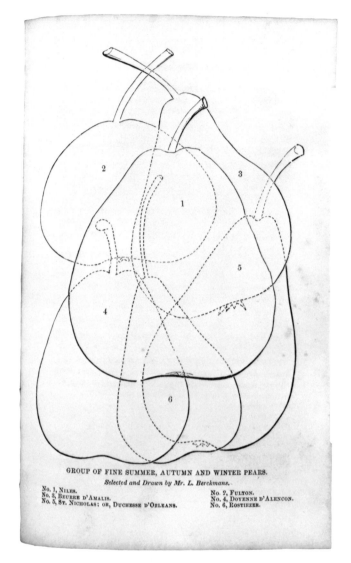

GROUP OF FINE SUMMER, AUTUMN AND WINTER PEARS.
*Selected and Drawn by Mr. L. Berckmans.*

No. 1, NILES.                     No. 2, FULTON.
No. 3, BEURRE D'AMALIS.           No. 4, DOYENNE D'ALENCON.
No. 5, ST. NICHOLAS; OR, DUCHESSE D'ORLEANS.   No. 6, ROSTIEZER.

T. W. FIELD's varied career began with teaching in Brooklyn, where he later established a
nursery garden called Weirfield (linking his first wife's surname and his own) in Bushwick
Avenue. His experience of growing fruit here led to his book on pears, but he wrote on many
other subjects too. The limping verses on the title-page of his pear book are presumably his own.
An important part of his large library was devoted to the history of the American Indians and
he published a bibliography of this subject before part of his collection was sold in 1875.

Another nursery in Brooklyn, established by André Parmentier when he arrived in America
in 1824, grew over two hundred varieties of pears in the six years before the owner's death in
1830. Many of these were imported from the Louvain nursery of Jean Baptiste Van Mons, who
began working on pears about 1785 and sent many new varieties from Belgium to the rest of
the world. The Berckmans nursery at Plainfield, New Jersey, established about 1850 by P.J.A.

224

Berckmans and his father Louis, was another source of Van Mons pears, and Field's book is dedicated 'To My Friend, Dr. Louis E. Berckmans, as a mark of affection and respect'. Dr Berckmans's little book, *Pear Culture for the South*, was published in 1859. Many other nurserymen responded to the popularity of pears and offered a good range for sale. Field's introduction explains this craze by the use of quince stocks for pears, producing grafted trees which began to bear fruit more quickly:

> The introduction of the French method of propagation upon the Quince stock has given such an impetus to the cultivation of the Pear, that the sales from a single nursery in this country reach the enormous number of half a million trees in one year . . . In the original introduction of the Pear as a fruit into this country, the French Huguenots bore a prominent part . . . This is evidenced by the multitude of aged trees (many of them producing fine varieties) in the immediate neighbourhood of their first settlements, particularly on Long Island and at New Rochelle . . . It is not a little curious to observe how the taste and preference for this fruit has survived in the countries through which the Huguenots passed in their flight, or where they temporarily sojourned. Belgium and Holland have produced more fine varieties, and more eminent cultivators, of this fruit than all the rest of the world.

Hedrick's *History of Horticulture in America* (1950, pages 235–36) tells us more about what he calls this 'mild mania':

> From about 1820 to 1870, the pear was the most popular fruit in the orchards of 'gentlemen farmers,' and nearly as popular as the peach and the apple in commercial orchards. The center of interest in pear culture was eastern Massachusetts, with the Massachusetts Horticultural Society, founded in 1829, as the clearing house for information and exhibits of the fruit. There was scarcely less interest in pear culture in the great estates along the Hudson, and in commercial orchards in western New York, in New Jersey, Delaware, Pennsylvania, with some large orchards in Maryland and Virginia . . . At the annual shows of the Massachusetts Horticultural Society, one reads of exhibits of pears beginning in the 1830's on to 1900 that numbered from 40 to more than 300 varieties. Several times we are told proudly in the horticultural papers that this or that show had a greater number of pears than had ever been displayed at the great shows of London, Ghent, or Paris.

## 85. 'AN AMATEUR'

The Illustrated Pear Culturist: containing plain, practical directions for planting, budding, grafting, pruning, training, and dwarfing the Pear Tree: also, Instructions relating to the propagation of new varieties, gathering, preserving, and ripening the fruit, together with valuable hints in regard to the locality, soil, and manures required for, and best arrangement of the trees in an orchard, both on the pear and the quince stock, and a list of the most valuable varieties for Dwarf or Standard Culture, accurately described, and truthfully delineated by numerous colored

engravings. By an Amateur. [wavy line 2.5 cm.] New-York: C. M. Saxton & Co., 140 Fulton Street. New-London: Starr & Co., No. 4, Main Street. [rule 1 cm.] 1858.

8° 23 x 14.5 cm. Collation irregular and unsigned *1–3* *4–106* then 'Specimens' section with 32 lithographs, each with an unnumbered page of description, followed by 24 blank leaves. There is also a folding frontispiece and 2 other plates.

BINDING: Brown publisher's cloth, gilt pears within gilt borders on sides; all edges gilt. An inscription on the fly-leaf reads 'Eliza M. French Gage. With respects of The Author'.

PLATES: Of the 32 coloured lithographs in the 'Specimens' section, two, Seckel and Forelle, are signed 'Boell Lith. N.Y.', that is William Boell, who worked in New York from 1854 to 1858 and in Philadelphia for the next ten years. He may also have been involved in printing at least some of the illustrations in A. J. Downing's *Fruits of America* (see page 158) and 17 of the Amateur's pears are identical to the Downing ones: Bartlett, Bloodgood, Beurré Bosc, Beurré d'Aremberg, Beurré Diel, Golden Beurré of Bilboa (which is reversed), Columbia, Dearborn's Seedling, Dix, Flemish Beauty, Forelle, Frederick of Wirtemburg [*sic*], Glout Morceau, Marie Louise, Seckel, Urbaniste, and Winter Nelis. The uncoloured folding frontispiece shows a woodcut silhouette of the gigantic California Pound Pear. There is a coloured lithograph of pyramid and dwarf trees facing page 45, an uncoloured engraving of an orchard plan opposite page 104 and diagrams of others in the text on pages 100 to 103.

T HIS BOOK is apparently another product of the current enthusiasm for growing pears. The anonymous author explained his book's background in its preface (pages 3–5):

This manual was not, originally, intended for publication. It originated in the mind of the writer, and was commenced as a private Note Book for his own study and convenience. But the further he proceeded, the more intensely interested he became in the subject, particularly in his collection of specimens and drawings, included in the plan. Having been referred to judicious friends, it was subsequently decided to increase somewhat its size, and give it publicity . . . To render it more useful and complete, many of the finer varieties of the fruit have been represented, which will contribute to the value and interest of the work. These have been obtained from various sources. A part of the original colored specimens were received from France;★ others have been collected from the various sources, from which the best drawings or specimens could be obtained; while some of them were drawn directly from the fruits themselves, either produced on our own grounds, or furnished us through the kindness of esteemed friends.

★After these specimens had been received and partly engraved, for the first time we examined a copy of Mr. Downing's "Fruits and Fruit Trees of America," *with colored plates*. They seem to be identical.

As the engravings exhibit only the most valuable popular kinds of our Pears, and amateurs and fruit growers are constantly increasing the number of new varieties, about a hundred blank pages are left at the close of the book, on which new varieties . . . may be added from time to time.

There is no further explanation of how the Downing illustrations came to be borrowed.

# PEACHES & SOFT FRUIT

Traité de la Culture des Pêchers. Deuxième Edition, revûe corrigée & augmentée. [vignette 2.5 x 5 cm.] A Paris, rue S. Jacques. Chez [bracket] Delaguette, Imprimeur-Libraire, à l'Olivier. Le Prieur, Imprimeur ordinaire du Roi, à la Croix d'Or. [double rule, upper one heavier]

M. DCC. L. Avec privilege du Roi.
12° 16 x 9.5 cm. a⁸ A–Q in alternate 8s and 4s R⁴ *i–ii* iii–xvi 1–198 *199–200*.

BINDING: Contemporary speckled calf.

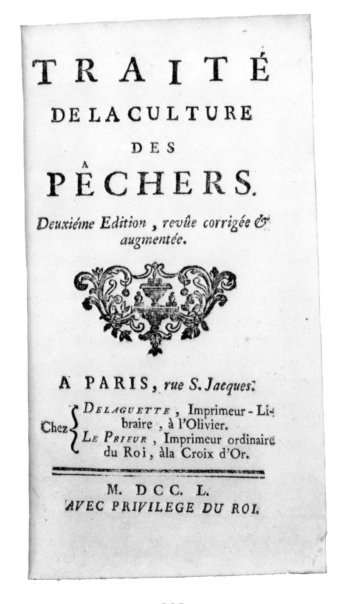

Title-page

THE de Combles family came from Lyons, though this anonymous member of it had a garden not far from Paris. The *Dictionnaire de Biographie française* suggests that the author may have been Jean de Combles, father of Charles-Jean (1741–1803), or one of his brothers. His little book on peach trees, first published in 1745, with a second edition in 1750 and a third in 1770, was the earliest in France devoted exclusively to this fruit. Its genesis is explained in the preface (pages iv, ix, xi):

> Le Jardinage est mon attrait: j'en fais depuis bien des années l'amusement de mon loisir, & la plus solide occupation de ma vie. . . . Une personne de la plus haute considération m'ayant demandé un jour quelque instruction sur la culture des Pêchers, dont elle aimoit particuliérement le fruit, je me fis un devoir de l'obliger, & je rédigeai toutes mes vûes par écrit. Ce petit Traité qui lui plût fort, ayant passé ensuite de ses mains, dans celles de plusieurs curieux, qui le trouverent de leur goût, on me pressa de le publier. . . . Quoique plusieurs Auteurs ayent déjà écrit sur cette matiere, je crois pouvoir dire qu'elle n'a jamais été qu'ébauchée, & qu'aucun d'eux n'en a fait une étude suffisante pour pouvoir servir de guide; cependant j'en excepte, a juste titre, M. de la Quintinie qui a donné des régles fort judicieuses fondées sur l'expérience & sur le bon raisonnement; mais il n'a pas donné un ordre a ses matieres qui mette le Lecteur à son aise, & il n'a pas dit tout ce que le sujet demande.

As well as advice on choosing, planting, pruning, and cultivating peach trees, there is a chapter on moving them, filled with the fruits of experience (pages 158, 159): 'J'en ai envoyé en Moscovie, & au fond de l'Italie, qui ont parfaitement réussi. . . . Lorsque vos Arbres seront heureusement arrivés au lieu de leur destination, il faut recommander qu'on ait soin de faire tremper les racines dans l'eau pendant deux jours avant de les planter.'

An anonymous English translation of the book appeared in London in 1768, possibly at the suggestion of the seedsman James Gordon, of Fenchurch Street, who is listed with the booksellers on its title-page. The translator 'having proved by experiment the superior excellence of the following Treatise' was 'induced to offer this translation of it to the public, in hopes of making the cultivation of peach trees better understood, and the art of pruning them practised upon more rational and more natural principles than it has hitherto been'.

De Combles also wrote *L'Ecole du Jardin potager*, which ran through six editions from 1749 to 1822, some of them including his treatise on peach trees too.

## 87.  BROWNE, Robert (*fl.* 1786)

A Method to Preserve Peach and Nectarine Trees from the Effects of the Mildew; And for destroying the Red Spider in Melon Frames, and other Insects, which infest Plants in Stoves, and Trees, Shrubs, &c. in the Open Garden. [rule] By Robert Browne, Gardener to Sir Harbord Harbord, Bart. at Gunton, in Norfolk. [rule]

London: Printed, by Subscription, for the Author, MDCCLXXXVI. [fist] Subscribers may have their copies of Mr. Walter, Bookseller, Charing-Cross.

8° 16 x 10 cm. a–b⁸ c–d² B–E⁸ F² i–vi vii–xl 1 2–65 66–68.

BINDING: Brown paper over boards.

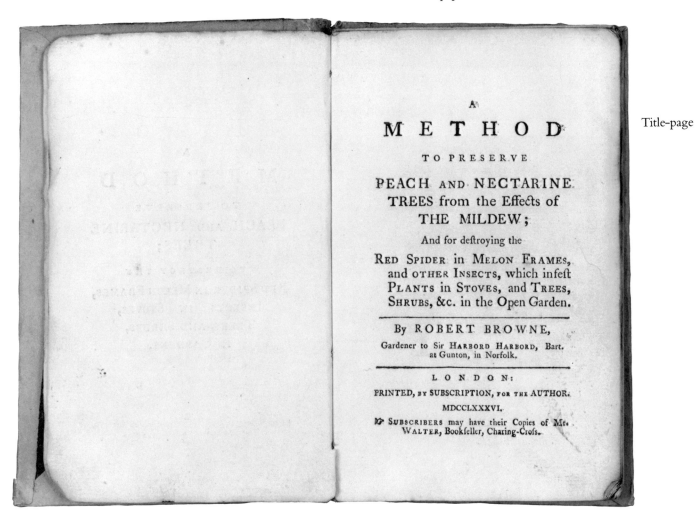

Title-page

ROBERT BROWNE was the gardener of Sir Harbord Harbord at Gunton Park, near Cromer, Norfolk. His little book, with very few widely spaced lines on each page, describes a fierce compound of soft soap, flowers of sulphur, wood ash, tobacco, lime, and water, to be brushed on to the leaves of the trees. A pirated edition of his directions appeared in Dublin the same year, appended to Speechly's *Treatise on the Culture of the Pine Apple* (see page 260).

Title-page

*Jno BSoutham*

A

**TREATISE**

ON THE

*IMPROVED CULTURE*

OF THE

𝕾𝖙𝖗𝖆𝖜𝖇𝖊𝖗𝖗𝖞, 𝕽𝖆𝖘𝖕𝖇𝖊𝖗𝖗𝖞,

AND

𝕲𝖔𝖔𝖘𝖊𝖇𝖊𝖗𝖗𝖞,

Designed to prove the present common Mode of Cultivation
erroneous, and the Cause of Miscarriage in Crops of Fruit;
also to introduce a cheap and rational Method of cultivating
the Varieties of each Genius, by which ample Crops of superior Fruit may be uniformly obtained in all Seasons, and
preserved beyond the usual Time of Maturity.

*SECOND EDITION.*

By THOMAS HAYNES,

*Of Oundle, Northamptonshire ;*

Author of

AN IMPROVED SYSTEM OF NURSERY GARDENING, ALSO INTE-
RESTING DISCOVERIES IN THE PROPAGATION OF ALL
FRUIT-TREES, SHRUBS, AND PLANTS, BY CUT-
TINGS, WITHOUT ARTIFICIAL HEAT, &c.

**LONDON:**
Printed by Plummer and Brewis, Love Lane, Eastcheap,
FOR B. AND R. CROSBY AND CO.
STATIONERS' COURT, LUDGATE STREET,
And Sold by all Booksellers.
1814.

## 88. HAYNES, Thomas (*fl.* 1790–1817)

A Treatise on the improved culture of the Strawberry, Raspberry, and Gooseberry, Designed to prove the present common Mode of Cultivation erroneous, and the Cause of Miscarriage in Crops of Fruit; also to introduce a cheap and rational Method of cultivating the Varieties of each Genius [*sic*], by which ample Crops of superior Fruit may be uniformly obtained in all Seasons, and preserved beyond the usual Time of Maturity. [swelled rule 1.5 cm.] Second edition. [swelled rule 1.5 cm.] By Thomas Haynes, Of Oundle, Northamptonshire; Author of An Improved System of Nursery Gardening, also Interesting Discoveries in the Propagation of all Fruit-Trees, Shrubs, and Plants, by Cuttings, without artificial heat, &c. [double rule, upper one heavier, 5 cm.] London: Printed by Plummer and Brewis, Love Lane, Eastcheap, for B. and R. Crosby and Co. Stationers' Court, Ludgate Street, And Sold by all Booksellers. [rule 1 cm.] 1814. 8° 22.5 x 14 cm. $A^4$ B–$G^8$ $H^4$ *i–iii* iv–vii *viii 1* 2–101 *102–104*.

BINDING: Original grey boards with labels on spine and front. Signature of Jno. B. Southam on title-page. 'A Catalogue of New Interesting Works . . . Now Publishing by B. & R. Crosby' bound in.

THOMAS HAYNES was a nurseryman at Oundle. The first edition of his little book on the strawberry and other soft fruit came out in 1812. He thought strawberries needed shade, as wild ones grow in cool soils and shady woods, therefore he had some novel ideas for shading them (page 36): 'To afford a more widely extended shade, roots of *Helianthus Tuberosus*, commonly called Jerusalem Artichoke, . . . from their broad foliage, will, in the hotter months of July and August, be found to afford a more cool and refreshing shade.' The same plant is recommended as shade for raspberries and gooseberries too.

Raspberries prefer damp, boggy soils, and temporary shade will help them, especially when they are blooming and setting fruit, 'but it will be in great danger of being devoured by thrushes and blackbirds . . . if unprotected by netting or other open covering freely admitting air' (page 72).

Gooseberries need rich beds as well as shade. 'It is easy to infer, that the very same sort of Gooseberry, by different soils and management, has produced very different-sized fruit, by the annual exhibitions in many countries' (page vii). Annual gooseberry shows are still held in several parts of the English Midlands, with individual berries being weighed and measured in carefully controlled competitions.

## 89.   THORY, Claude Antoine (1759–1827)

Monographie ou Histoire naturelle du genre Groseillier, contenant la description, l'histoire, la culture et les usages de toutes les groseilles connues, Avec 24 Planches coloriées. Par C.-A. Thory. [swelled rule 4.5 cm.] A Paris, Chez P. Dufart, Libraire de son altesse royale Monseigneur le duc de Bourbon, Quai Voltaire, N° 19. [decorated rule 0.5 cm.] 1829.
8° 22 x 14 cm. π² a⁸ 1–9⁸ 10⁴ [4] *i* ii–xvi *1* 2–152 and a frontispiece and 24 plates.
BINDING: Original paper wrappers; uncut and unopened.

PLATES: The frontispiece is an uncoloured, unsigned, lithograph portrait of Thory. Another uncoloured lithograph, opposite page 8, showing fruit and floral parts, is signed by A. M. Canneva. All the other plates, lithographs coloured by hand, were drawn by L. A. Canneva, who also engraved numbers 18 to 24. Plates 2 to 17 were engraved by Antoine Pascal, who had worked with Redouté and in 1836 published a little book about the great man's methods. All the plates were printed by Langlumé.

THORY was an amateur botanist who wrote the text for Redouté's *Roses* (1817–1824) and published a *Monographie du genre Rosier* (1820) as well. In his gardens at Belleville and later at his country house at Clamart-sous-Meudon he grew roses and many other plants too. In the anonymous editor's preface to his posthumous little book on gooseberries, his interest in this humble fruit is justified: 'Les soins . . . ne lui faisaient pas négliger le modeste, mais utile Groseillier: il s'appliquait depuis longues années à étudier sa nature, ses moeurs, à réunir, à classer méthodiquement les espèces et les variétés connues tant en France qu'à l'étranger.' After a descriptive catalogue of varieties bearing green, red, or buff fruit, the final section talks about

C. A. THORY
*Monographie ou Histoire naturelle du genre Groseillier* 1829 plate 15 An amber gooseberry, drawn by L. A. Canneva and engraved by Antoine Pascal

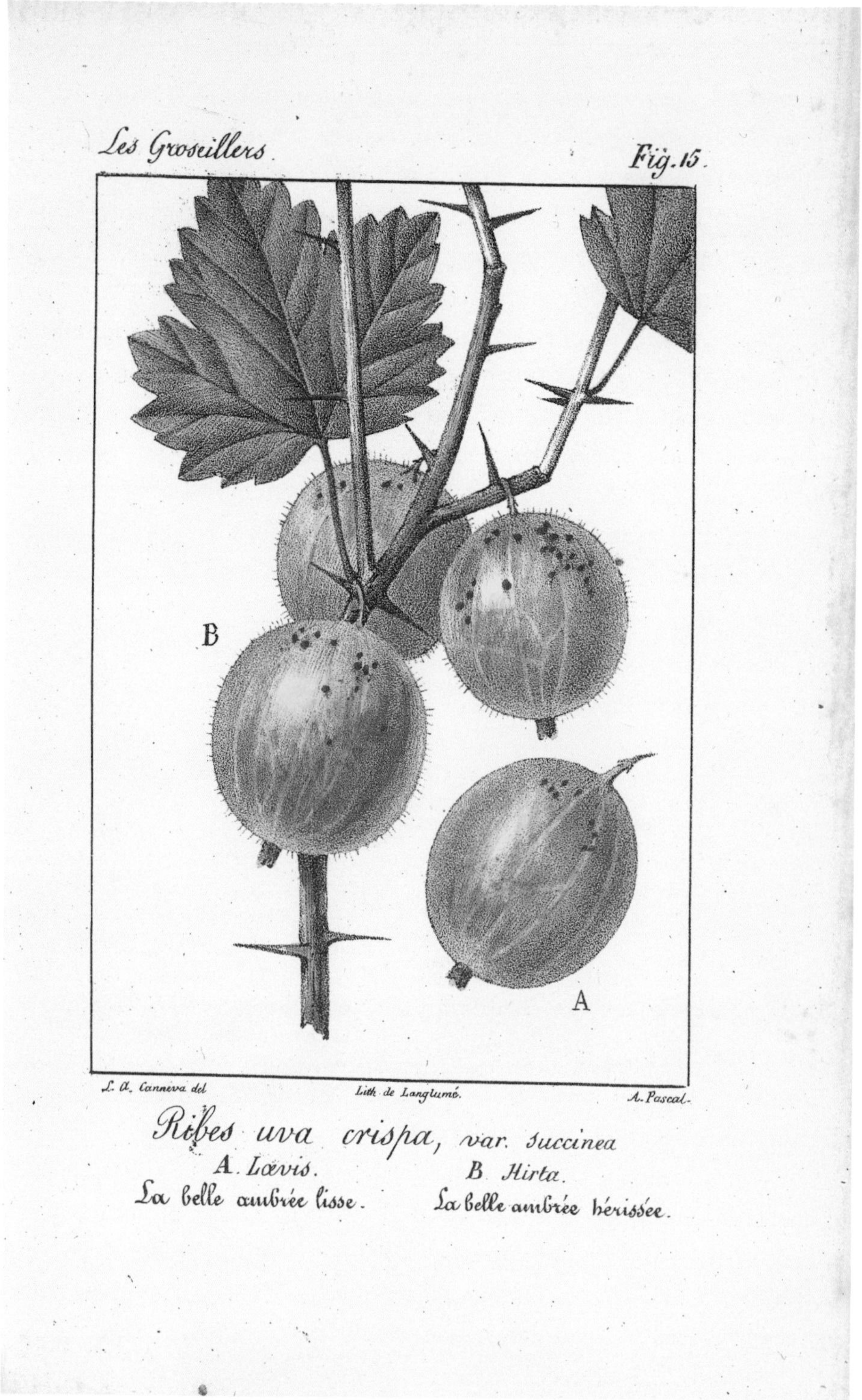

*Les Groseillers.*     *Fig. 15.*

L. A. Canneva del.     Lith. de Langlumé.     A. Pascal.

*Ribes uva crispa,* var. *succinea*
A. *Lævis.*     B. *Hirta.*
*La belle ambrée lisse.*     *La belle ambrée hérissée.*

the value of gooseberries in the garden and quotes references to them in early herbals. Then there are recipes, some from other hands, for gooseberry sauce, gooseberry jam, gooseberry fool, gooseberry ice, and even gooseberry wine in imitation of champagne.

The gooseberry has always been less popular in America than it is in Europe, perhaps because it is easily attacked by mildew there. Fewer varieties are available, and they usually have smaller and less attractive fruit. In areas where white pines are grown gooseberries may also be dangerous, as they are hosts to a blister rust that attacks these trees. They may also have been involved in the spread of the chestnut blight which almost wiped out the native chestnut tree in eastern North America. In Europe the gooseberry is a less troublesome plant. In the Midlands of England, especially Cheshire, annual competitions for single dessert or culinary gooseberries are still lovingly conducted, each plump fruit in perfect condition being weighed and measured before being compared with its rivals.

## 90.  WHITE, Joseph J. (*fl.* 1870–1885)

Cranberry Culture by Joseph J. White, a practical grower. Illustrated. New York: Orange Judd Company, 751 Broadway. [1870.]
12° 18.5 x 12.5 cm. 1–5¹² 6⁶ *1–2* 3–126, including six pages of advertisements.

BINDING: Maroon publisher's cloth, blind-stamped sides.

JOSEPH WHITE lived in Juliustown, Burlington County, New Jersey, the second state in which the commercial planting of cranberries was started about the middle of the nineteenth century. Massachusetts preceded it, for on Cape Cod attempts at the culture of this difficult plant began about 1810. By the time White was writing, 'Every possessor of waste swamp land is interested to know whether, by planting it in cranberries, he may not "make it to blossom as the rose," and, at the same time, increase his revenue . . . The proper location for a meadow, as regards its soil and surroundings, is a matter of the utmost importance . . . The Cranberry is peculiar in its tastes and habits. On some soils it cannot be made to thrive, while upon others it is very hardy, and easily propagated' (page 25).

The cranberry's demands include a peaty bog and plenty of water to flood its territory. Only in parts of North America is it found growing wild, and William Penn described it in 1683 as one of the new fruits in the country's woodlands.

By 1890 over a hundred named varieties, not all of them very well defined, were being cultivated. Their classification was based on shape, colour, high or low growth, earliness, and the glossiness of the berries. The handful of woodcut illustrations in White's book show the

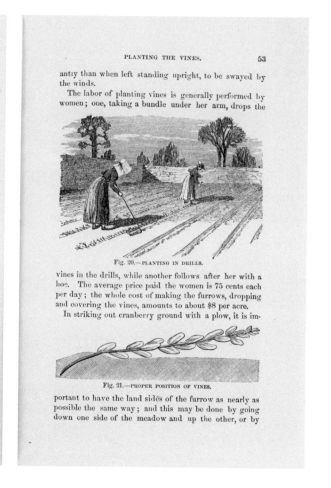

three main varieties—bell, bugle, and cherry—as well as details of soils, cultivation, and pests. His instructions were not the first ones published, for B. Eastwood's *Complete Manual for the Cultivation of the Cranberry* appeared in 1856, but White's book was popular enough to go into a second edition, with five extra pages, in 1885. On page 3 of his introduction to the 1870 edition he explained why he wrote: 'In view of the rapidly increasing demand for a reliable guide, or text-book for the cranberry culturist, we have attempted, with the liberal aid of some of our most successful growers, to prepare such a work . . . The business has increased enormously within the last ten years, and knowledge and experience have kept pace with that increase. The insufficiency of the works upon this subject, which we have hitherto taken as books of reference, is very apparent.'

# GRAPES

# 91. A SOCIETY OF GENTLEMEN

[within a border of double rules] Essays, for the month of December, 1716. To be Continued Mon[t]hly. [rule] By a Society of Gentlemen. [rule] For the Universal Benefit of the People of England. [double rule] London: Printed for J. Roberts, near the Oxford-Arms in Warwick-Lane. MDCCXVI.

8° 20.5 x 13 cm. A–C⁸ D² *1–2 3–51 52* and 4 engravings.

BINDING: Vellum spine, grey boards. 'P. 37 Grapes.' on front cover and an illegible inscription on front pastedown, with 'p. 17 augurs' in pencil on flyleaf and 'Plats' jewel house of art & nature London 1653—p. 211—' in ink on back pastedown.

PLATES: All are unsigned and one appears at the start of each essay, the first showing a grinding mill and a potter's shop, the second the manufacture of balls of coal and mud and their burning in a fireplace, the third brick-making, and the fourth grape-vines trained on walls.

Plate facing page 37
Vines trained on walls

ESSAY IV on pages 37 to 51 is devoted to grapes, making a case for vineyards in England on the usual grounds that the climate is as good as several other parts of Europe in which good wine is produced. '*England* wants *Wine of her own*, not through any *Defect* in her *Climate*, but the Omission of due *Industry* in her negligent *Natives*' (page 40). In recent years the natives have made good this negligence, and a number of vineyards have been established in the southern half of England.

An 'Advertisement' on the last page of the *Essays* makes their intention clear:

All who wou'd have these Books brought Monthly to their Houses, paying only a *Shilling for each Book*, at the *Delivery*, which in the whole is a Charge of but Twelve Shillings a Year, may be furnish'd with them, upon giving Notice to the *Beadles* of their respective *Parishes*: For our Design being nothing but the *Publick Good*, we chuse that way of *spreading our Essays*, that Rich and Poor may have them without Trouble; and the *Good* we aim at, may, by that Means, also spread as wide as possible.

Another set of essays for January 1717 is in the British Library, but the series survived no longer.

## 92.

The Vineyard: being a Treatise shewing   I. The Nature and Method of Planting, Manuring, Cultivating, and Dressing of Vines in Foreign-Parts.   II. Proper Directions for Drawing, Pressing, Making, Keeping, Fining, and Curing all Defects in the Wine.   III. An Easy and Familiar Method, of Planting and Raising Vines in England, to the greatest Perfection; illustrated with several useful Examples.   IV. New Experiments in Grafting, Budding, or Inoculating; whereby all Sorts of Fruit may be much more improv'd than at present; Particularly the Peach, Apricot, Nectarine, Plumb, &c.   V. The best Manner of raising several Sorts of compound Fruit, which have not yet been attempted in England. [rule] Being the Observations made By a Gentleman in his Travels. [rule] London: Printed for W. Mears, at the Lamb, without Temple-Bar. MDCCXXVII.

8° 19.5 x 12 cm. A–N⁸ *i–xvi 1* 2–192 and an engraved frontispiece.

BINDING: Contemporary calf, sides bordered with gilt rules. Inscribed on front pastedown 'This Book I Give My Nephew Ward Mary Mears'; it may have been a gift from a member of the publisher's family. The fly-leaf is stamped 'HENRY ★ NICKOLL. BARHAM' and inscribed 'Henry Denne Embridge House Littlebourne Kent And of Denne Hill Margate Thanct Feb!ʸ 1818'. On the back pastedown is the armorial bookplate of Alured Barkley Denne, inscribed 'to Eustace H. Denne November 1917'.

PLATE: A frontispiece showing a vineyard scene with grapes being harvested, drawn by R. Cooper and engraved by Henry Fletcher.

THERE IS a strong possibility that this book was the work of Richard Bradley (d. 1732), a prolific writer on all aspects of gardening and a Fellow of the Royal Society, who was also the first professor of botany at the University of Cambridge, from 1724 until his death. He certainly visited France in 1714 and 1719, paying special attention to vineyards on his second visit. Many of his books were also published by W. Mears, who issued *The Vineyard*. A book with this title is listed among Bradley's publications in John Nichols's *Literary Anecdotes* (1812, volume I, page 450) where it is dated 1728.

The dedication to James Brydges, Duke of Chandos (1673–1744) is signed by 'S.J.' but Bradley was certainly acquainted with the Duke, for he had worked on the huge formal garden at Canons, near Edgware, Middlesex, that was begun by this nobleman in 1713. Bradley's contribution to its growth ended in 1717, when he was dismissed.

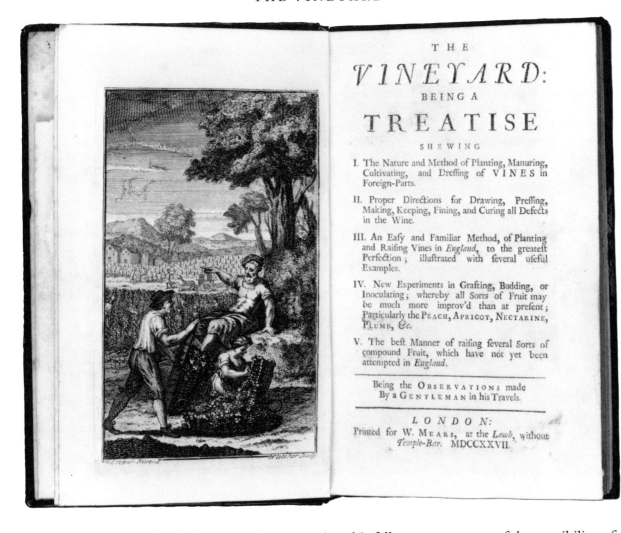

THE
## VINEYARD:
BEING A
## TREATISE
SHEWING

I. The Nature and Method of Planting, Manuring, Cultivating, and Dreſſing of VINES in Foreign-Parts.

II. Proper Directions for Drawing, Preſſing, Making, Keeping, Fining, and Curing all Defects in the Wine.

III. An Eaſy and Familiar Method, of Planting and Raiſing Vines in *England*, to the greateſt Perfection; illuſtrated with ſeveral uſeful Examples.

IV. New Experiments in Grafting, Budding, or Inoculating; whereby all Sorts of Fruit may be much more improv'd than at preſent; Particularly the PEACH, APRICOT, NECTARINE, PLUMB, &c.

V. The beſt Manner of raiſing ſeveral Sorts of compound Fruit, which have not yet been attempted in *England*.

Being the OBSERVATIONS made
By a GENTLEMAN in his Travels.

LONDON:
Printed for W. MEARS, at the *Lamb*, without *Temple-Bar*. MDCCXXVII.

*The Vineyard* 1727 Frontispiece, drawn by R. Cooper and engraved by Henry Fletcher, and title-page

The author, in his dedication, tries to convince his fellow countrymen of the possibility of growing wine at home: 'The Natives of our Island . . . have Annually remitted vast Sums of Specie to purchase this exhillerating Liquor from Foreigners, which we might as well raise at home with a little Industry, and by a right Application.' He collected many observations of French ways of cultivating grapes and making wine, concentrating on champagne and burgundy, 'since those Wines are allow'd to be preferable to all other Wines in France'. A woodcut figure on page 83 illustrates one of the stages in the manufacture of champagne, showing twin casks and the bellows used to move the wine from one to the other with the least possible disturbance.

The 'compound fruits' described look rather unlikely, from olive-grapes to damson-almonds, and the author seems convinced that only bad management stops oranges flourishing out of doors in England.

## 93. LOCKE, John (1632–1704)

Observations upon the Growth and Culture of Vines and Olives: the Production of Silk: the Preservation of Fruits. Written at the request of the Earl of Shaftesbury: to whom it is inscribed: by Mʳ. John Locke. Now first printed from the original manuscript in the possession of the present Earl of Shaftesbury. London: Printed for W. Sandby, in Fleet Street. M DCC LXVI.

8° 16 x 10 cm. A⁸(–A1) B–E⁸ F⁴(F4+1) *iii–v* vi–xv *xvi* *1* 2–73 *74*.

BINDING: Tan calf. Armorial bookplate of William Gilstrap and bookplate of Rachel McMasters Miller Hunt (1882–1963).

IN 1663 King Charles II granted the land now known as Carolina (from Carolus, the Latin form of the king's name) to eight 'lords proprietors', one of whom was John Locke's patron, Anthony Ashley Cooper, later the first Earl of Shaftesbury. For nine years Locke acted as secretary to the proprietors, even drawing up 'a plan of government' for the province. He also drew on the observations he had made in France during his stay in Montpellier, in the warm south, from the end of 1675 to the spring of 1677, to compile some advice on the cultivation of grapes and other useful products of the region. Lord Shaftesbury, an enthusiastic gardener, had been sent interesting plants from Locke in France, and he commissioned this compilation, which the author dedicated to him, from Christ Church, Oxford, on 1 February 1679. The philosopher was hardly a francophile, for the dedication reads:

> The country where these observations were made hath vanity enough to over-value every thing it produces: and it is hard to live in a place and not take some tincture from the manners of the people. Yet I think I should scarce have ventured to trouble your Lordship with these French trifles, had not your Lordship yourself encouraged me to believe, that it would not be unacceptable to you, if I took this way (for I ought all manner of ways) to express that duty and observance.

Locke's manuscript remained with the Shaftesbury papers for nearly ninety years before being published by Gregory Sharpe (1713–1771), one of the friends of the fourth Earl of Shaftesbury, who is described in Sharpe's introduction as 'an active and zealous Trustee for the colony of Georgia, from which, in time, we may expect a considerable quantity of raw silk will be imported into England'. This hope was not to be fulfilled. Sharpe also explained his purpose in publishing Locke's observations:

> However populous and great, industrious and rich, the settlements in the vast continent of America may hereafter become, this the mother country may for ever be connected with it more intimately than the southern nations, by encouraging the growth and produce of Vines and Olives, Silk and Fruits, which cannot advantageously be raised in England: and sound policy will always engage the subjects in England and America not to be rivals in trade, by setting up such manufactures in one county as must necessarily distress the other.

OBSERVATIONS UPON
THE GROWTH AND CULTURE
OF VINES AND OLIVES:
THE PRODUCTION OF SILK:
THE PRESERVATION OF FRUITS.

WRITTEN AT THE REQUEST OF
THE EARL OF SHAFTESBURY:
TO WHOM IT IS INSCRIBED:
BY MR. JOHN LOCKE.

NOW FIRST PRINTED FROM THE
ORIGINAL MANUSCRIPT IN
THE POSSESSION OF THE
PRESENT EARL OF
SHAFTESBURY.

LONDON:
PRINTED FOR W. SANDBY, IN FLEET STREET.
M DCC LXVI.

JOHN LOCKE *Observations . . .* written in 1679, printed in 1766 Title-page

The first and largest section of the *Observations* deals with wine, from planting and pruning vines (with Languedoc varieties described) to the transformation of their fruit. Then comes oil, that is, olive oil, treated in similar detail. A section on fruit comes next, listing local varieties of plums, peaches, and pears, and describing how some kinds are dried. The last and shortest part is about the treatment of silkworms and the manufacture of silk, a process encouraged in Virginia in the seventeenth century, and in Georgia and other states in the eighteenth.

## 94. SPEECHLY, William (1734–1819?)

A Treatise on the Culture of the Vine, exhibiting new and advantageous Methods of Propagating, Cultivating, and Training that Plant, so as to render it abundantly fruitful. Together with New Hints on the Formation of Vineyards in England. [rule] By William Speechly, Gardener to the Duke of Portland. [double rule, upper one heavier] York: Printed for the Author, by G. Peacock; and sold by G. Nicol, Bookseller to His Majesty, Pall-Mall; J. Debrett and J. Stockdale, Piccadilly; and E. Jeffery, near Carleton-Place, London. [rule 1.5 cm.] MDCCXC.
4° 29 x 22 cm. $a^4$ $b^4$ $\pi^2$ A–L$^4$ M$^4$(M2 + 1, M4 + 1) N–2E$^4$ *i–v* vi–xvi *xvii–xx 1* 2–92 [2] 93–96 [2] 97–224 and

5 engravings, 3 of them folding. The unnumbered leaves between pages 92 and 93 and pages 96 and 97 contain the explanations of plates I and II.

BINDING: Modern half red leather, marbled paper sides. A large-paper copy, uncut, part unopened.

PLATES: All five are engraved by James Basire. The first three, all folding, are taken from the author's own drawings and show plans and diagrams; the fourth is from a drawing by S. H. Grimm, and the fifth from one by Hayman Rooke.

SPEECHLY followed his book on pineapples (see page 260) with another on the vine, also the result of his work at Welbeck for the third Duke of Portland, to whom the book was dedicated. Once again it was printed in York, under the eye of Alexander Hunter, as the preface (page xvi) makes clear: 'My most grateful acknowledgments are due to my very excellent, worthy, and truly-learned friend Dr. A. Hunter. His obliging and assiduous attention to the work during the time it was in the press, has greatly contributed towards rendering it more worthy of the public approbation.'

Of the five plates, the first three show a plan for a stove suitable for pineapples and vines, a section of a heated wall designed to speed up the ripening of grapes, and the author's preferred way of pruning and training vines. The fourth, from a drawing by Samuel Hieronymus Grimm, shows a 'remarkable vine growing at Northallerton' in Yorkshire, and the last, from Hayman Rooke's drawing, a terraced landscape planted with vines. In the same year Rooke produced a book of his own about the oaks at Welbeck.

Speechly's *Treatise on the Vine*, like his similar book on the pineapple, was also pirated in Dublin in 1791, before the official, extended, second edition appeared in London in 1805. A third, combined with the *Treatise on the Culture of the Pine Apple*, was published in 1821. The pairing of these two books shows the esteem in which the two noble fruits were held by the employers of the gardeners who needed advice on their cultivation. George Brookshaw, writing in the introduction to his *Pomona Britannica* (1812; see page 104) was less pleased with Speechly's account of the vine, saying that his 'description of the grape is as vague, incorrect, and deficient, as any of the old writers'.

The book was published by subscription, and the list of subscribers is a rich one, including, among others, 'Wm. Aiton, Gardener to His Majesty at Kew . . . William Hanbury, Esq; 2 copies . . . James Lee, Nurseryman at Hammersmith . . . Humphrey [*sic*] Repton, Esq; . . . John

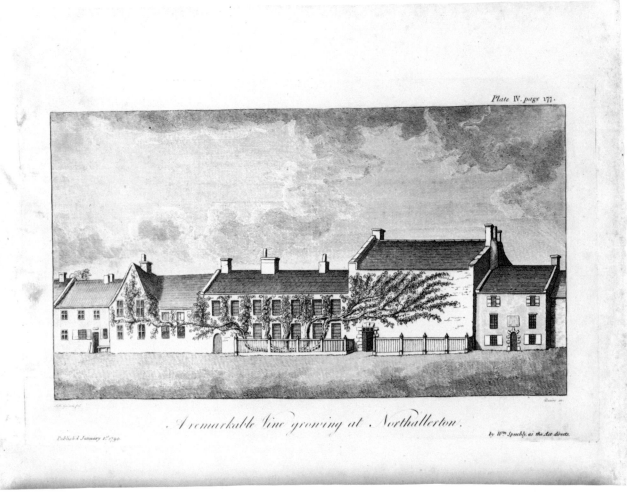

WILLIAM SPEECHLY
*A Treatise on the Culture of the Vine* 1790 plate IV 'A remarkable Vine growing at Northallerton' in Yorkshire, drawn by S. H. Grimm and engraved by James Basire

Sibthorpe, M.D. Professor of Botany (Oxford) . . . The Philosophical Society at Derby [i.e. Erasmus Darwin and his friends]' and quantities of noblemen and their gardeners, led by the Duke of Portland, the dedicatee, who ordered twenty copies.

## 95. KERNER, Johann Simon (1755–1830)

Le Raisin, ses espèces et variétés, dessinées et colorées d'après nature par J. S. Kerner, Conseiller aulique et Professeur, etc. [wavy rule 9 cm.] I$^{ère}$ Livraison. [wavy rule 9 cm.; vignette 18 x 20 cm. of Bacchus handing a bunch of grapes to Flora seated beneath a tree; wavy rule 19.5 cm.] Stoutgart chez l'Auteur, 1803.
1° 57 x 43.5 cm. Title-page, 2 leaves text, and 12 watercolours.

. . . Seconde Livraison. [wavy rule 9 cm.; vignette 18 x 20 cm. of a butterfly and a bunch of grapes; wavy rule 19.5 cm.] Stoutgart chez l'Auteur, 1805.
Title-page, 1 leaf text, and 12 watercolours, as in the following parts.

. . . Troisième Livraison . . . [vignette 17 x 15 as in Seconde Livraison] . . . 1807.

J. S. KERNER *Le Raisin*
fifth part 1809 Forment
grape, drawn by the
author

Forment

. . . Quatrième Livraison . . . [vignette 15 x 14 cm.] . . . 1808.

. . . Cinquième Livraison . . . [vignette 15 x 16 cm.] . . . 1809.

. . . Sixième Livraison . . . [vignette 17 x 18 cm.] . . . 1810.

. . . Septième Livraison . . . [vignette 13 x 14 cm.] . . . 1811.

. . . Huitième Livraison . . . [vignette 20 x 19 cm.] . . . 1811.

. . . Professeur, Membre de plusieurs Académies et Sociétés, etc. . . . Neuvième Livraison . . . [vignette 18.5 x 15 cm.] . . . 1812.

. . . par J. S. de Kerner, Chevalier de l'Ordre royal civil de Wurtemberg, Conseiller de la Cour, Professeur, Membre de plusieurs Académies et Sociétés, etc. . . . Dixième Livraison . . . [vignette 17 x 15 cm.] . . . 1813.

. . . Onzième Livraison . . . [vignette 16 x 18 cm.] . . . 1814.

. . . Douzième Livraison . . . [vignette 15 x 15 cm.] . . . 1815.

BINDING: Red morocco, broad gilt borders; all edges gilt. The 12 parts are bound in two volumes.

PLATES: The illustrations of grapes—144 of them—and the title-page vignettes—12 of them—are all watercolours by Kerner, *not* engraved and printed reproductions.

STOUTGART CHEZ L'AUTEUR, 1808.

J. S. KERNER *Le Raisin* fourth part 1808 Title-page vignette: Vitis vulpina (the American fox grape) and Papilio Ulysses, drawn by the author

FROM 1780 Kerner was a professor of botany at the Hohe Karlschule, that is, the university, in Stuttgart, where he was also in charge of the botanic garden and its herbarium. He wrote floras of the Wurttemberg region and books about economic plants, as well as publishing three illustrated by his own original watercolours: one on melons in 1810, with over thirty illustrations, *Hortus Sempervirens* (the evergreen garden) from 1795 to 1830, with eight hundred and fifty-one drawings, and *Le Raisin*, illustrating a hundred and forty-four grape varieties, with fruit, foliage, and usually a piece of the stem. Given the method of production, it is hardly surprising that not many copies of these three books were issued.

Each drawing in the grape book has the name of the variety inscribed at the bottom—Spanish, Portuguese, German, and even English grapes, as well as French ones. Written descriptions to go with the drawings were promised in the introductions to parts I, VI, and XII, but they were never published:

> Conformement à la promesse cette première livraison aurait dû être accompagnée de déscriptions de chaque espèce de raisin; mais des obstacles imprévus en ayant arrêté l'impression . . . la caractéristique n'a pû être imprimée avec cette livraison . . . Une déscription complette de chaque sorte sera donnée avec la sixième livraison . . . Les figures déjà données et faites d'après nature, seront suivies dans un an, de descriptions complètes de ces Espèces et variétés de la vigne, fondées sur des observations et des expériences de quarante ans; elles formeront un petit volume, et compleront [sic] ainsi l'ouvrage.

Each title-page vignette after the first shows a butterfly and a bunch of grapes; both fruit and insect are identified in the introduction to each part.

J. S. KERNER *Le Raisin* ninth part 1812 Title-page vignette: Raisin-pêche and Papilio Eurilochus from Surinam, drawn by the author

STUTTGART CHEZ L'AUTEUR, 1812.

250

## 96. PRINCE, William Robert (1795–1869) and
## PRINCE, William (1766–1842)

A Treatise on the Vine; embracing its history from the earliest ages to the present day, with descriptions of above two hundred foreign, and eighty American varieties, together with a complete dissertation on the establishment, culture, and management of vineyards. [rule 1.5 cm.] "The vine too, here her curling tendrils shoots, Hangs out her clusters glowing to the south, And scarcely wishes for a warmer sky." [rule 1.5 cm.] By William Robert Prince, aided by William Prince, Proprietor of the Linnæan Botanic Garden, Vice-President of the New-York Horticultural Society; Member of the Linnæan Society of Paris; of the Horticultural Societies of London and Paris; of the Imperial Society of the Georgofili at Florence; Honorary Member of the Massachusetts Horticultural Society, etc. etc. [double rule, upper one heavier, 1 cm.] New-York: Published by T. & J. Swords, G. & C. & H. Carvill, E. Bliss, Collins & Co. G. Thorburn & Sons, New-York; Judah Dobson, Philadelphia; J. B. Russell, Boston; Gideon B. Smith, Baltimore; James Winston, Richmond; and Joseph Simmons, Charleston, S.C. [rule 1.5 cm.] 1830. 4° 22 x 13.5 cm. 1–44⁴ 45² *i–v* vi–viii *9* 10–355 *356* and a lithographed frontispiece.

BINDING: Modern tan calf. Stamp of the Mercantile Library Association, New York, on title-page and first page of text.

PLATES: The frontispiece, showing a bunch of grapes of *Vitis labrusca* var. Isabella, was drawn by William Prince, who introduced the variety, and lithographed by Pendleton.

WILLIAM ROBERT PRINCE belonged to the fourth generation of nurserymen in his family, which established gardens at Flushing, Long Island, in 1737. Until the middle of the nineteenth century, the Linnæan Botanic Garden and Nursery was a leader in its field, offering for sale a greater number of varieties of fruit trees and other plants than any of their competitors. William Robert was a botanist and plant-collector, as well as a nurseryman. He travelled with Torrey and Nuttall in the eastern states, and in 1849 and 1850 brought back plants from California to the family nursery. He also spent a great deal of time experimenting with vines, trying out all the European ones he could find. Eventually he concentrated on improving and distributing promising varieties of native American grapes.

Hedrick, the historian of American horticulture, says firmly that 'A Treatise on the Vine was the first good work to appear on viticulture in America.' It was dedicated to Henry Clay, of Kentucky, who 'more than thirty years ago, united with many of our fellow citizens in forming an association for promoting the cultivation of the Vine in our country'. The book starts with the history of vine-growing, comments on suitable soils and settings, then provides a catalogue of varieties, first European and then American, with an attempt to elucidate some of the problems of confused nomenclature. William Bartram's account is reprinted in describing American vines. The last part of the book gives practical advice on growing vines, with several comments from correspondents in various parts of America, the longest being a letter from Edward H. Bonsall about the vineyard he started in 1825 in Germantown, near Philadelphia. A catalogue of grapes available from Prince's vineyard at the Linnæan Botanic Garden offers 'above

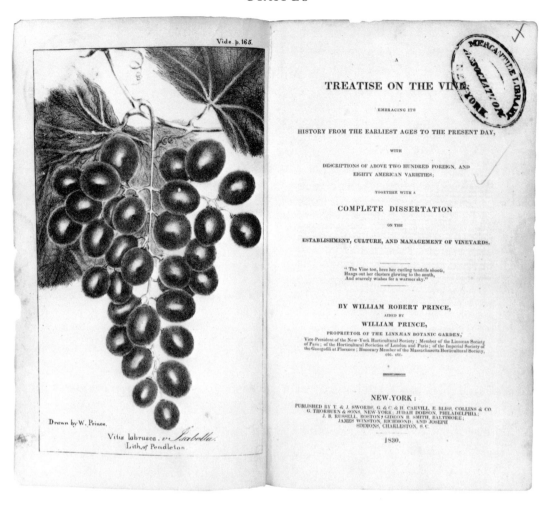

W. R. PRINCE *A Treatise on the Vine* 1830 Frontispiece showing the Isabella grape, drawn by William Prince and lithographed by Pendleton, and title-page

Drawn by W. Prince.

Vitis labrusca. *v.* *Isabella.*
Lith. of Pendleton

A
TREATISE ON THE VINE;
EMBRACING ITS
HISTORY FROM THE EARLIEST AGES TO THE PRESENT DAY,
WITH
DESCRIPTIONS OF ABOVE TWO HUNDRED FOREIGN, AND
EIGHTY AMERICAN VARIETIES;
TOGETHER WITH A
COMPLETE DISSERTATION
ON THE
ESTABLISHMENT, CULTURE, AND MANAGEMENT OF VINEYARDS.

" The Vine too, here her curling tendrils shoots,
Hangs out her clusters glowing to the south,
And scarcely wishes for a warmer sky."

BY WILLIAM ROBERT PRINCE,
AIDED BY
WILLIAM PRINCE,
PROPRIETOR OF THE LINNÆAN BOTANIC GARDEN;
Vice-President of the New-York Horticultural Society; Member of the Linnæan Society
of Paris; of the Horticultural Societies of London and Paris; of the Imperial Society of
the Georgofili at Florence; Honorary Member of the Massachusetts Horticultural Society,
etc. etc.

NEW-YORK:
PUBLISHED BY T. & J. SWORDS, G. & C. & H. CARVILL, E. BLISS, COLLINS & CO.
G. THORBURN & SONS, NEW-YORK; JUDAH DOBSON, PHILADELPHIA;
J. B. RUSSELL, BOSTON; GIDEON B. SMITH, BALTIMORE;
JAMES WINSTON, RICHMOND; AND JOSEPH
SIMMONS, CHARLESTON, S. C.

1830.

two hundred varieties which are the identical kinds which were cultivated at the Royal Garden of the Luxembourg at Paris, an establishment formed by royal patronage for the purpose of concentrating all the most valuable fruits of France, and testing their respective merits'.

Prince planned a second volume of his *Treatise*, called *The Particular History of the Vine*, which he advertised on page 353 of the first volume, promising publication 'as soon as a sufficient number of subscribers is obtained'. This stage seems never to have been reached. The second part was to have comprised 'a Topographical Account of all the known Vineyards throughout the World, and including those of the United States; with the modes of culture, and . . . every particular necessary to render any one a complete Vigneron. This work will comprise all the important information contained in the new edition of Duhamel.' The *Nouveau Duhamel* (see page 82) had been completed about ten years earlier, describing and illustrating many more grapes than the earlier version.

# MELONS

Pl. XXX

P. J. JACQUIN *Monographie complète du Melon* 1832 plate XXX Four melons

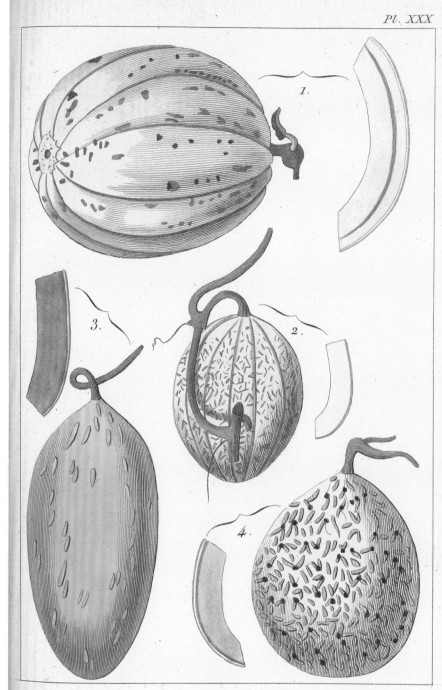

1. *Melon Sageret fond blanc.*
2. *Melon de Mequinez.*
3. *Melon de Candie.*
4. *Melon de Rio-Janeiro.*

Monog. des Melons.

# 97. JACQUIN, Pierre Joseph (1779?–1856)

Monographie complète du Melon, contenant la culture, la description et le classement de toutes les variétés de cette espèce, suivies de celles de la pastèque a chair fondante, avec la figure de chacune dessinée et coloriée d'après nature. Par M. Jacquin aîné, membre de plusieurs sociétés horticulturales françaises et etrangères. [swelled rule 3.5 cm.] Paris, Rousselon, Libraire-Éditeur, rue d'Anjou-Dauphine, N° 9. Jacquin Frères, Marchands Grainiers, quai de la Mégisserie, N° 14. [rule 0.5 cm.] 1832.
8° 22 x 14 cm. π⁴ 1–9⁸ 10★⁸ 11–12⁸ 13⁴ [4] *i* ii–iv *1* 2– 199 *200* and 33 engravings bound in a separate volume.

BINDING: Quarter leather, rebacked; patterned paper sides. Bookplate of the Horticultural Society of New York, Bequest of Kenneth K. Mackenzie, October 1934.

PLATES: The engravings, coloured by hand, show several varieties on most plates, with sections showing the colour and texture of the flesh as well as the outside of the fruit. In all, over 90 varieties are illustrated on the 33 engravings, which are not signed.

P. J. JACQUIN was a Paris nurseryman who set out to give a full account of the range of melons available for cultivation in the open or under glass, in favourable or more difficult climates—melons with rough or smooth, plain or patterned, green or buff skins, and pale green, yellow, or orange flesh. A few watermelons are also described and illustrated. A four-page prospectus bound with the plates summed up Jacquin's intentions:

Un ouvrage de culture ne peut obtenir du succès qu'autant qu'il répond à un besoin, et qu'il est le résultat d'une pratique eclairée. La confusion, qui règne parmi les nombreuses variétés de Melon, nous a inspiré l'idée d'y mettre de l'ordre; nous avons pensé, à juste titre sans doute, que notre travail serait utile aux cultivateurs comme aux amateurs de cet excellent fruit . . . Notre but est donc de faire connaître, en détail et méthodiquement, l'espèce Melon, si féconde en variétés; d'indiquer les caractères distinctifs de chacune; de designer celles qui, par l'excellence de leurs fruits, méritent la préférence; d'exposer les modes de culture le plus convenables pour obtenir, sans trop de frais, ces diverses variétés pendant huit mois de l'année, . . . enfin de débrouiller leur synonymie si confuse, et de nommer les variétés nouvelles.

Over half the text is occupied with the culture of this temperamental fruit; the rest covers its history, from Pliny on, with a classification of the multitude of varieties—over ninety of them—and a description of each one.

The prospectus, which is not dated, says that the monograph will be issued in six parts, each containing thirty-two pages and five or six plates, the first to appear the following December and the rest to follow at monthly intervals. The wrapper of the first part, dated 1832, is also bound with the prospectus. If the book was issued as planned it should perhaps be dated

1832–1833, as December 1832 would have been the month the first part was published and the later ones could not have appeared until the following year. There is also a possibility that the prospectus was distributed in 1831, referring to the issue of the first part in December of that year, which would indicate a date of 1831–1832 for the whole book.

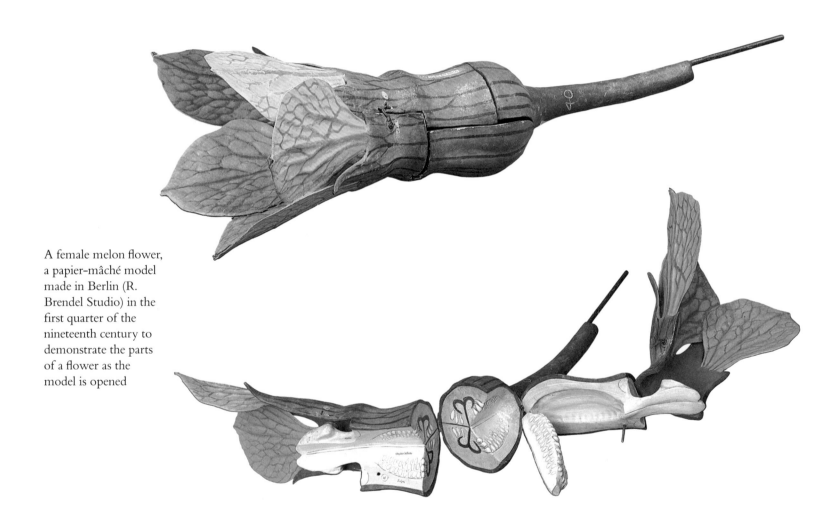

A female melon flower, a papier-mâché model made in Berlin (R. Brendel Studio) in the first quarter of the nineteenth century to demonstrate the parts of a flower as the model is opened

# TROPICAL FRUIT

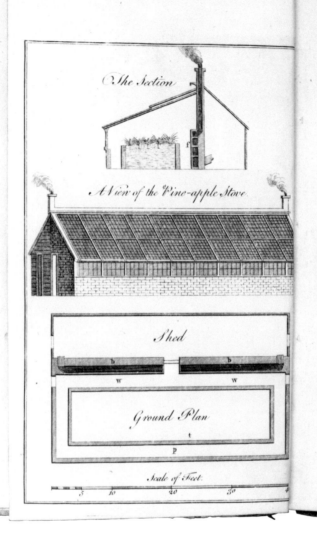

*The Section*

*A View of the Pine-apple Stove*

*Shed*

*Ground Plan*

*Scale of Feet.*

5    10    20    30    4

# ON THE

# CULTURE

OF THE

# ANANA,

OR

## PINE-APPLE PLANT.

THE excellency, fragrancy, and
flavour of the fruit which this
plant produceth needs no commendation, as it is well known to excel all the
fruits hitherto cultivated ; so that it is
no wonder every gentleman of taste and
fortune is fond of this polite article of
gardening.

The pine-apple plant is a native of Surinam, one of the hottest countries of
South-America, and of some inland parts
of Africa. There they grow in such quantities,

B

# 98. GILES, John (1726?–1797)

Ananas: or, A Treatise on the Pine-Apple. In which The whole Culture, Management, and Perfecting this most excellent Fruit, is laid down in a clear and explicit Manner. To which is added, The true Method of raising the finest Melons with the greatest Success: shewing the whole Process of their Management, from sowing the Seeds to ripening the Fruit. The Whole deduced from many Years Practice and Observations; and containing various Improvements in the Culture of these Plants never before published. Illustrated with a Curious Copper-Plate, in which is exhibited at one View, a Stove, &c. peculiarly adapted for raising the Pine-Apple Plant. [rule] By John Giles, Gardener, At Lewisham, in Kent. [rule] Experientia docet. ['Experience teaches'; double rule, upper one heavier] London: Printed for the Author; and sold by S. Bladon, in Paternoster-Row, and S. Noble, in Carnaby-Street. [1767].

8° 21.5 x 12 cm. A–H⁴ *i–iii* iv–viii *1* 2–56 and 1 engraving.

BINDING: Quarter calf, marbled paper-covered boards. 'Earl of Macclesfield' written on front pastedown, perhaps indicating the ownership of Thomas Parker, third Earl of Macclesfield, who held the title from 1764 until his death in 1795.

PLATE: The single plate, engraved by John Lodge, shows a section, a view, and a ground plan of a pineapple stove.

THE publication date of 1767 is given by J. C. Loudon in his *Encyclopaedia of Gardening* (1822, page 1275). At this time John Giles was a gardener employed by Lady Boyd at Lewisham, now part of London, then a village in Kent. It was the first of several manuals giving directions for the cultivation of the temperamental pineapple. Melons were popular too. Among the enthusiastic gardeners who spent a great deal of time and attention on their melon frames was Gilbert White of Selborne.

Later in his life, in 1777, Giles became a foreman in a local nursery run by a man called Russell.

Although the pineapple was introduced to England from Holland as early as about 1690, it did not become exceedingly fashionable in Britain until well into the eighteenth century, once a reliable method had been found to make it bear fruit there. Henry Telende, gardener to Sir Matthew Decker at Richmond Green, managed this achievement about 1712, using a brick-lined hot-bed filled with tanner's bark, an innovation later adopted by Philip Miller at the Chelsea Physic Garden to germinate the seeds of delicate tropical plants. Special hot-houses for pineapples were built in many of the richer gardens, and the skill of those in charge of them was valued by their employers. By 1754 at least two nurserymen, Henry Scott, of Weybridge, Surrey, and James Scott, of Turnham Green, near London, were specializing in the provision of both plants and fruit. As late as 1822, Loudon still said firmly that the pineapple 'is the first of dessert fruits'.

Title-page

A
TREATISE
ON THE
CULTURE
OF THE
PINE APPLE
AND THE
MANAGEMENT
OF THE
HOT-HOUSE.
TOGETHER
WITH A DESCRIPTION OF EVERY SPECIES OF
INSECT
THAT INFEST HOT-HOUSES, WITH EFFECTUAL METHODS
OF DESTROYING THEM.

By WILLIAM SPEECHLY,
GARDENER to the DUKE of PORTLAND.

To which is added,
A METHOD TO PRESERVE
PEACH AND NECTARINE TREES,
FROM MILDEW, &c.

By ROBERT BROWNE.

DUBLIN:
Printed for LUKE WHITE, No. 86, DAME-STREET,
M,DCC,LXXXVI.

## 99.  SPEECHLY, William (1734–1819?)

A Treatise on the Culture of the Pine Apple and the Management of the Hot-House. Together with a Description of every Species of Insect that infest Hot-Houses, with effectual Methods of destroying them. [rule] By William Speechly, Gardener to the Duke of Portland. [rule] To which is added, A Method to Preserve Peach and Nectarine Trees, from Mildew, &c. [rule] By Robert Browne. [rule; swelled rule 3.5 cm.] Dublin: Printed for Luke White, No. 86, Dame-Street. [rule 2 cm.] M,DCC, LXXXVI.

8° 19 x 11.5 cm. a⁴ π² b⁸ A–M⁸ N⁴ [2] *i–iii* iv–v *vi* [2] *vii* viii–xvii *xviii 1* 2–186 *1–2* 3–18 and 2 unsigned engravings. The pages between gatherings a and b contain explanations of the plates.

BINDING: Bound with Samuel Hayes, *A Practical Treatise*

*on Planting*, 1794, in contemporary calf. Gilt coat of arms with the motto *Semper fidelis* on front and back.

PLATES: A folding one of 'A Plan of an approved Pine and Grape Stove' is adapted from the drawing used for plate I of Speechly's *Treatise on the Culture of the Vine*, 1790 (see page 246).

WILLIAM SPEECHLY learned his trade at Milton Abbey in Dorset and Castle Howard in Yorkshire before becoming head gardener to the third Duke of Portland at Welbeck Abbey, near Worksop, Nottinghamshire, in 1767. Here he stayed until 1804 and then turned to farming, later moving to Oxfordshire, where he died at Great Milton. His improvements to the garden at Welbeck earned him a reputation as one of the best fruit and kitchen gardeners of his time, and the Duke sent him to Holland in 1771 to study Dutch methods of raising fruit. As the knowledge needed to produce pineapples had been brought to England from Holland, it seems appropriate that it was this visit that led to the construction at Welbeck of the stove or heated greenhouse for pineapples and grapes, which was built to Speechly's design and under his supervision. His *Treatise on the Pine Apple* was first published in 1779 at York, presumably on the advice of Alexander Hunter, the editor of an enlarged edition of Evelyn's *Silva* who lived there and who is thanked in the preface. Speechly also contributed a description of the way Welbeck's woods and plantations were run to Hunter's *Silva*. His pineapple book, with its advice on hot-house insects and how to get rid of them, was pirated in Dublin in 1786, with the addition of *A Method to Preserve Peach and Nectarine Trees from Mildew*, by Robert Browne, which had been published on its own in London earlier in the year (see page 232). An official second edition of Speechly's book appeared in 1796, and a third, combined with his *Treatise on the Culture of the Vine*, in 1821.

## 100. ABERCROMBIE, John (1726–1806)

The Hot-House Gardener on the General Culture of the Pine-Apple, and Methods of Forcing Early Grapes, Peaches, Nectarines, and other choice Fruits, in Hot-Houses, Vineries, Fruit-Houses, Hot-Walls, &c. with Directions for raising Melons and early Strawberries. [swelled rule 4.5 cm.] By John Abercrombie, Author of Every Man his own Gardener; The Universal Gardener's Kalendar; The Complete Kitchen Gardener; and the Garden Vade Mecum. [swelled rule 4 cm.] Illustrated with five Copper Plates, representing the Pine-Apple, Grapes, Peaches, Nectarines, Cherries, Melon, and Strawberries, —Coloured from Nature. [swelled rule 4.5 cm.] London: Printed for John Stockdale, opposite Burlington-House, Piccadilly. M.DCC.LXXXIX.

8° 25.5 x 16 cm. A–Q⁸ *i–iii* iv–xvi *1* 2–238 *239–240* (the last two pages containing advertisements) and 5 coloured engravings.

BINDING: Contemporary boards, uncut. Bookplate of Arpad Plesch (1890–1974).

PLATES: The unsigned engravings are printed in red and coloured by hand. The first and fourth ('Sugar Loaf Pine Apple' and 'Cantaloupe Melon') are dated August 1 1789, the other three ('Muscat of Alexandria', 'Royal George Peach, Roman Nectarine', and 'May Duke Cherry, Scarlet Strawberry') March 26 1789.

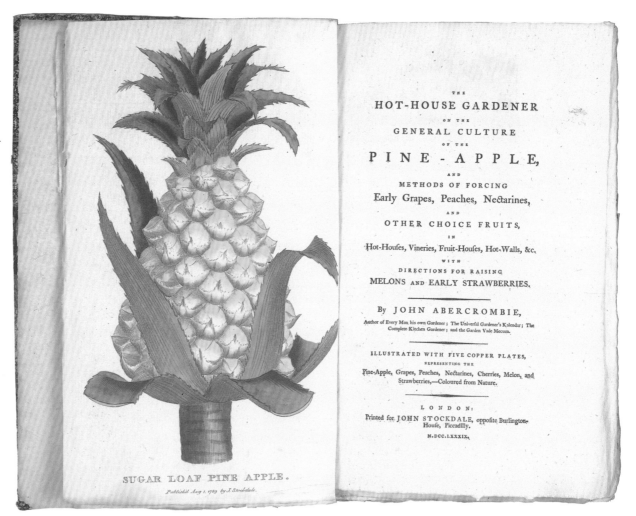

JOHN ABERCROMBIE
*The Hot-House Gardener*
1789 Frontispiece and
title-page

SUGAR LOAF PINE APPLE.

*Published Aug 1. 1789 by J. Stockdale.*

THE
HOT-HOUSE GARDENER
ON THE
GENERAL CULTURE
OF THE
PINE-APPLE,
AND
METHODS OF FORCING
Early Grapes, Peaches, Nectarines,
AND
OTHER CHOICE FRUITS,
IN
Hot-Houses, Vineries, Fruit-Houses, Hot-Walls, &c.
WITH
DIRECTIONS FOR RAISING
MELONS AND EARLY STRAWBERRIES,

By JOHN ABERCROMBIE,
Author of Every Man his own Gardener; The Universal Gardener's Kalendar; The
Complete Kitchen Gardener; and the Garden Vade Mecum.

ILLUSTRATED WITH FIVE COPPER PLATES,
REPRESENTING THE
Pine-Apple, Grapes, Peaches, Nectarines, Cherries, Melon, and
Strawberries,—Coloured from Nature.

LONDON:
Printed for JOHN STOCKDALE, opposite Burlington-
House, Piccadilly.
M.DCC.LXXXIX.

TEN YEARS after publishing *The British Fruit-Gardener* (see page 92) John Abercrombie supplemented it with another book about a handful of the most demanding fruits. *The Hot-House Gardener* concentrates on the pineapple and other 'highly-esteemed fruits' needing protection and extra heat, like grapes, peaches, nectarines, and melons. Although these subjects were treated in general gardening books, the author felt that, in more comprehensive works, 'there is not the opportunity, as in a distinct Work of this kind, of giving the thorough practical process . . . The Author's evident intention in this Work is to render the methods of practice clear and instructive to those who may wish for information in these particular branches of gardening.' These directions were delivered in a 'plain unadorned stile of writing', with an apology hardly needed from a writer who, by the date of this book, was already a best-seller, with several popular books to his credit.

INDEX

# INDEX

*Page numbers in italics refer to illustrations or their captions*

COMPOSED AND PRINTED BY

MERIDEN-STINEHOUR PRESS, LUNENBURG, VERMONT

DESIGNED BY MARK ARGETSINGER

BOUND BY ACME BOOKBINDERY, CHARLESTOWN,

MASSACHUSETTS. THE PHOTOGRAPHY IS

BY GREG HEINS